Salon des Femmes

Conversations about Women, Men, Sex, Love, Relationships,
Becoming a Pragmatist of Femininity and Many, Many Other Things

Gary M. Douglas

Based on a Series of Teleclasses
with Gary Douglas and a Gathering of Eighteen Powerful and Amazing
Women

ACCESS
CONSCIOUSNESS®
PUBLISHING

Published by
Access Consciousness Publishing, LLC
www.accessconsciousnesspublishing.com

Printed in the United States of America

Ease, Joy and Glory

DISCLAIMER

Please don't take any of this seriously or make it significant.

My heart's desire here is to create more ease and peace with females and males.

It is not to create separation or judgment.

What if you lived in a world where everybody was kind to each other?

What if you were the one that could assist in creating that?

Contents

Foreword

During the 17th and 18th centuries in France, salons were places where smart, forward-looking women met, talked together and exchanged ideas, just as smart, forward-looking men did.

In the spirit of those salons, I hosted a series of fourteen tele-classes with groups of amazing women where we talked about women, men, sex, relationships, men's and women's roles, creating the future and many, many other subjects. This book is based on those conversations.

Throughout the discussions that follow, there may be some words and concepts you have never encountered before. We have tried to define them all in a glossary at the end of the book.

You will also find the clearing statement we use in Access Consciousness®. It's a short-speak that addresses the energies that are creating the limitations and contractions in your life. When you first read it, it may twist your head around a little bit. That's our intention. It's designed to get your mind out of the picture so you can get to the energy of a situation.

Basically, with the clearing statement, we're addressing the energy of the limitations and barriers that keep us from moving forward and expanding into all of the spaces that we would like to go.

The Access Consciousness Clearing Statement is "Right and Wrong, Good and Bad, POD and POC, All Nine, Shorts, Boys and Beyonds®." There is a brief explanation of what the words mean at the end of the book.

You can choose to use the clearing statement or not; I don't have a point of view about that, but I do want to invite you to try it and see what happens.

1

Pragmatic Feminism

*I have one thing in mind and that's to get you to total awareness.
If you really don't want to have that,
then you'd better put up your guard or else I am going to take you on a
wild ride.*

Gary:

Hello ladies. For years, Dr. Dain Heer and I held sex and relationships workshops with groups of men and women. On Thursday night, all the men would come together and get rid of their judgments of women. On Friday night, all the women would come and get rid of their judgments about men, and then they would go out and have a slumber party and build a new pack of judgments. They became judgmental of men once again, and the men were scared to death because they knew that they could have their testicles cut off by these angry women.

An Operative State of Living

Why were the women so angry about the men? Because they had created an operative state of life and living as women.

When you have an operative state of living, the same thing shows up over and over again, and you wonder why things keep happening in the same way. If you keep having conflicts with men or if you keep getting bored or you keep thinking that something needs to be different from what it is, you have an operative state that keeps things showing up the same way.

If you really want to change your relationship with the other sex or with your sexual partner, you have to change the way you look at things.

Salon Participant:

I am always in a fight against masculine or feminine.

Gary:

There should be no fight between masculine and feminine. That's what I am trying to create here. When I did the Gentleman's Club the first time, the men didn't feel they had to fight for the right to be men, and they didn't feel they had to fight against women to have themselves. They could just be themselves and women could choose them or not as they wished.

Salon Participant:

I feel like I am in competition with men.

Gary:

That's an operative state. An operative state is a place you try to function from. It's a choice you make. You're not willing to have something different. You've concluded, "This is the way it is, this is the way I will always do it, and this is what's going to happen."

Instead, you could ask yourself:

- What would I truly like to choose?
- What could I be or do different that would change all this?

How many judgments do you have to put into place to have an operative state? A lot, a little, megatons, or more than God knows? More than God knows!

Everything that is times a godzillion, will you destroy and uncreate it all? Right and Wrong, Good and Bad, POD and POC, All Nine, Shorts, Boys and Beyonds.

What stupidity are you using to create the operative state of life and living as a female are you choosing? Everything that is times a godzillion, will you destroy and uncreate it all? Right and Wrong, Good and Bad, POD and POC, All Nine, Shorts, Boys and Beyonds.

And what stupidity are you using to create the feeling of a constant state of conflict between masculine and feminine are you choosing? Everything that is times a godzillion, will you destroy and uncreate it all? Right and Wrong, Good and Bad, POD and POC, All Nine, Shorts, Boys and Beyonds.

Salon Participant:

At the end of those processes, you asked, "Are you choosing?" I tend to say, "That you are choosing." I realize you don't say that. Can you tell me why?

Gary:

"That you are choosing" justifies your reason for choosing. It's a fixed point of view. It is saying, "I am choosing this because ____." You would prefer to believe you are choosing for a *reason* rather than *just choosing*. I am trying to get you to see that there is no reason for what you choose—you just choose. That's why I ask, "Are you choosing?"

Salon Participant:

I love you, Gary! That eliminates so much little energy, so much crap.

Salon Participant:

I have a question. Are men actually mean and vicious?

Gary:

No, in reality, men are not mean and vicious.

Salon Participant:

So, why does it seem like they are?

Gary:

Because they have bought the lie that being mean and vicious is masculine. How many lies have you bought about men that are screwing up your lives? A lot, a little, or megatons?

How many lies about men have you bought that are locking up your life and living? Everything that is times a godzillion, will you destroy and uncreate it all? Right and Wrong, Good and Bad, POD and POC, All Nine, Shorts, Boys and Beyonds.

Salon Participant:

My dad was supportive of me going to a good college and getting a good internship. Yet he ridiculed women. He laughed at women who were crying. And when my sister was dying, he chose not to go to see her. I developed a really skewed idea of what men are.

Gary:

Well, pretty much everyone does that, even men.

What stupidity are you using to create the conflict between male and female are you choosing? Everything that is times a godzillion, will you destroy and uncreate it all? Right and Wrong, Good and Bad, POD and POC, All Nine, Shorts, Boys and Beyonds.

Salon Participant:

If one side is maintaining the conflict and the other side is in interesting point of view about it, does that have the capacity to defuse the conflict?

Gary:

It defuses the conflict to a certain extent, but it doesn't keep the relationship going in the long run. I did that with my ex-wife. I would go into interesting point of view. I would not be in conflict, so there would be no conflict, but that didn't change anything in her world. The problem is that most women, rather than seeing a man for who he is, have the point of view that if they change him, he will turn into a good man.

How many times have you taken a man and seen him as a perfect picture? Everything that is times a godzillion, will you destroy and uncreate it all? Right and Wrong, Good and Bad, POD and POC, All Nine, Shorts, Boys and Beyonds.

Choosing a Man You Want to "Fix"

Salon Participant:

I have a question about that. What is it that creates the dynamic of choosing a man you want to fix or change?

Gary:

As a kid, you were taught that you had to find a 'good' bad boy. All romance novels are about a man who is considered a bad boy, and because he falls in love with you, you tame the beast in him, and he is your lover.

Everywhere you are trying to tame the wild beast, will you destroy and uncreate it all? Right and Wrong, Good and Bad, POD and POC, All Nine, Shorts, Boys and Beyonds.

Salon Participant:

Is it also about saving him? "I can help him, I can fix him, I can make him better." Is it a mother thing, a mother instinct about saving?

Gary:

It's not a mother thing. It's a female thing. You have been taught that your job is to be a support and to sit behind the throne—not *beyond* the throne. It's to be in charge without being in charge. You're supposed to pretend that you are just a sweet young thing who doesn't know anything. These roles given to women are not true. They have nothing to do with what a true woman is.

> Everything that is times a godzillion, will you destroy and uncreate it all? Right and Wrong, Good and Bad, POD and POC, All Nine, Shorts, Boys and Beyonds.

Some Day My Prince Will Come

Do you ever look at these things and say, "That's nuts! Why would I choose that?" Some of you do. You say, "Never mind, I won't even bother to have a relationship." Others of you say, "Well, someday the right man will come, someday my prince will take me away from being the Cinderella."

> Everything that is times a godzillion, will you destroy and uncreate it all? Right and Wrong, Good and Bad, POD and POC, All Nine, Shorts, Boys and Beyonds.

Salon Participant:

What if you have both of those going on at once?

Gary:

Most of you do have both of them going on at once. You are taught that this is how it's going to be. Eventually the right man will come along and everything will work out. No, none of that is real! Would you, as an infinite being, have only one true love?

Salon Participant:

No!

Gary:

It doesn't make sense. Because as an infinite being, you would have oneness as the thing you desire, not *one* as the thing you desire.

Everything that is times a godzillion, will you destroy and uncreate it all? Right and Wrong, Good and Bad, POD and POC, All Nine, Shorts, Boys and Beyonds.

As a kid, you are taught there is one true love for you. You are taught that someday you will find your prince. Someday the right man will come along and he will love you the way you should be loved. And someday everything will be perfect. Someday never arrives because someday is never today. Someday is something that has never existed, will never exist and can never exist.

How many somedays are all of you still trying to bring to fruition? Everything that is times a godzillion, will you destroy and uncreate it all? Right and Wrong, Good and Bad, POD and POC, All Nine, Shorts, Boys and Beyonds.

Are any of you beginning to notice a lot of charge on this area?

Salon Participant:

Yeah!

Gary:

This stuff maintains the insanity of this reality. The conflict between male and female, the idea of relationship and marriage, The idea that sex is supposed to be beautiful, wonderful and blah-blah-blah. In reality, does any of that exist?

What stupidity are you using to create the non-existent sex life, romance life, marriage and relationship life that never existed in any reality are you choosing? Everything that is times a godzillion, will you destroy and uncreate it all? Right and Wrong, Good and Bad, POD and POC, All Nine, Shorts, Boys and Beyonds.

It's like you never ask a question. You go to, "He is so beautiful, wonderful, and kind," but you never ask, "Is this really going to work for me?" You come to a conclusion about what you are supposed to have instead of choosing what will actually work.

I want you to be the pragmatist of femininity, not the fighting Irish, the fighting Nordics, the fighting Vikings, the fighting Hispanics and every other nationality of women you think you have to be.

Everything that is times a godzillion, will you destroy and uncreate it all? Right and Wrong, Good and Bad, POD and POC, All Nine, Shorts, Boys and Beyonds.

Salon Participant:

I also feel a constant conflict, a constant fighting between man and woman. It keeps me in a constant conflict with me.

Gary:

Yeah, because you have been a man and a woman. All things should be available to you. There isn't anything you haven't been or done in one lifetime or another. Everything that you have ever been or done should be accessible to you, but in an attempt to define yourself as a woman or a man, you cut off half of what is available to you. If you define yourself as a man, you have to cut off your feminine side. If you define yourself as a woman, you have to cut off your masculine side. You buy into points of view about men and points of view about women so you can define who you are, but those definitions have nothing to do with you, the being.

Salon Participant:

Yeah, it's like I am fighting against men and I go into wrongness of me for doing that.

Gary:

What stupidity are you using to create the conflict between male and female that you are choosing? Everything that is times a godzillion, will you destroy and uncreate it all? Right and Wrong, Good and Bad, POD and POC, All Nine, Shorts, Boys and Beyonds.

If you were a male in your last lifetime and you thought being a female was easier and better and you come into this lifetime as a female, you'll say, "Wait a minute, it's not easier being a female. It's better being a male," and you'll go into a conflict with your decisions and your choices, which gives you how much choice?

Salon Participant:

Zero.

Gary:

And how much judgment does it give you? Megatons.

Everything that is times a godzillion, will you destroy and uncreate it all? Right and Wrong, Good and Bad, POD and POC, All Nine, Shorts, Boys and Beyonds.

Homage to Relationship vs. Homage to Vagina

One of the things I want you to get from this Salon des Femmes is to be able to have your feminine side without the necessity of making it a problem with men. Nothing should be a problem with men. Everything should be a choice.

What stupidity are you using to create the eternal homage to relationship are you choosing? Everything that is times a godzillion, will you destroy and uncreate it all? Right and Wrong, Good and Bad, POD and POC, All Nine, Shorts, Boys and Beyonds.

The male version of that is:

What stupidity are you using to create the eternal homage to vagina are you choosing? Everything that is times a godzillion, will you destroy and uncreate it all? Right and Wrong, Good and Bad, POD and POC, All Nine, Shorts, Boys and Beyonds.

Both sides of this are playing on everybody, and that creates a lot of opposition. You want *him* to worship your vagina, and *you* want to worship your relationships. Women are trained to the idea that everything is about relationship—your relationship to your kids, your relationship to your spouse. Women and men are worshipping different gods and wondering why they can't get it together!

What stupidity are you using to create the eternal homage to relationship are you choosing? Everything that is times a godzillion, will you destroy and uncreate it all? Right and Wrong, Good and Bad, POD and POC, All Nine, Shorts, Boys and Beyonds.

What stupidity are you using to create the eternal homage to vagina are you choosing? Everything that is times a godzillion, will you destroy and uncreate it all? Right and Wrong, Good and Bad, POD and POC, All Nine, Shorts, Boys and Beyonds.

Salon Participant:

Is there also an eternal homage to not having relationships? Or is that a different side of the same coin?

Gary:

Yes, it is a different side of the same coin.

If you are doing homage of any kind, you are not being present with choice, possibility and question. We have to get rid of the homage to relationship, either for or against, and we have to get rid of the homage to the vagina, for or against. Both of them create a problem where you end up with an oppositional point of view.

Salon Participant:

Ah, right.

Gary:

What stupidity are you using to create the eternal homage to relationship are you choosing? This can be either side. Everything that is times a godzillion, will you destroy and uncreate it all? Right and Wrong, Good and Bad, POD and POC, All Nine, Shorts, Boys and Beyonds.

What stupidity are you using to create the eternal homage to vagina are you choosing? Everything that is times a godzillion, will you destroy and uncreate it all? Right and Wrong, Good and Bad, POD and POC, All Nine, Shorts, Boys and Beyonds.

Salon Participant:

Gary, the second question, "What stupidity are you using to create the eternal homage to the vagina are you choosing?" is strong for me. Can you explain that?

Gary:

At some point in some lifetime, you probably decided you wished you had a vagina.

Salon Participant:

Me, being a man in that lifetime?

What Constitutes Masculine and Feminine, Anyway?

Gary:

Yeah, the whole idea of being for or against a point of view is hysterically funny to me. There isn't anything you haven't been or done in one lifetime or another. What constitutes masculine and feminine, anyway?

Salon Participant:

That was my next question!

Gary:

Well, I've got a process for that too.

What stupidity are you using to create you as the concubine of MEST reality, physical reality and psychological insanity are you choosing? Everything that is times a godzillion, will you destroy and uncreate it all? Right and Wrong, Good and Bad, POD and POC, All Nine, Shorts, Boys and Beyonds.

When you make you a concubine, it's like being the mistress of MEST reality (the reality of matter, energy, space and time), physiological reality and psychological insanity, because in this world, don't you become a slave and servant to that? It's like the creation of sex to most people. For instance, how many times have you had a relationship in this matter, energy, space and time reality that has been joyful for you?

Salon Participant:

Ha–ha–ha.

Gary:

Hardly ever! And how many of those relationships have been about your physiological reality? How many of the people you have had sex with actually enjoyed sex? How many of them think that you are beautiful, wonderful and fabulous—because you are?

Salon Participant:

Not many.

Gary:

And then there is psychological insanity, which is where most people function from in relationships of all kinds. Most people use judgments to create sexual excitement. Judgment is not a way to create an expansive world. It can only create a contractive one. Does that help?

Salon Participant:

My whole body is a struggle now. The energy is all messed up.

Gary:

That's why we are running this. We've got to straighten out your bodies so you can have greater ease with them and everything you choose in life. This teleclass is to get you to a place where you can have ease with being a female, ease with choosing to act like a male, ease with creating as a male does and ease with creating as a female does. Right now most of you are struggling for or against one side or the other, which doesn't give you total choice. Do you guys get that?

Nothing in this reality is about choosing and creating your sexual identity and reality. It's about buying into everything you are told and sold, everything out there in the world that tells you, "This is how it is supposed to be."

Everything that is times a godzillion, will you destroy and uncreate it all? Right and Wrong, Good and Bad, POD and POC, All Nine, Shorts, Boys and Beyonds.

Salon Participant:

Gary, you mentioned the freedom to create as a man or woman. Will you talk about that?

Manipulation and Knowing

Gary:

The thing about men is that they tend to be quite straightforward. They are more direct than most women. Boom, boom, boom. They also lie well. If you are a woman, you learn that men will lie, and you try to confront them, control them or manipulate them to get them to tell the truth. Actually, you shouldn't try to get them to tell the truth. You just want to know what the truth is, because that gives you control over the situation.

Part of being a woman, part of womanology, is having a sixth sense. You have an awareness of things that men don't have, but that is not encouraged in this reality. Your innate ability to know is not encouraged. You are supposed to give up your knowing in favor of manipulation, as though manipulation is going to be ultimate source of control instead of awareness. No. With awareness, you can have control over anything.

Salon Participant:

Can you talk a little more about manipulation and knowing? If I understood correctly, you're saying I use manipulation rather than knowing the lie is there and using it to my advantage.

Gary:

Yes, that's what we are taught in this reality. We're taught to cut off our awareness at every opportunity. Were you taught to believe everything your father said? Yes. You were taught that you could trust your father. So, every man becomes someone you can trust, right?

Salon Participant:

Or the opposite, actually!

Gary:

It goes in both directions. Neither one can give you the freedom of awareness. We are looking for how you get to awareness—not the place where you trust and have blind faith.

How many of you have tried to create blind faith in men? Everything that is times a godzillion, will you destroy and uncreate it all? Right and Wrong, Good and Bad, POD and POC, All Nine, Shorts, Boys and Beyonds.

And how many of you have tried to create blind faith in women? "This woman is my sister; she will take care of me." When you cut off your awareness, women will be as mean and vicious as men if they are given the opportunity. How do you give someone that opportunity? By cutting off your awareness.

you destroy and uncreate it? Right and Wrong, Good and Bad, POD and POC, All Nine, Shorts, Boys and Beyonds.

Being a female pragmatist is seeing how you can use the things available to your advantage. For example, you have cleavage. Can you use that to an advantage with a man who is not too bright?

Salon Participant:

Yeah!

Gary:

Can you use it with a man who is very bright?

Salon Participant:

Yeah!

Gary:

Can you use it with a man who is aware?

Salon Participant:

Yeah.

Gary:

No, you can't. Because he knows you are using it. That creates a different reality.

What stupidity are you using to create the feeling of conflict between feminine and masculine are you choosing? Everything that is times a godzillion, will you destroy and uncreate it all? Right and Wrong, Good and Bad, POD and POC, All Nine, Shorts, Boys and Beyonds.

I don't know whether you have noticed, but all of these processes have a lot of charge on them. Your points of view about these things are one of the primary ways we keep this world in conflict. They're one of the ways we keep this war going. Now that you guys are changing your points of view about these things, the war will cease.

You may be a little stronger than you think!

Stupidity vs. Awareness

When I talk about stupidity, I am talking about all the places you make yourself unaware enough to be stupid about something. You have to make yourself unaware in order to choose stupidity over total awareness. If you have total awareness, you can walk down the street and say, "That guy would be fun to have sex with. That guy would be really boring. That guy would be great to have a relationship with, but he would be boring in bed." You will have awareness of what your choices are and you will be able to choose accordingly.

As a woman, you have more choices than men do. I know you don't think so, but the reality is you do. Because you're a female, you have been given a pedestal to stand upon. Or you have been given the choice to slide off the pedestal. Or you have been given the choice to control the man utterly. You have those three choices as the beginning context to create anything with a man. Most of you don't see that.

Salon Participant:

Most of us seem impelled to choose the one who won't choose us.

Gary:

Exactly. That's the way most people function. Men do that too, but they have learned over time that they get chosen by the female. Females keep looking for the men who will choose them but in actuality, women have the choice because if they say, "Come here," the man says, "Yes!" But if the man says, "Come here" to the woman, the woman says, "F--- you!"

Everything that is times a godzillion, will you destroy and uncreate it all? Right and Wrong, Good and Bad, POD and POC, All Nine, Shorts, Boys and Beyonds.

"I Let My Guard Down"

Salon Participant:

In my first marriage, I was doing "I will change you." That didn't work out, and I immediately went into another relationship. He didn't want me and I wanted him, so that one didn't work out either. I went into my third relationship saying, "Whatever comes my way, I am keeping an open mind and going with it." I finally found a relationship that I am very happy and comfortable with. That's because I let my guard down and I don't place a judgment on what the relationship is going to be.

Gary:

The most important thing you said there was, "I let my guard down." Most women don't see that they are guarding against men most of the time.

Salon Participant:

I've learned through Access Consciousness tools to let things go, and I've found that when I do let go, everything flows to me easily. There's a greater sense of freedom and I feel more secure with who I am.

Gary:

The purpose of this call is to get you to a point where that's always the choice you have. You never have to put up your guard again, because when you put up a guard against someone, you also have to put up a shield against awareness.

Everywhere you have put up a guard against someone and everywhere you have cut off your awareness, which makes you stupid enough to make wrong choices, will you destroy and uncreate all of that? Right and Wrong, Good and Bad, POD and POC, All Nine, Shorts, Boys and Beyonds.

Salon Participant:

I'm feeling mad at you.

Gary:

Was it something I said?

Salon Participant:

You, the man, telling me, the woman, that I have more choices.

Gary:

I am not a man. I am an infinite being.

Salon Participant:

Ha-ha-ha! Thank you!

Gary:

How dare you call me a man? I'm an infinite being.

Salon Participant:

Gary, that's awesome. I see that I put my guard up to you because I was doing the man-woman thing with you.

Gary:

Yeah, we do that with all the people we come into contact with. We are always on guard, we always have a protection, we always put up walls and barriers rather than realizing that we always have total awareness.

How many walls are you choosing to keep you away from total awareness and everything that you desire? Everything that is times a godzillion, will you destroy and uncreate it all? Right and Wrong, Good and Bad, POD and POC, All Nine, Shorts, Boys and Beyonds.

If I were you, I would put up your guard against me because I am a really bad person. I have one thing in mind and that's to get you to total awareness. If you really don't want to have that, then you'd better put up your guard or else I am going to take you on a wild ride!

What stupidity are you using to create the feeling of conflict between a male and female are you choosing? Everything that is times a godzillion, will you destroy and uncreate it all? Right and Wrong, Good and Bad, POD and POC, All Nine, Shorts, Boys and Beyonds.

Fairy Tales

Salon Participant

In my reality, you have to worship a man, and he is the one who chooses you. As in all fairy tales, he is the one who falls in love with the woman. He is always the smartest and the brightest, and I am not worthy of that kind of man, so how can he possibly choose me?

Gary:

Wow, what kind of chocolate are you putting on that pile of crap? It must be some seriously good chocolate if you are buying that stuff!

Salon Participant:

Yeah, that's why I want to clear it now.

Gary:

Here is a process:

What stupidity am I using to create the fairy tale life and living that never works am I choosing? Everything that is times a godzillion, will you destroy and uncreate it all? Right and Wrong, Good and Bad, POD and POC, All Nine, Shorts, Boys and Beyonds.

It's like women's lib took away men's role. And fairy tales take away women's role. Fairy tales are "It's all going to work out in the end and I will live happily ever after." How many people do you know who live happily ever after? That's not living! You can't just do happily ever after. You have to create and generate the relationship that works for you, and that's the one thing most of us are never taught.

This is the place we want to get to—a place where you can create and generate what works for you. I'll be talking more about this as we get further along. But first, I need to get some charge off you guys, as you are locked in cages. You talk about women being a burden and being locked in a cage, and that's pretty much the way you try to function when you are functioning from this reality's point of view about male and female.

Everything that is times a godzillion, will you destroy and uncreate it all? Right and Wrong, Good and Bad, POD and POC, All Nine, Shorts, Boys and Beyonds.

Salon Participant:

If women are ingrained with the point of view, "Someday my prince will come," then what are men taught or ingrained with as far as choosing a relationship or a mate?

Gary:

First of all, the man is not taught to choose a relationship. He is taught to choose for sex—because his job is to provide the seed of the next generation.

Salon Participant:

What about "Find a good woman and settle down"? What's that?

Gary:

Are you from the 1950s?

Salon Participant:

Yes!

Gary:

Okay, good! Because in the 1950s, that was the point of view.

Salon Participant:

So, you don't think that exists anymore?

Gary:

I know it doesn't exist. I grew up in the 1950s, and I saw people sowing their wild oats, getting married and having kids. Then they got divorced. Kids, wives and husbands all were miserable; nobody was happy. Where was the happily ever after? Happily ever after doesn't occur unless you are willing to become pragmatic about your choices.

I noticed that in my age group, people would choose to have a great relationship, but they would not look at the person they were with to see whether that person wanted the same thing they did. Pragmatic feminism is recognizing what you truly would like to have and being willing to create that even though it doesn't fit anybody else's reality.

Everything that brought up for everyone times a godzillion, will you destroy and uncreate it all? Right and Wrong, Good and Bad, POD and POC, All Nine, Shorts, Boys and Beyonds.

This MEST reality is created with the idea that there is something right about it. You are supposed to be subjected to it and live for it.

What stupidity are you using to create you as the concubines of MEST reality, physical reality and psychological insanity are you choosing? Everything that is times a godzillion, will you destroy and uncreate it all? Right and Wrong, Good and Bad, POD and POC, All Nine, Shorts, Boys and Beyonds.

What stupidity are you using to create the feeling of conflict between male and female are you choosing? Everything that is times a godzillion, will you destroy and uncreate it all? Right and Wrong, Good and Bad, POD and POC, All Nine, Shorts, Boys and Beyonds.

The War between Men and Women

One of the reasons the conflict between masculine and feminine or between the sexes has been created is to produce powerless people. It's a way to keep everyone powerless. If you were willing to be everything that you are as a man or as a woman, nobody would be powerless. And being powerless is not in anybody's best interest. Yet how many of you have noticed that you feel powerless in front of certain kinds of men or certain kinds of women?

What stupidity are you using to create the powerlessness of men and women are you choosing? Everything that is times a godzillion, will you destroy and uncreate it all? Right and Wrong, Good and Bad, POD and POC, All Nine, Shorts, Boys and Beyonds.

Salon Participant:

Is this conflict creating the war on the planet?

Gary:

Yeah, and it's certainly creating war between men and women. Women tell men things that make the men feel powerless, and men tell women things that make the women feel powerless.

Early on in my first marriage, I had a six-month-old baby and a wife in the house, and a guy came to visit that I hadn't seen in years. He told me that he was wanted by the police for having hired the Mexican mafia to kill his brother so he could inherit all the money in his family. Then he invited me out for dinner.

I immediately knew I needed to get rid of him. I said, "I really don't want to go for dinner, but you are welcome to use my car." I knew if I gave him my $2,000 car that he would go away, and from my point of view, that was much better than having a guy who was willing to kill stay in the house with me, my wife and child.

My wife went ballistic on me. She said, "You are a coward. You're no good and useless. I hate you." She could not see from my point of view how you get a killer out of your house without getting killed. I am more pragmatic than confrontational.

Everything that is times a godzillion, will you destroy and uncreate it all? Right and Wrong, Good and Bad, POD and POC, All Nine, Shorts, Boys and Beyonds.

Creating and Generating Your Life

Salon Participant:

If we were to stop referring to ourselves as women or men and we began to see men and women as infinite beings, even if they were not behaving that way, how would that change the dynamics?

Gary:

Well, you can still refer to yourself as a woman or man. It's not bad; it's not about eliminating the referral point. It's about recognizing that this other person is an infinite being and looking at whether this infinite being is functioning in a way that is going to expand his or her life—and yours. Most of you choose people you can control or people you think can control you or people you think are going to make you feel or look better for some reason.

You choose an operative state of living as though it is going to create and generate what you desire. It doesn't. An operative state of living can only institute what already exists. All operative states are ways we create autopilots that seem like they're going to work. When you are in an operative state, you are not operating on an aware level. You are operating on autopilot.

Salon Participant:

How do we get rid of these operative states? What question do we ask? What do we have to be?

Gary:

You have to be pragmatic.

Salon Participant:

What's pragmatic? I have never been pragmatic in my life.

Gary:

Yes, you have. It's being practical. You are always pragmatic about making sure you make money.

Salon Participant:

Yes, that's the place I am not bored. I love money, I love my body and I love nature. I am bored with everything else.

Gary:

You are not creating and generating your life. You're living and instituting the operative state of life and living you are choosing. You already have everything handled from your point of view. Of course you are bored: You are not going beyond to a different reality.

Salon Participant:

Okay. How, when, where, what, please?

Gary:

It's not what, where, when, how. It's: I would not choose this for what reason?

Salon Participant:

I have been asking this question!

Gary:

Have you asked: What can I choose beyond boredom?

Salon Participant:

Wow, that one I haven't asked!

Gary:

You are bored, so choose beyond boredom. If you are in a bad relationship, ask: Who can I choose so I am not bored in this relationship anymore? If you are bored in your life, ask: What can I choose beyond boredom?

Salon Participant:

I am lightened a whole lot, Gary!

Gary:

Good! That's why I gave it to you.

Salon Participant:

I love you, Gary, thank you!

Gary:

What stupidity are you using to create the operative state of life and living are you choosing? Everything that is times a godzillion, will you destroy and uncreate it all? Right and Wrong, Good and Bad, POD and POC, All Nine, Shorts, Boys and Beyonds.

When something keeps showing up again and again, you have to go to: What operative state am I trying to live by?

When you're doing, "It's not working, I am not happy with it, I would really like something different, but I can't seem to choose anything different," you have to realize that this is an operative state of living. It's not that you can't choose something different; it's that you won't.

What stupidity are you using to create the operative state of life and living are you choosing? Everything that is times a godzillion, will you destroy and uncreate it all? Right and Wrong, Good and Bad, POD and POC, All Nine, Shorts, Boys and Beyonds.

The operative state is to get to death as soon as possible by having a couple of affairs on the way there. Everything that is times a godzillion, will you destroy and uncreate it all? Right and Wrong, Good and Bad, POD and POC, All Nine, Shorts, Boys and Beyonds.

Your Body Is Inside of You

Salon Participant:

You're talking about creating and generating our lives and choosing something differet, yet we are still in a female body.

Gary:

Why did you say that as though it's a limitation you can't overcome?

You say, "I am *in* a female body." Are you in a female body—or is the female body *inside* of you? You aren't in a body. Your body is inside of you. It's what you created this lifetime to give you something to do. Now, what you chose it for and how you created it to get that result—that part I don't get to know—only you do.

Salon Participant:

What's the difference between me being inside this body or it being inside me?

Gary:

You are an infinite being. There are no edges to you, but there are outside edges to your body.

Salon Participant:

So, my body is inside me?

Gary:

Could you be a bigger being who couldn't get bored, with her body or without her body or anything else?

Salon Participant:

Yes! Thank you!

Gary:

What stupidity are you using to create the operative state of life and living are you choosing? Everything that is times a godzillion, will you destroy and uncreate it all? Right and Wrong, Good and Bad, POD and POC, All Nine, Shorts, Boys and Beyonds.

This is what I want you to run until the next call. You need to get clear about where you are operating from. Most of you are not looking at creating for something greater. You are operating from a state you think you have to function from rather than having a choice or a possibility. You are trying to create from a place, the female body, as though that's the only choice there is rather than asking: What creation would I have available to me here if I was willing to embrace the female and not reject the male? And not reject my infinite being?

Everything that is times a godzillion, will you destroy and uncreate it all? Right and Wrong, Good and Bad, POD and POC, All Nine, Shorts, Boys and Beyonds.

How many of you are looking for your soul mate, your significant other, your twin flame, your other half or your matching energy in male body?

Salon Participant:

Someone to complete me!

Gary:

There! Huge!

Everything that is times a godzillion, will you destroy and uncreate it all? Right and Wrong, Good and Bad, POD and POC, All Nine, Shorts, Boys and Beyonds.

Would an infinite being need completion? Or would an infinite being be willing to have sex or relationship with anybody they chose to have relationship with?

Salon Participant:

Absolutely, any time any place.

Gary:

You keep trying to create all these operative states you can function from.

How many operative states of limitation are you choosing? All of those times a godzillion, will you destroy and uncreate it all? Right and Wrong, Good and Bad, POD and POC, All Nine, Shorts, Boys and Beyonds.

Salon Participant:

What are the elements for true enjoyment of embodying being a woman?

Gary:

Get rid of all judgments about being a woman or a man.

Salon Participant:

In the past, you have talked about all the decisions, judgments, computations and conclusions impelled at our bodies. Can you talk about how those elements play in here?

Gary:

When you cut off your awareness, you make yourself stupid enough to not be aware of what people are projecting at your body, and those things lock into your body and hurt it. You have to be willing to be aware of what's going on. You have to have the awareness, "This guy is looking at me with lust. Does my body like that? Oh! My body likes being lusted after. Interesting!" At least your body can enjoy the lust. That's being pragmatic about being a woman.

You recognize the difference between when someone looks at you with lust and your body enjoys it and when you think you have to do something about it. Most people look at someone and look away because they think if they look at someone for too long it means they have to do something. No! It just means you are looking.

I've found a way around that. When I look at a woman for too long and she gets uncomfortable, I say, "Wow, great shoes, great purse. Where did you get them?" With guys you can say, "Do you work out a lot? You are doing a good job!" or "Wow, you must drink a lot of beer!" You have to be willing to recognize what's going on.

Salon Participant:

What is going on when men and women who don't know each other walk by each other and look the other way? Are they trying to avoid discomfort?

Gary:

It is conflict.

What stupidity are you using to create the feeling of conflict between the male and female you are choosing? Everything that is times a godzillion, will you destroy and uncreate it all? Right and Wrong, Good and Bad, POD and POC, All Nine, Shorts, Boys and Beyonds.

Please note that I am talking about this as male and female. Those are the elements that define what happens when you take on a male body or a female body. You should be willing to recognize, "I am wearing this body, but that doesn't equal who I am."

"Wow, I Never Thought of That"

Salon Participant:

I am currently working in a male-dominated corporate environment and I'm still new to the business. I have two male managers in particular whose duty it is to constantly point out where I am falling short in my role. I feel like I'm creating the relationship I had with my dad when I was a teenager, which, by the way, has changed dynamically since I started this crazy stuff called Access Consciousness. I feel stumped at this point. What can I be or do different that would have these gents become putty in my hands?

Gary:

You have to get that they are trying to be teachers to you. If you want someone to think highly of you, always ask a question that you already know the answer to. Then say, "Wow, I never thought of that. That's brilliant. I am so grateful."

They will start giving you breaks and feeding you information instead of trying to correct you. Their point of view is that they have to set up a youngster to do a better job. It has nothing to do with your being a woman. That's the problem. You haven't asked them a question that proves you already know what you are talking about.

Every Choice Creates

Salon Participant:

I grew up with a lot of rules about what you need to do as a woman in a relationship: You have to be always ready for your man. You have to be pretty, cook well, keep the house clean, keep the clothes arranged and make sure the man is comfortable. You have to have right words, the right attitude and the right answers to cheer him up, in order to keep him.

Gary:

Apparently you too grew up in the 1950s!

Salon Participant:

All of that makes us women very dependable because in some part of the story, we were taught that we cannot make money, that a man is the only thing, and that it all takes a lot of work to keep the relationship. This is where I cut myself off and divorce me. So, I've decided not to be involved in a relationship ever again.

Gary:

Now, let's see. Is that a decision, a judgment, a computation or a conclusion? Yes, you make those. That's not being the pragmatist of the feminine reality.

Everything that is times a godzillion, will you destroy and uncreate it all? Right and Wrong, Good and Bad, POD and POC, All Nine, Shorts, Boys and Beyonds.

Salon Participant:

That's why I am on this call. I still don't want to have a relationship. I want to be me and enjoy myself. I don't want to take care of anyone, including my children. But I want to clear this area. I am sure it will open a highway that I am shutting off now, because I keep doing things for others rather than putting me first. I still don't know how to think of me first and do for me first.

Gary:

First of all, it's not about thinking of you first or doing for you first. Can you be first in oneness? That will be a *no.* It's about being aware that every choice creates. When you choose, ask: Will this be good for me *and* everyone else?

If you are trying to be first in oneness, you are in competition. But who are you in competition with? How many of you are in competition with men instead of being in a cohesive union with men?

Everything that is times a godzillion, will you destroy and uncreate it all? Right and Wrong, Good and Bad, POD and POC, All Nine, Shorts, Boys and Beyonds.

Salon Participant:

How can I get rid of the point of view that I am fat and ugly? I have been POD and POCing it, but it still sticks. And what is my reaction to resist hearing "I love you"?

Gary:

If you actually heard "I love you," you'd have to receive—and you'd rather not receive. You'd rather hold onto.

What stupidity are you using to create the physiological reality you are choosing? Everything that is times a godzillion, will you destroy and uncreate it all? Right and Wrong, Good and Bad, POD and POC, All Nine, Shorts, Boys and Beyonds.

Here is a good process for anyone who has a question about his or her body—because you have chosen a physiological reality. You have created it, so you think you have to keep it. No, you don't have to keep it. You have choice.

What physical actualization of physiological reality beyond this physical reality am I now capable of generating, creating and instituting? Everything that doesn't allow for that to show up times a godzillion, will you destroy and uncreate it all? Right and Wrong, Good and Bad, POD and POC, All Nine, Shorts, Boys and Beyonds.

So how are you all doing?

Salon Participant:

Awesome. This is really awesome.

Gary:

Great! I am grateful all you ladies are here. I would like to get you to the place where you can have you as the kindness to you that you can be because you have this idiocy that you have to be kind to others—and not to you. You have to be kind to others *and* you at the same time. Not for any reason, just because it makes your life easier, and that's pragmatic feminism.

I want you to become pragmatic feminine people, not feminists, not chauvinists. If you hate men, you are doing chauvinism towards men. None of that is really necessary.

I want to stop this place where men and women fight one another. Then women won't have to make their men prove that they are brave, and men won't have to prove their women are wrong, and everyone can have a sense that they actually have a choice. War would be a nice thing to end. We may be able to do it between all of us. Thank you all so much.

2

Choosing to Alter Reality

*What if you are capable of altering reality—
and you are not choosing that?*

Gary:

Hello ladies.

Soul Mates and Twin Flames

Dain and I did a show on the Puja Radio Network today about soul mates and twin flames, which is very funny, because the metaphysical community considers soul mates and twin flames to be the proper thing to happen in this reality. The amount of charge on them was freaking unbelievable. I am going to use the processes we used on the show today with you guys because I think they are going to help you all.

What stupidity are you using to create the twin flame, soul mate, significant other, mythical creature, prince or princess, perfect person for you and perfect complement for you are you choosing? Everything that is times a godzillion, will you destroy and uncreate it all? Right and Wrong, Good and Bad, POD and POC, All Nine, Shorts, Boys and Beyonds.

Apparently when you were kids, some of you read way too many stories about Cinderella, Rapunzel, and all those creatures you were supposed to become but you never could become because you weren't as repulsive as any of those creatures were.

What stupidity are you using to create the twin flame, soul mate, significant other, mythical creature, prince or princess, perfect person for you and perfect complement for you are you choosing? Everything that is times a godzillion, will you destroy and uncreate it all? Right and Wrong, Good and Bad, POD and POC, All Nine, Shorts, Boys and Beyonds.

This is the idea that the purpose of relationship is finding the perfect one for you. Would an infinite being truly have a perfect complement—or would an infinite being have multiples of those?

How many of you have had multiples who you keep trying to find the perfect one of? Everything that is times a godzillion, will you destroy and uncreate it all? Right and Wrong, Good and Bad, POD and POC, All Nine, Shorts, Boys and Beyonds.

In reality, you are looking for the perfect one who doesn't exist. Would that require you to judge you—or to choose you?

Salon Participant:

Judge.

Gary:

Everywhere you have judged you for not finding the perfect one for you, will you destroy and uncreate all that? Right and Wrong, Good and Bad, POD and POC, All Nine, Shorts, Boys and Beyonds.

Live From Loving—*Not* Love

In the conversation Dain and I had on the show today, I realized that the opposite of love is not hate. The opposite of love is judgment. Love does not require hate as its opposition; it requires judgment as an oppositional point of view.

The oppositional forces in our life are 1) love and judgment, 2) caring and hate, and 3) stupidity and receiving. Those three oppositional forces create confusion and do not allow you to choose something that works for you.

Salon Participant:

When you say love and judgment are oppositional forces, are you saying that because I have love in my life, I have judgment? Could you explain this?

Gary:

Loving—not *love*—is what you want to live from. As long as you are loving, you cannot have judgment. When you are truly loving, you have gratitude for what the person does. You don't judge the other person or yourself.

Don't try to live from *love*. Live from *loving*. When you function from loving, caring and receiving, you don't function from judgment. In order to stop loving, you have to do judgment; otherwise, you are just loving.

Gary:

What stupidity are you using to create the oppositional forces of love and judgment, caring and hate, and stupidity and receiving are you choosing? Everything that is times a godzillion, will you destroy and uncreate it all? Right and Wrong, Good and Bad, POD and POC, All Nine, Shorts, Boys and Beyonds.

This process is a little more intense than I thought it would be. Let's run it again.

What stupidity are you using to create the oppositional forces of love and judgment, caring and hate, and stupidity and receiving are you choosing? Everything that is times a godzillion, will you destroy and uncreate it all? Right and Wrong, Good and Bad, POD and POC, All Nine, Shorts, Boys and Beyonds.

Salon Participant:

I have not had a relationship without judgment.

Gary:

Most of you haven't, because relationship without judgment is not "normal" in this reality. Why do we consider relationship with judgment more real than relationship without judgment? You know why? Because relationship with judgment is more intense. We define that intensity as love, and we look for that rather than the joy and possibility that loving is. True loving is to embrace the joy and possibility—not the judgment.

Salon Participant:

I have a partner who doesn't judge me according to what this reality sees relationships should be, but I tend to create judgments with him to make our relationship fit into what this reality sees a relationship should look like.

Gary:

Good call. That's what every one of us does in order to create the sense of love according to this reality. It's about the intensity of judgment, not about the awareness of possibility we create with our partners.

Everything that all of you have done to create that in you and your partner, will you destroy and uncreate that? Right and Wrong, Good and Bad, POD and POC, All Nine, Shorts, Boys and Beyonds.

Love is a conclusion; *loving* is an action. You have to stop trying to function from love and instead function from loving. When you are with somebody, look at what would be a loving act today, an action of loving today. Asking, "How can I express my love today?" is a loving action.

Recognize that *loving* is an active particle in the world and that *love,* as a judgment, is by necessity, a completed particle in the world. If you are in the act of loving, you cannot be in the act of judging.

If you love, you are operating from the idea that you have completed everything. You think, "That's enough. That's all I have to do." I see people do this a lot. They say, "I love this person," and then they stop creating the relationship any further than that. They stop being in the action of loving. They have loved; therefore, it's complete and they don't have to do anything else.

When you do completion—"I love him"—then it's a done deal, and no creation happens from that point forward. All you can have is love/hate. You can't have total joy and possibility.

When you say, "I love this person," what do you mean, anyway? One of the greatest difficulties is that love has eight trillion godzillion definitions.

All the definitions you have about love that have nothing to do with loving, will you destroy and uncreate it all? Right and Wrong, Good and Bad, POD and POC, All Nine, Shorts, Boys and Beyonds.

Salon Participant:

Often when I talk to people about relationships, they describe a whole string of what's not working. I ask, "What's the value of this? Why are you holding on to this?"

They say, "But I love him."

I ask, "What does that mean? I don't understand." Can you explain this?

Gary:

Most people decide that when they love, everything should turn out right, but the idea that you love and it turns out right is a judgment. It's not an awareness.

What awareness are you missing to create the judgment you are stressing? Everything that is times a godzillion, will you destroy and uncreate it all? Right and Wrong, Good and Bad, POD and POC, All Nine, Shorts, Boys and Beyonds.

You have to start creating from the pragmatic point of view and ask: What would I like to create? Do you ever look at that when you are in a relationship? I never did. I looked at, "Oh, I want to make her happy. I want her to know how much I love her," which means "I lack of her knowing how much I love her." All I was doing was feeding the lack. How many of you have spent your life trying to feed the lack of relationships instead of the possibilities of relationships?

Everything that is times a godzillion, will you destroy and uncreate it all? Right and Wrong, Good and Bad, POD and POC, All Nine, Shorts, Boys and Beyonds.

Salon Participant:

It always seems to me that when people say, "I love this person," what they really mean is, "I need something and I'm expecting to get it from the person I have decided I require." But when you talk about loving, it has the energy of an outpouring of gratitude rather than a "give me" quality.

Salon Participant:

What you just said about love and loving was brilliant. Thanks.

Gary:

I want to thank all of you for your questions, because with them, you have opened the door to a level of possibilities that have never existed for the women on this planet. Please know this. You are opening a door to greater possibilities for men and women than have ever existed on this planet Earth by the fact that you are willing to look at these things and change the stupidity you are functioning from. This is what I wanted to create with these calls, and this is what is happening. I am grateful for each of you for being here.

Salon Participant:

Thank you!

Gary:

What stupidity are you using to create the oppositional forces of love and judgment, caring and hate, and stupidity and receiving are you choosing? Everything that is times a godzillion, will you destroy and uncreate it all? Right and Wrong, Good and Bad, POD and POC, All Nine, Shorts, Boys and Beyonds.

"What Is This?"

Salon Participant:

I have been looking at relationships between men and women. It takes two to tango, right? When there are judgments, does it matter whether it's the men or the women judging? What does it look like if I have a relationship with somebody and it brings up judgments? What is my role there?

Gary:

Most people don't get that they have to create from *what is* and not what they think *ought to be.* You have to function from "What is this?" not "What judgment do I have of this?"

It's not about the judgments; it's about loving what expands your life. It's about pragmatic relationships. It's a whole different universe. Pragmatic relationship is:

- What's going to work here?
- How do I make this work for me, the other person and everyone involved?

If you don't function from pragmatic relationship, you function from judge-able relationships, which are about "I love him" or "I don't love him." It's like pulling the petals off a flower and saying,

"He loves me; he loves me not." You pull off the petals to come to a conclusion about whether he loves you or doesn't love you.

What if you had a relationship that was loving, caring and receiving—and not unaware, not hating and not judging? But that's not how this reality works. Without that judgment, hate and stupidity, you couldn't have fallen in love at all. You couldn't have trauma and drama and all the things considered the most valuable products of this reality.

You have to create a pragmatic relationship that works for you. Instead of doing that, you try to create relationships based on somebody else's point of view.

Everything you have done to create your relationships based on other people's points of view and not your own, will you destroy and uncreate it all? Right and Wrong, Good and Bad, POD and POC, All Nine, Shorts, Boys and Beyonds.

You all have been doing a lot of that!

Salon Participant:

Are you at a point in your reality where you are not judging anymore—or you are instantly aware when you judge and do you POD and POC it?

Gary:

Mostly I'm instantly aware of where I start judging.

A while back I looked at having a relationship with somebody who was perfect for me, and I asked a question, "Would the relationship work for her?" I said, "Wow, no!" because what would work for me and what would work for her were two different things. That's looking at a pragmatic relationship: Is this really going to work for the other person? It's not: Is this going to work for me?

Most of us do this. We look at a relationship in terms of "Can I make it work for the other person?" or "How can I make it work for me?" as the two points of view. What if there is a third point of view you could have?

Everything that doesn't allow you to perceive, know, be and receive the extremely pragmatic points of view that would allow everything to work for everyone, will you destroy and uncreate it all? Right and Wrong, Good and Bad, POD and POC, All Nine, Shorts, Boys and Beyonds.

Salon Participant:

In getting to that third point of view, I guess both parties should come up with questions to see what would work for them?

Gary:

Only one person has to come up with questions, and that person has to be willing to look at:

- What is this?
- What can I do with it?
- Can I change it?
- How can I change it?

Say you decide to get into a relationship with somebody. They have a family. Is the family involved in the relationship?

Salon Participant:

Yes.

Gary:

Does the family have a point of view about relationships? Oh yeah! Do they project and expect certain things out of you because of your relationships?

Salon Participant:

Oh, yes.

Gary:

So, do you actually have true choice—or do you have to alter your choices based on how you have to include other people in your relationship?

Salon Participant:

The latter.

Creating Future

Gary:

You have to be willing to recognize how every choice is going to create the future you would like to create. Most of us never look at creating future because this is not a reality for most everybody on this planet.

I started reading a book about risk called *Against the Gods*. It talks about the idea that risk is created by certain things and that there are *probabilities* that will create the future—rather than *possibilities* that will create the future.

Probability is the idea that you can determine mathematically what is most likely to occur in agreement with everybody else's point of view. It is based on your judgment and everybody else's judgments rather than the idea that choice and possibility can actually alter reality.

You have to recognize that choice literally creates possibilities. What if you are capable of altering reality—and you are not choosing that?

How many places have you chosen to avoid creation based on choice of possibility in favor of the probability of what everybody else will accept, align and agree with? Everything that is times a godzillion, will you destroy and uncreate it all? Right and Wrong, Good and Bad, POD and POC, All Nine, Shorts, Boys and Beyonds.

If you are choosing from possibilities, you can see that there could be a different creation that has not yet existed. I am asking you ladies to be willing to create beyond the limitations of this reality.

"What is the possibility here of a different future?" is a point of view that does not occur in relationships, sex and copulation, or in your own life. Here is a brand new process I have never used on anybody. You are the first.

What stupidity are you using to create the probabilities of actualizing future are you choosing? Everything that is times a godzillion, will you destroy and uncreate it all? Right and Wrong, Good and Bad, POD and POC, All Nine, Shorts, Boys and Beyonds.

Your Point of View Creates Your Reality

We make choices without realizing how those choices create our future in every way. Every choice we make creates. I have been talking for a long time about how choice is creation. Choice is not a rightness or wrongness but a creation. It is the creating element of all things on planet Earth. Every choice you make creates something. Your point of view creates your reality; your reality does not create your point of view. Have you ever chosen to have a relationship with somebody who was not good for you?

Salon Participant:

When you talk about all this, what's coming up for me is the energy of space that I haven't been willing to choose. I don't choose from space because I don't have a reason, justification or clue of what it's going to create.

Gary:

Yes, because you are trying to look for the probability.

Salon Participant:

Yes, wow! Thank you.

Gary:

You, as a woman, are no less than a man. You are just different than a man. Not in a bad way, not in a good way, just different. You have equal choices. In fact, you have more choice than men do— because a man, in order to prove he is a man, must prove he is not feminine and not gay. I know that doesn't make sense to you, but it's true. I had a lady come to my office the other day and she said, "Dain is gay, isn't he?"

I said, "No, actually, he is not. What makes you think he is gay?"

She said, "When I cut my finger, he put a Band-Aid on it, and he was so kind and loving about it. He couldn't possibly be straight, because a straight man would just slam the Band-Aid on you and say, "How's that?"

Because the man is caring, he is gay? No. That's a total judgment and a decision, and unfortunately it is not true. Trust me, there would be a lot of men who would be glad for Dain to be gay, but he is not. You, as women, if you are not totally kind and caring, are not considered feminine. That's just insanity.

Make Every Choice as a Source of Possibility

Salon Participant:

Are you saying that as a woman, acknowledging that I have more choice is acknowledging that every choice is a creation that will open up things for me?

Gary:

Yes, every choice will open the doors to possibility. Every choice creates multiple possibilities. Every possibility and choice creates a set of possibilities. Every time you choose, you create a set of possibilities.

Just by imagining the idea, you create choice and ten possibilities open up. Then, you choose again and another ten possibilities open up. In the first, one choice creates a set of possibilities and in the second, another set of possibilities tie together two of the choices you created as possibilities. That's how you start creating the cobwebs of the future to actualize, to come into reality the existence of a different possibility.

When you start to perceive those places where multiplicities have connected to one another every time you create a choice, you see what contributes to creating a line of different possibility to a different future that perhaps never existed for you or anybody you know.

Salon Participant:

Thank you, that was brilliant. When you said that when you make a choice, ten possibilities show up and you choose one of those ten possibilities and they tie together, there was such a strong energy on that. Whatever that is, I am not willing to know what it and the web of it all is. I like to pretend that I don't know what I really know.

Gary:

Let's try this:

What stupidity are you using to create the lack of awareness of the web of possibilities that the choice you choose creates are you choosing? Everything that is times a godzillion, will you destroy and uncreate it all? Right and Wrong, Good and Bad, POD and POC, All Nine, Shorts, Boys and Beyonds.

Every choice creates a multiple set of possibilities. We keep trying to come to conclusion, thinking that's going to solidify the choice we make and create a "correct" point of view to get a result we desire.

All of you have had the experience of getting into a relationship with somebody, taking a fixed point of view, and having it fall apart. Why do you think it fell apart? It fell apart because you weren't willing to create and generate beyond the choice, "I love him."

When you find a so-called soul mate or see someone as your significant other, you create from a strange point of view that has nothing to do with you, and you are no longer able to create what's possible.

That's the place where you make your choice the end of creation. Don't make any choice as an end of creation. Make every choice as a source of possibility.

What stupidity are you using to create the twin flame, soul mate, significant other, mythical creature, prince and princess, perfect person for you and perfect complement for you are you choosing? Everything that is times a godzillion, will you destroy and uncreate it all? Right and Wrong, Good and Bad, POD and POC, All Nine, Shorts, Boys and Beyonds.

What stupidity are you using to create the blood, sweat and tears of relationship are you choosing? Everything that is times a godzillion, will you destroy and uncreate it all? Right and Wrong, Good and Bad, POD and POC, All Nine, Shorts, Boys and Beyonds.

A lot of you have made yourself wrong for not choosing to have a relationship. What if not choosing a relationship was the smartest thing you ever chose for you?

What stupidity are you using to create the wrongness of not choosing a relationship are you choosing? Everything that is times a godzillion, will you destroy and uncreate it all? Right and Wrong, Good and Bad, POD and POC, All Nine, Shorts, Boys and Beyonds.

You have the point of view that you're wrong for not having a relationship because your mother or your sisters or your girlfriends are always encouraging you to have a bad relationship. You don't really want a relationship, which is why you keep choosing bad relationships. If you truly wanted a relationship, you'd create a good one.

If you don't really want a relationship, there's nothing wrong with it. You're not wrong to not want a relationship!

Relationship is a concept; it's not a reality. You don't need somebody to complete you. You are complete as a soul unto yourself. You don't need a relationship, family, children, group or any of that kind of stuff to complete you. You are a complete entity, a being unto thyself. To thine own self be true.

Everything you have done to make you not true, will you destroy and uncreate it? Right and Wrong, Good and Bad, POD and POC, All Nine, Shorts, Boys and Beyonds.

So, What Is Relationship?

Salon Participant:

Can I ask you what relationship means to you?

Gary:

Relationship is a pragmatic living together that expands both of your realities and both of your agendas. Relationship is some place where you can live comfortably together without judgment. It's a place you can live together in the possibilities, not in the necessities of, "You are not cleaning your share," "You are not doing your share," "You are not sharing." Sharing is a concept that creates a space where you judge someone, not where you live with someone.

The moment you go to judgment, you, as a being, cease to exist. A being and judgment cannot exist in the same universe. A being is an element of gratitude; a judgment is an element of destruction. You cannot have gratitude and destruction in the same universe. One is creation; the other is destruction.

Salon Participant:

It's almost like I want to get rid of the word *relationship.* I want to call it something else. I don't want to have "relationship."

Gary:

"I don't want to have relationship" means you don't lack of a relationship, which means you have a whole lot of relationships, and most of them are bad.

Salon Participant:

Yes.

Gary:

So, why are they bad?

Salon Participant:

I am not showing up. I am not being everything I am in any of my relationships.

Gary:

Why are you not being everything you are in your relationships?

Salon Participant:

I am not received by other people or they can't get me.

Gary:

Why do you expect them to get you? What would it be like if you were willing to have everything that's possible for you without a need to have anybody else?

Salon Participant:

That would be awesome.

Gary:

Yeah, that would create something entirely different. You have to be willing to look at a different possibility.

What stupidity are you using to create a lack of a totally pragmatic relational reality are you choosing? Everything that is times a godzillion, will you destroy and uncreate it all? Right and Wrong, Good and Bad, POD and POC, All Nine, Shorts, Boys and Beyonds.

I want all of you to put this on a loop and listen to it for at least thirty days. If you do this, it will clear that area and you will erase your stuck points and go on to other possibilities with greater ease. Put this clearing on your computer and play it low over and over again while you're sleeping. It's kind of like subliminal programming—except it's subliminal *deprogramming*.

What stupidity am I using to create a lack of a totally pragmatic relational reality am I choosing? Everything that is times a godzillion, I destroy and uncreate it all. Right and Wrong, Good and Bad, POD and POC, All Nine, Shorts, Boys and Beyonds.

What stupidity are you using to create the twin flame, soul mate, significant other, mythical creature, prince and princess, perfect person for you and perfect complement for you are you choosing? Everything that is times a godzillion, will you destroy and uncreate it all? Right and Wrong, Good and Bad, POD and POC, All Nine, Shorts, Boys and Beyonds.

Copulation by Choice

I am going to say something that may be totally offensive to many of you. Most of you are looking for a relationship—and what your body actually wants is copious amounts of copulation. Your body would rather have copulation than relationship, but you have determined that being female requires relationship, not copulation.

Everything that is times a godzillion, will you destroy and uncreate it all? Right and Wrong, Good and Bad, POD and POC, All Nine, Shorts, Boys and Beyonds.

Salon Participant:

Why do I resist copulation so much?

Gary:

Have you resisted it?

Salon Participant:

Yeah.

Gary:

Because if you were willing to have lots of copulation, you wouldn't be considered a female. In this reality, desire of copulation is a masculine trait, not a feminine trait.

Everything you determined and decided about that, will you destroy and uncreate it all? Right and Wrong, Good and Bad, POD and POC, All Nine, Shorts, Boys and Beyonds.

Salon Participant:

I have a question about copulation. All my life, I have had the desire of copulation until I came to Access Consciousness and realized it was not a necessity but a choice, and the desire kind of fizzled. I lost interest.

Gary:

Copulation by choice, rather than the necessity of copulation. The more you begin to realize that people use judgment to create copulation, the more there is sense that somehow you are missing something if you go directly to copulation and you do it without judgment.

Salon Participant:

I don't understand.

Gary:

Let's say you have a man in your life who you would like to copulate with and you are not doing judgment. If he is doing judgment to create his hard-on, then he cannot get a hard-on, because you are not doing enough judgment of the wrongness of what you are doing to get him sexually excited.

So, you have a choice: How much judgment do you have to put into his universe to make him get hard—or how much control do you have to use to get him so excited he can't stop himself?

Everything that brought up or let down will you destroy and uncreate it all? Right and Wrong, Good and Bad, POD and POC, All Nine, Shorts, Boys and Beyonds.

Judgment is a system of control. Do you all get that? You have a choice. You can let the person do judgment, you can create judgment for him, or you can create enough control that his judgment is not positioned to overcome your demand of his body—not him, his body.

Salon Participant:

What kind of control are you talking about here?

Gary:

You have to be willing to look at him and ask, "What's it going to take to control this guy so he is so freaking horny that he has no choice but to deliver anything I want any time I want it?"

There is a particular kind of energy you have to be. It requires the man to deliver whether he desires it or not. You have to override his system of desire rather than buying in to what will make him desire you for. That's the level of control women have been told they are not allowed to have—and they shouldn't have.

Everywhere you bought that you should not have that control, you should not do that control, you cannot have that control, you have no idea what that control is and even if you have that control, you wouldn't choose it because that would be so not feminine, will you destroy and uncreate all that? Right and Wrong, Good and Bad, POD and POC, All Nine, Shorts, Boys and Beyonds.

Salon Participant:

Is that what has been judged as domination—and that's why we are excluded?

Gary:

Yes, you have tried not to be the dominant species because you have been told that men are the dominant species. Is that really true? And is there really dominant species? Or is there a moment in which each of us needs to be dominant according to our needs, desires and requires?

Everything that doesn't allow you to choose that will you destroy and uncreate it all? Right and Wrong, Good and Bad, POD and POC, All Nine, Shorts, Boys and Beyonds.

Total Sexualness

For example, those women out there who think it would be fun to do some gay play, please be willing to do that if that's what your body says is going to work for you. You cannot have the point of view, "There is gay and there is straight." That's a judgment, and if you have judgment, you can't be loving, which means you can't have caring.

You have to get that there is a whole world available to you as a creature of no judgment. Total sexualness is an omnisexual reality, which would be "I have no real sexuality. I have no point of view. I could do anything." You could also say it's pan-sexuality, which means you do all of it. Androgyny is not omnisexual. It's not omnisexuality, as that would be a judgment.

It's about being the sexual energy you and your body are, which is about being. It's a choice; it's what you choose to receive.

Everything that is times a godzillion, will you destroy and uncreate it all? Right and Wrong, Good and Bad, POD and POC, All Nine, Shorts, Boys and Beyonds.

Salon Participant:

What would it take to stop harshly judging women who let their spouses or partners make decisions and who always go with what men think is right over their own awareness or desires? What contribution can I be to changing this? And an infinite being would choose that for what reason? Do you think that's a judgment?

Gary:

No, darling, it's not a judgment; it's an awareness. I love you, and you are aware. It is insane to divorce you to make your partner happy. Is that making you happy? If it is, become more of it. If it isn't, then do something different.

Everything that is times a godzillion, will you destroy and uncreate it all? Right and Wrong, Good and Bad, POD and POC, All Nine, Shorts, Boys and Beyonds.

Your Body Has a Point of View

Salon Participant:

Why, as an infinite being, do I have a dual personality, my spirit me and the physical me?

Gary:

It is not a dual personality. It is just that your body has one point of view and you have another. You are not willing to see that your body has a different point of view than you. Your body is inside of you; you are not inside of your body. So, it's not a dual personality. It's that your body experiences life from a physiological perspective, and you are experiencing it from a psychological perspective. Here are a couple of processes for all of you to put on a loop:

What stupidity am I using to create the lack of physiological reality I am choosing? Everything that is times a godzillion, will you destroy and uncreate it all? Right and Wrong, Good and Bad, POD and POC, All Nine, Shorts, Boys and Beyonds.

What physical actualization of a totally different physiological reality am I now capable of creating, generating and instituting? Everything that doesn't allow for that to show up times a godzillion, will you destroy and uncreate it all? Right and Wrong, Good and Bad, POD and POC, All Nine, Shorts, Boys and Beyonds.

Salon Participant:

I would love to regenerate my reproductive system for body health and more pleasurable sex. What question can I ask?

Gary:

Why are you choosing for body health and more pleasurable sex? Why aren't you going for something that would create a life that is more joyful and more fun for you? That's a question.

What can I be, do, have, create or generate today that will create more fun, ease, sex and pleasure in my life for all eternity? Everything that doesn't allow for that to show up times a godzillion, will you destroy and uncreate it all? Right and Wrong, Good and Bad, POD and POC, All Nine, Shorts, Boys and Beyonds.

Sex and Receiving

Salon Participant:

Is it because we divorce parts of ourselves that we lose interest in sex?

Gary:

It's because you lose part of receiving. Sex can only occur when you are totally receiving.

What part of receiving are you diminishing with such intensity that you are eliminating the sex and joy of copulation you could be choosing? Everything that is times a godzillion, will you destroy and uncreate it all? Right and Wrong, Good and Bad, POD and POC, All Nine, Shorts, Boys and Beyonds.

Salon Participant:

Is it a choice I am making, not wanting or desiring to have sex?

Gary:

Yes, it's a choice, and it's usually based on the place where you decided or concluded that if you have sex with a particular person, you have to have a monogamous relationship. Monogamous means one. If you are in a monogamous relationship, there is only one in the relationship, which is the other person, not you. You want a polygamous relationship in which you are included in the relationship.

Abusive Relationships

Salon Participant:

Please talk about how to recognize when a relationship becomes abusive, especially when it gets so subtle that you may not recognize it as abuse.

Gary:

That's pretty much the way it is with all abusive relationships. When you come to the conclusion that you love somebody, you never ask questions as to what they are doing.

When somebody criticizes you, that is not loving. It's a conclusion, not a possibility. You have to go to awareness and be willing to ask questions. I was in a relationship where I was judged every day. I actually tried to go to a hypnotist so I would stop withdrawing every time this person touched me. Every time she would reach out for me, I would withdraw. I didn't know why I was withdrawing.

It was only after the relationship ended that I realized it wasn't me withdrawing; it was my body withdrawing from the abuse. You have to be really clear about where you have been abused in a relationship. When you think you no longer wish to have sex or you use the other person's judgments to create sexual desire, you are in an abusive relationship. When it is more fun to be with other people than it is to be with your spouse or your partner, you are in an abusive relationship. You are getting into an abusive relationship when you think the other person is smarter than you. No one is smarter or more aware than you. Ever. Ever. Ever. Please get this.

Salon Participant:

Sometimes when I touch my partner or he touches me, I feel a painful, intense sensation in my hands, arms and body.

Gary:

Is it pain? Or is it a level of intensity or awareness that you don't want to have? Are you aware of the pain in his body? Do you want to have that awareness?

You are trying to avoid the awareness, which is why you call it pain. Whenever you label something as pain or suffering, as a problem or as trauma or drama, you are trying to avoid it. Instead of avoiding it, you need to ask:

- What is this?
- What can I do with this?
- Can I change it?
- How can I change it?

That's the place you have to go to. What if you knew that the only way you could change it was to have sex with him? Would you be willing to do that?

Salon Participant:

Would that be caring for me?

Gary:

What does this have to do with the Kingdom of Me and the Kingdom of We?

Salon Participant:

What is the difference between the Kingdom of Me and the Kingdom of We?

Gary:

The Kingdom of Me and the Kingdom of We are totally different universes. The Kingdom of *Me* is where you try to come to conclusion. The Kingdom of *We* is the awareness of how each and every thing will interact with another thing.

Salon Participant:

Is that what I'm doing when I try to be responsible with everything?

Gary:

You're doing the Kingdom of Mc. You're saying you're the only person who exists in the universe, and the Earth revolves around you. How is that working for you? You can choose something else.

Sexual Healing

Salon Participant:

Can we talk more about Kingdom of We with sex?

Gary:

A lot of you don't want to know this, but you are sexual healers. If you felt lighter when you heard me say that, you are a sexual healer. You will start to feel better if you acknowledge it.

When you don't acknowledge that you are a sexual healer, you start to use that as a weapon against you to create pain. You have to acknowledge it. If you don't, instead of choosing a relationship with somebody who will make things better, you will always choose a man who needs sexual healing, and you exclude you in the computation of your own reality.

Salon Participant:

Are you saying that if you acknowledge you are a sexual healer, you won't choose somebody who you have to heal?

Gary:

Yes.

Salon Participant:

How does that work?

Gary:

Your judgment is that you shouldn't be a sexual healer. When you don't acknowledge you are a sexual healer, what you will find exciting are people who need sexual healing. You will tend to make the choice to have sex with somebody rather than looking at what else is possible. When you have a capacity for sexual healing and you don't acknowledge it, you always have to pick somebody who uses you and takes from you, not somebody you choose to be with.

When you acknowledge you are a sexual healer, you can ask:

- Does this person need sexual healing?

- Is this the only choice I have?

Salon Participant:

Say you acknowledge that you're a sexual healer and you meet somebody you would like to have sex with. You ask, "Does this person require sexual healing?" If you get yes, you ask, "What else is possible?" Is it possible to have copulation with that person without giving him the sexual healing he requires?

Gary:

No. The way you asked the question was the weasel clause you tried to put in it. The question you didn't ask is: Do I really want to do this?

Here is an example of how asking questions work in subtle ways. A lady called me and said, "I can get you in to see Obama."

I said *no.*

She said, "It's only such-and-such amount of money."

I said *no.*

She asked, "Why?"

I said, "I don't have the money to do that."

She said, "I will loan you the money if you want."

I said, "That's not the point."

She asked, "If you met him, would that change the world?"

I got a yes, and I said, "Okay, I will do it." After paying the money, I went to Austin, Texas with the idea of meeting President Obama. But our plane was delayed three hours, and we couldn't make it in time to see him.

I said to myself, "Oh, this was the energy I was aware of in the first place, but I didn't acknowledge it when I went to the questions, 'Would meeting him change the world? Would my paying the money be okay?' I didn't ask, 'Will I actually be able to get there?'" It was actually a no from the beginning, but I didn't notice because I wasn't willing to ask the extra questions.

That's the reason you have to ask the question, "If I have sex with this person, will that actually heal him?" He might need it, but it doesn't mean he is going to receive it. Do most people you have sex with actually receive you—or do they take from you? They think you are going to heal them, so they are not contributing. You have to get that you have the ability to heal sexually and that your need of healing others doesn't necessarily mean they are going to receive it.

"Good Sex" vs. Expansive Sex

Salon Participant:

After sex, my husband bounces around and I just want to get back into bed.

Gary:

For him, sex is generative, and for you, it is a completion. You are more like a man. How much adrenaline are you using to create sexual orgasm? A lot, a little, or megatons?

Salon Participant:

Megatons comes up, but that doesn't make sense.

Gary:

Everything that is times a godzillion, will you destroy and uncreate it all? Right and Wrong, Good and Bad, POD and POC, All Nine, Shorts, Boys and Beyonds.

It doesn't make sense because it's not about *logical* sense. Most people create orgasm by creating an adrenaline pump. Apparently your husband is not creating an adrenaline pump to create the orgasm. He is expanding out and becoming more present with his life. Sex and copulation is the gift you can be if you are willing to be it, but if you are trying to fulfill his needs or do something in particular, the easiest way to reach "orgasm" is by creating an adrenaline pump, which exhausts your body. That's what most people have learned is "good sex".

Adrenaline is the greatest source for creating contraction. It's the way you supposedly get into flight or fight mode. If you contract, you withdraw into yourself so you're ready to fight everyone else. And if you use contraction to create orgasm, you're not with your partner. You separate from your partner, and you're not expanding his sex and your sex. You're contracting from the sex in order to create the completion of it as though sex should be a completion. When you do that, at the end of the sex, rather than feeling really energized and ready to go to work, you get exhausted and fall asleep. Most men have learned that's what they're supposed to do by watching porn flicks. They're taught that if they contract, they create the orgasm—and then they fall asleep, which is infuriating to most women. Whereas, if you function from a place of expanding out to achieve orgasm, the end result is you're ready to go to work, you're ready to get up and play.

Everything that is times a godzillion, will you destroy and uncreate it all? Right and Wrong, Good and Bad, POD and POC, All Nine, Shorts, Boys and Beyonds.

Salon Participant:

Could you talk more about the expansive element of sex, Gary?

Gary:

The expansive element of sex is about recognizing that the purpose of sex is not creating the adrenaline that causes orgasm but creating the orgasmic quality of life and living, which is about the joy and choice of possibilities.

You not only have to get you off but you also have to get your partner off as well. What if you were looking to get your partner to a place of greater possibility through sex? Sex and copulation should be about creating greater possibilities, not about getting completion.

What you get with the adrenaline pump has been sold by the French as the best you can get.

Salon Participant:

When I do confrontation or judgment, it seems like I am not acknowledging that I am a healer.

Gary:

If you are not acknowledging total awareness, you will try to use confrontation to create awareness in others. What if you were totally aware and in question instead of coming to conclusion or judgment? You are trying to enforce receiving when you come to that place of confrontation. A lot of people do that in sex and copulation as well as relationships. They tend to enforce awareness through confrontation and they try to use force to get the other person to receive. You have to ask the question: What can this person receive that I have to offer?

You have to be willing for your consciousness to permeate reality. In Dain's book, *Being You, Changing the World,* he talks about how when you are totally being you, you permeate the space and change everybody around you. What if you did that in sex and copulation, relationships and everything else in life? What if you were permeating and being all of you into a different reality?

Salon Participant:

I have had moments of that permeation and they were delicious.

Gary:

Can I ask you a question? Why do you not live the delicious life all the time?

Salon Participant:

Judgments came up. Judgments keep me from living the delicious life.

Gary:

Judgments are just judgments. Choose deliciousness whether anyone else chooses it or not. Choose the deliciousness of living instead of other people's judgments, because the deliciousness of living and the permeability of consciousness go beyond judgments and create possibilities. It's a choice one has to make, not a place one has to live. When you function from judgment, you go to the place where one has to live—not to the choice of possibility.

Everything that is times a godzillion, will you destroy and uncreate it all? Right and Wrong, Good and Bad, POD and POC, All Nine, Shorts, Boys and Beyonds.

Thank you ladies, you are awesome. I would really like you to get how phenomenal you are, because you can change the world being that. Talk to you next week. Bye!

3

Realizing Who You Truly Are

You chose a woman's body.
Does that mean you are a woman? Or are you an infinite being
with a woman's body?
If you're an infinite being with a woman's body,
shouldn't you take advantage of what that gives you as a weapon
and as a tool?

Change vs. Doing Something Different

Gary:

Hello ladies. I'd like to begin by talking about the difference between *change* and *doing something different,* because unfortunately for most women, when they have a relationship, they try to fix or change what doesn't work with the man, rather than doing something entirely different

One day Dain was talking about a situation in life. He asked, "What am I going to do to change this?"

I said, "Why would you bother to change it? It's not working. Do something different."

Dain said, "You don't do that. You fix what isn't working."

I said, "What?!"

This conversation changed all of Access Consciousness, because I had been functioning from the assumption that what people wanted was something different, not that they wanted to fix or change something that wasn't working.

As a female of the species, you were trained that you have dolls, you change their clothes and then they're different. Well, they are not different. They just have different clothes.

Women have learned to look for *change*—not *different*. When you have a situation with a mate, you will try to get him to change. You never ask the question that will create what you want, which is: What can I be or do different that would make all this a different reality? It's about functioning from a different place.

Salon Participant:

What's the difference between the definition of *change* and the definition of *difference*?

Gary:

Change your position in your chair.

Salon Participant:

To me that means move.

Gary:

Change is about move. *Different* is about a different possibility, a different reality, a different choice and a different question.

If you want to create a different reality with someone, you have to be or do whatever you have to be or do different in order to create a different reality. So, with a relationship in particular, you ask: What can I be or do different to create a different reality?

It's not about getting him to change so he's happy. If you have the idea that you have to get somebody to change, you are trying to make him happy, or you're trying to make him sad or you're trying to make him confront something. No, you don't want to make him *change;* you want to create a different reality—a different possibility.

Salon Participant:

In the last call when you talked about controlling a man to get what you want, you said it's an energy you be. Could you talk about what you mean by that?

Gary:

You have to be willing to do and be *different,* not *differently.* *Differently* is still trying to change something. You have to be willing to be or do whatever it takes to be different enough to get what you're asking for.

You can ask: What can I be or do different today that would create a different reality here with this man, where I have the control, where I have what I'm asking for, where I get what I would really like to have?

Confrontation Doesn't Work

Salon Participant:

Please, can you assist me in massively changing whatever it is that keeps me hesitant and shrinking from confrontation? I would love to happily be me and expand who I am rather than shrinking or contracting with fear. Sometimes I feel almost paralyzed.

Gary:

You are not good at confrontation because you are not willing to be the demon bitch from hell and you are not willing to see how you can choose something different that does not require confrontation.

Confrontation doesn't work. It requires you to go into fight or flight. Shrinking from confrontation is what confrontation is all about. You have no fear; you are not paralysed, okay?

Use the question: What can I be or do different that would make all this a different reality?

Women Want Copious Amounts of Sex

Salon Participant:

Last week you said that most women don't actually want a relationship; they want copious amounts of sex. I said, "Wow. Yes! That rings so true." How does that work pragmatically, since that's not what we're told?

Gary:

Why are you buying all the things you have been told?

Salon Participant:

That's an excellent question. Now that I realize I would like to have a lot of sex and not a relationship, what does that look like out in the world?

Gary:

The easiest way is to find a man who is at least twenty years younger than you are. He will have sex with you and be grateful for it because girls his age won't have sex with him. They want to get married. After you have sex with him, say, "Wow, that was wonderful. I hope I can have some fun with you again another time."

He will say, "Really?" and he'll be available when you call.

You can also ask: What could I be or do different that would create and generate copious amounts of sex without commitment?

Salon Participant:

Do you suggest saying something up front like, "I'm looking for sex and not relationship"?

Gary:

No. Never be honest with a man. What is the matter with you people?

Salon Participant:

That's why I'm asking. This is new for me.

Gary:

Yes, I understand that. You have all been taught that honesty is the best policy. No. Lying is the best policy. Tell them what they want to hear. Don't tell them what you think they ought to hear.

If you tell them what you think they ought to hear, you're telling them your point of view, your truth, your reality. Every time you tell them your truth and your reality, they have to run away. They don't have any space for that. If you tell them what they want to hear, they have space for it, and they recognize that they might have a different possibility or a different choice with you.

You have to be aware of what people are going to choose. That's the reason you ask the question: What are these people capable of hearing?

Don't ask, "What do I want?" That is not a question. "What would I like from this guy?" is not a question. Instead ask:

- Would this be fun?
- Would this be easy?
- Would this work for me?

Those are real questions. But instead of asking real questions, we keep trying to look for somebody to fulfill some fantasy or ideal scene we have about what is so.

What stupidity are you using to create the romantic utopian ideal of romance, sex, copulation and relationship are you choosing? Everything that is times a godzillion, will you destroy and uncreate it all? Right and Wrong, Good and Bad, POD and POC, All Nine, Shorts, Boys and Beyonds.

An ideal scene is an idea about what must come to fruition. You have to judge it into existence to make it so. If you're doing utopian ideals, you're doing judgment. Why would you use judgment as a source of creation for a relationship? Because that's normal on planet Earth. It doesn't work, but it is normal.

Judgments and Conclusions

Salon Participant:

What do you do to break the conclusion game in your head during sex?

Gary:

What stupidity are you using to create the conclusions you are choosing? Everything that is times a godzillion, will you destroy and uncreate it all? Right and Wrong, Good and Bad, POD and POC, All Nine, Shorts, Boys and Beyonds.

This morning when I woke up, I was having a judgment about sex. I asked, "What the heck is this?" Then I remembered I had shown a picture of my nine-month-old grandson to a woman. He was naked, crawling on the floor with his testicles hanging down. This horrified her. She was still in my head, going on about what a horrible thing it was to show a picture of this naked little kid with his testicles hanging down.

She doesn't care for men, so that was probably hard for her to take. But it's the fact that someone can get in my head with a point of view, and if I don't acknowledge that their point of view actually isn't mine, I keep trying to think it is mine and I keep trying to come to conclusion.

What stupidity are you using to create conclusion of the conclusion that the conclusion you are choosing is a creation of the conclusion you should be concluding are you choosing? Everything that is times a godzillion, will you destroy and uncreate it all? Right and Wrong, Good and Bad, POD and POC, All Nine, Shorts, Boys and Beyonds.

If you should be concluding it, is that a judgment or a choice? It's a judgment.

"Have You Tried This? I Just Love That!"

Salon Participant:

When you have partners who judge you or themselves in bed, how do you find the space within you to ask them to do what you would like to have from them?

Gary:

First of all, don't ask them for what you would like to have. You have to say, "Have you ever tried this? I just love that!" Most men are trying to do what's going to please you. They have been taught that doing for a woman is what makes them valuable and real. That's what their job is. All you have to do is ask, "Have you ever tried this?" If they say *yes,* just say, "Gosh, I love it when people do that." That's manipulation without demand.

If you ask the man, "Will you go down on me?" and he says, "I don't like to go down on a woman," you're not going to get anywhere because he has come to conclusion. Of course, if you ask a man to go down on you and he says he doesn't like it, you can always get rid of him.

Salon Participant:

I feel uncomfortable going down on a man. I've done it a few times but I haven't enjoyed it. I feel like I am being bad or dirty.

Gary:

It has been considered a wrongness for years. Going down on a man has been considered the greatest wrongness you could do. However, many women find it enjoyable because it's one of the few things some men will actually allow themselves to receive.

Unfortunately, though, about eighty percent of men won't allow themselves to receive it when a woman goes down on them. And you are also not receiving when they go down on you.

What stupidity are you using to create the fellatio and cunnilingus you are choosing? Everything that is times a godzillion, will you destroy and uncreate it all? Right and Wrong, Good and Bad, POD and POC, All Nine, Shorts, Boys and Beyonds.

Ladies, how many lifetimes were you men and you had a woman go down on you and she choked or she vomited or she spit it out, and you decided that was one of the most disgusting things you could ever make anyone do? Everything that is times a godzillion, will you destroy and uncreate it all? Right and Wrong, Good and Bad, POD and POC, All Nine, Shorts, Boys and Beyonds.

You have to make the choice to be unaware of what your choice creates. Whichever way you're going, you have created something around it, which has a good deal of charge.

Turning Men On

Salon Participant:

In the last call, you talked about using control to get a man sexually excited. You've also said that most people use judgment to create sexual excitement. Would you speak about turning men on sexually, using control rather than judgment?

Gary:

Men like to be controlled. Women say, "Honey, will you do this for me?" That is what they have been trained to do their whole lives. But you have to be selective about what you ask men to do. And don't call them "honey." Call them "lover.". When you do that, they start to deliver because you're turning them on sexually with the control of how you deliver to them.

You want to deliver to a man as though he is a stallion. You have to go out and see how stallions are bred. The handlers walk a stallion up to a mare who doesn't want him. Next, they walk him up to another mare, and she doesn't want him either, and they walk him up to another one, and the mare and stallion get all excited. Then they take the stallion to the mare that is willing to have him. The moment they take him to the mare that's willing to have him, he suddenly becomes erect. He's ready to go and he delivers.

You have to see the man like he's a stallion. You have to tease him. Take your man out, walk down the street and say, "Would you like to have sex with that girl? She's kind of cute. She's kind of pretty. She seems sexy." By the time you've gone 150 yards, he'll be ready to go to bed, and you can take him home and use him.

Salon Participant:

Can you talk some more about controlling the man's turn-on without judgment?

Gary:

The greatest turn-on to most people is somebody who looks at them without judgment. However, there are men who need judgment to get off. I had a friend who, without the woman's judgment to determine what he was supposed to do, couldn't get a hard-on. For him, her judgment was a source of sexual excitation.

You have to be willing to look at the man you're with and see "Does this guy need judgment to turn on? What judgment can I give him that will turn him on harder than a rock?" That's where you have to recognize that you are the operative person in the relationship or the sex. You're the one who creates what occurs. Most women don't want to think that they're in control, they're in charge, they're the aggressor.

I know so many women, who after they get married, ask, "Why doesn't my husband come after me anymore?"

I ask, "Did he really come after you in the first place?"

They say, "Well, not exactly."

I ask, "So why do you assume he will do it now?"

They say, "Because he should."

What question is "he should"? It's not a question! "What's it going to take to turn the boy on big time?" is a question. You have to look at the person you're with and see what it's going to take to turn him on.

Women Are the Most Competitive Creatures on the Planet

Salon Participant:

Can you please explain about what appears to be a particular kind of competitiveness that women have with each other when men are around?

Gary:

You, as a woman, are more competitive than a man. Women are the most competitive creatures on the planet. It's a primal instinct they come in with. Why? In part because they are genetically impelled to compete for the best mate, so they can make the best progeny to create the expansion of the species. Men are just sperm donors. Women always pick the best men. In the animal kingdom, the mates are chosen not by the men, but by the women.

When men come around, women get even more competitive and backstabbing with one another. I've never seen it fail to happen. I've seen women communicating with each other, being friendly, kind and loving to one another, and when the men come around, that's gone and there is stiff competition. That's the way it works.

There is nothing you can do about this except acknowledge it and then you get to choose: Okay, do I want to hang out with these women when they are doing this? The other thing you can do when a man comes around is to start talking to the women as a group and call them "ladies". When you do that, they will have to change the way they function in front of the man to prove that they are ladies. It's called controlling the group without control.

Male and Female Programming

Salon Participant:

What questions can I ask that will unlock all male programming as well as the vulnerability I have to being a female?

Gary:

We choose the male side or the female side depending on our experience in the world about being woman or being man. You've been male in some lifetimes; you've been female in other lifetimes. Sometimes the male programming will kick in when you're around certain people—and the female programming will kick in when you're around other people. Different people stimulate your male or female programming. If you eliminated all the programming, you'd be in a place where you could create in the moment, for the fun of it.

What stupidity are you using to avoid being the woman you truly could be choosing? Everything that is times a godzillion, will you destroy and uncreate it all? Right and Wrong, Good and Bad, POD and POC, All Nine, Shorts, Boys and Beyonds.

You chose a woman's body. Does that mean you are a *woman?* Or are you an *infinite being* with a woman's body? If you're an infinite being with a woman's body, then shouldn't you take advantage of what that gives you as a weapon and as a tool? You tend not to use those weapons and tools because you have decided, concluded and judged what it means to be a woman, what you should be as a woman, and what you aren't as a woman.

What judgment do you have of being a woman? Everything that is times a godzillion, will you destroy and uncreate it all? Right and Wrong, Good and Bad, POD and POC, All Nine, Shorts, Boys and Beyonds.

What judgment do you have of you, with being a woman? Everything that is times a godzillion, will you destroy and uncreate it all? Right and Wrong, Good and Bad, POD and POC, All Nine, Shorts, Boys and Beyonds.

What judgment do you have of sex, with being a woman? Everything that is times a godzillion, will you destroy and uncreate it all? Right and Wrong, Good and Bad, POD and POC, All Nine, Shorts, Boys and Beyonds.

What judgment do you have of you with sex, with being a woman? Everything that is times a godzillion, will you destroy and uncreate it all? Right and Wrong, Good and Bad, POD and POC, All Nine, Shorts, Boys and Beyonds.

Salon Participant:

I get that I'm an infinite being in a woman's body, yet there is a separation for me between the two.

Gary:

Have you defined *infinite being* as having sexuality, sexualness or a body? Or have you defined *infinite being* as having no body? If you have no body, you can't have a relationship. And you can't have a relationship with you, because that means you can't have you. *No body* means not even you.

Whose Judgment Is This?

Salon Participant:

I had always thought that I was contractive in sex only to realize that I had picked partners who were contractive, and I was aware of their contraction.

Gary:

How often do you assume that a judgment is yours? If you feel a judgment, if you're aware of a judgment, you automatically assume it's yours. You don't go into question and ask:

- Whose judgment is this?
- What do I do here?
- What do I want to do here?
- What's this going to look like?
- What choices do I have here?

Here's why it's so important to ask these questions: Question creates possibility, and choice creates potential. When potential intersects possibility, a new reality can get created.

What choice and what question are you not asking that would create a new reality around sex, copulation and judgment? Everything that is times a godzillion, will you destroy and uncreate it all? Right and Wrong, Good and Bad, POD and POC, All Nine, Shorts, Boys and Beyonds.

You create a question, which creates a number of possibilities. Every time you intersect a new possibility, you create new choices. When you choose something with that new possibility you've created by the question you've asked, you have a moment in which you can create a new reality. Question creates multiple possibilities.

You've been taught to conclude, "A man is blah-blah-blah." Is that really what a man is? No.

What judgment do you have of men? Everything that is times a godzillion, will you destroy and uncreate it all? Right and Wrong, Good and Bad, POD and POC, All Nine, Shorts, Boys and Beyonds.

What judgment do you have of you with regard to men? Everything that is times a godzillion, will you destroy and uncreate it all? Right and Wrong, Good and Bad, POD and POC, All Nine, Shorts, Boys and Beyonds.

What judgment do you have of sex with men? Everything that is times a godzillion, will you destroy and uncreate it all? Right and Wrong, Good and Bad, POD and POC, All Nine, Shorts, Boys and Beyonds.

What judgment do you have of you with regard to sex with men? Everything that is times a godzillion, will you destroy and uncreate it all? Right and Wrong, Good and Bad, POD and POC, All Nine, Shorts, Boys and Beyonds.

Now I understand why sex and copulation are so hard for the human race. Everybody acts like they're doing it, and nobody is doing it. The majority of the world claims to be having sex, but they are not having sex. It's all a pretense.

Pain and Intensity

Salon Participant:

When you were running the judgment processes, all the answers related to me as pain. How can I get out of that?

Gary:

What stupidity are you using to create intensity as pain are you choosing? Everything that is times a godzillion, will you destroy and uncreate it all? Right and Wrong, Good and Bad, POD and POC, All Nine, Shorts, Boys and Beyonds.

We tend to have this weird point of view that if something is intense, it's pain. It's the idea that intensity equals pain. We try to create it as that—but intensity doesn't have to be pain. You probably don't get that you're intensely aware. Is intense awareness painful? Yes. Why? Because you've *defined* it as pain. Not because it *is* pain.

Everything you've defined as pain that actually isn't, will you destroy and uncreate all that? Right and Wrong, Good and Bad, POD and POC, All Nine, Shorts, Boys and Beyonds.

Huge numbers of people see anything that's intense as painful. Why would that be valuable or viable?

Would you like to know why? The way you maintain the intensity of a problem and a pain is by not looking at *what is* and by trying to look at what you've *decided is.* That's a conclusion. You are trying to come to conclusion about what it is and you talk about your conclusion rather than looking at what it is that could be different. You want to change it, but you don't want to do something different. You try to *change* the pain so it is less painful rather than *doing something different* that would create a different reality in which pain would not have to exist. Don't try to change it. You want a *different* reality. Changing it makes it less of what it is; it's not about having something different show up in your life. You are not able to create a reality that's different from that point of view. Instead, ask: What can I do or be different that would create a different reality here?

That question will make your life so much easier. Most people don't realize that's what is going to make their life easier, which is why they don't choose it.

You have to be willing to have the awareness of what you are choosing. Ask:

- What am I doing here?

• What can I choose to be different?

That's the way to get out of thinking that you're doing something different when all you're doing is changing something.

Salon Participant:

If you're willing to have more and more intensity, what does that create?

Gary:

It creates more and more possibilities. The intensity is a question, not a conclusion.

Salon Participant:

What is intensity? I don't think I have intensity.

Gary:

You are very intense. Just ask these people if they think you're a pain in the arse. When you do intensity to the point where it becomes painful, it can be painful to others or it can be painful to you. Intensity is one of the ways in which you make sure that you don't have to lose anything.

> What stupidity are you using to create the probability structure of future, rather than the possibility systems of future you could be choosing? Everything that is times a godzillion, will you destroy and uncreate it all? Right and Wrong, Good and Bad, POD and POC, All Nine, Shorts, Boys and Beyonds.

So much of what goes on in the world is about avoiding loss. When you get into a relationship, you want to avoid loss. If you had the point of view that you could lose this person in a heartbeat, then he would always want to stay with you. When you have the point of view that you don't wish to lose people, you try to hold onto them intensely, which drives them away. This is how we get into trouble. We go into *demand* about things instead of the *choice* of them.

If you create an intense demand of a man, you are going to drive him away. If you say, "You're not having sex with me, and I want you to have sex with me," he is going to go away. He is going to be less willing to have sex, not more.

Creating a Demand for a Man's Body

Salon Participant:

Is that different from what you said about creating a demand for a man's body?

Gary:

Yes. Creating a demand for a man's body and putting it into his universe is saying, "Ooh, I love the way you move. I love the way you look. Could you just take off your clothes and let me look at you?" Or it's getting him to do something that you particularly admire. I've noticed that women admire different parts of men's bodies. Some women like legs. Some women like butts. Some women like biceps. Some women like triceps. Some women have other things that they like. You have to ask to see the part you like. I knew a lady who loved to see her lover twist to the right, but not to the left. So, when he was standing there, she would put something out to the right and say, "Can you just do this for me, please?" He would do it, and she would say, "I love it when you do that. That's so sexy. All I can think about is sex when I see you do that." That man was horny all the time. That's where you create the demand for his body instead of a demand for him to change to fit what you want.

Salon Participant:

When you say to a young guy, "Hey, thanks for the great sex," he receives it completely. When you say the same thing to an older guy, he doesn't receive it. Where is the older guy going with that? Why doesn't he receive it in the same way the young guy does?

Gary:

The young guy is looking at it from the point of view of, "Wow. I must be good." The older guy thinks, "Oh my God. I wonder if I am not committed to something I didn't know I was committed to." Old guys assume that if you give them a compliment, it means they have to do something or they have to deliver something, whether they can or not.

Salon Participant:

With a young guy, it's like you were just playing Frisbee. What's another way to say, "Thanks for the great sex" when you're saying goodbye?

Gary:

You say, "That was so much fun. I'm grateful you're so young." Then he'll think, "Wow, I'm still a stud," which is what most men have a hard time with.

Salon Participant:

I realize that I have so many judgments about men.

Gary:

You're not looking at what's in front of you. You're looking at everything through the filter of judgment that you've entrained to. How many of you women realize you've been entrained to dislike men? Did your mother like men? Did your aunts like men? Did your grandmother like men? Or did they all have a basic feeling that liking men was all wrong?

Most women do not like men. You can tell whether a woman likes a man if she likes the smell of his different body parts.

Salon Participant:

I really like the smell of different body parts on men...well, most men.

Gary:

The ones you like the smell of are the ones you want to hang out with. Not the other ones.

Salon Participant:

Does that mean I actually like men?

Gary:

Unfortunately, yes, you do. Sorry.

Salon Participant:

Is this where I get called a slut?

Gary:

I hope so. Sluts have way more fun than uptight virgins. I don't think there are any of those on this call, anyway.

Salon Participant:

I possibly require having some sex for that to be the case.

Gary:

No, you don't have to have sex to be a slut. And you can have all the sex you want if you're willing to choose it.

Salon Participant:

Is the sense of smell another form of awareness? Is it a judgment? There are certain smells I am sensitive to. If my lover doesn't have a shower, I can't stand the smell. Do I hate men? Can this be changed?

Gary:

Smell is part of awareness. You have to be pragmatic. Just take your lover into the shower with you before you have sex.

"I Turn into a Giggling Schoolgirl"

Salon Participant:

Whenever I am around a guy that I would like to have sex with, I seem to turn into a giggling schoolgirl.

Gary:

When it comes to having sex with a man, ask: Who would be easy and who could I learn from?

If you turn into a giggling schoolgirl around men, you are probably choosing what you would have chosen when you were a schoolgirl. How many of those men actually turned out to be somebody that you would want to know?

What stupidity are you using to create the giggling schoolgirl you are choosing? Everything that is times a godzillion, will you destroy and uncreate it all? Right and Wrong, Good and Bad, POD and POC, All Nine, Shorts, Boys and Beyonds.

You're Not Responsible for Everything That People Choose

Salon Participant:

Can you talk about how you choose and create something? For example, if someone is being mean or cruel, I ask, "How am I choosing and creating this?" I go into where I am doing everything wrong.

Gary:

You're trying to change that reality, so you're looking for what you did wrong to try to change the fact that someone else was mean. No. That person was mean. That's it. You're trying to look for the reason and justification for things as though if you know why it occurred, it won't occur again.

Instead of doing that, ask: What could I be or do different that would create a different reality?

Salon Participant:

When someone is vilifying or judging me, I go into reaction. I go into, "I've created this."

Gary:

You haven't created it. You've been trying to take responsibility for everything and everyone your whole life. The good news is you are a god—but you're a really bad one, because instead of judging *them,* you've judged *you.* You might as well give that up and become an infinite being who recognizes you're not responsible for everything that people choose. Everything is choice. Choice is the ultimate source of all creation. Every choice you make creates something. Why would you choose to assume that you're responsible for everything that occurs?

Notice that you don't have an answer. But you will go out and search to find a reason why you're responsible for everything, which is a creation.

What stupidity am I using to create the stupidity of me I am choosing? Everything that is times a godzillion, will you destroy and uncreate it all? Right and Wrong, Good and Bad, POD and POC, All Nine, Shorts, Boys and Beyonds.

Salon Participant:

Can you please expand on the concept of kindness and how I can allow myself to be kind to me and others without being hurt and playing the fool.

Gary:

There is a problem here. You are creating caveats. You are looking for all the reasons why people are not going to understand you, why they are going to think you're an idiot and why they're going to think you're stupid. You think they're going to wonder why they

chose you and why they continue to choose you. This is what you
do when you're not willing to be in total allowance.

You're not doing something different. Ask: What can I be or do
today to allow me to be kind to me and everyone I touch with total
ease?

I highly recommend you listen to the *Ten Commandments* CD set.
It is the key to your freedom.

Taking Down the Barriers to Receiving

Salon Participant:

Can you talk a bit about how to take down the barriers to receiving people and how to deal with the possible rejection?

Gary:

If you are worried about receiving rejection, you are going to
pull in somebody who will reject you, because you'll have a big sign
over your head that says, "reject me." It's like when you were a kid
and you put a "kick me" sign on the back of somebody. Everybody
would kick the person and you thought it was terribly funny.

If you realize you're putting a "reject me" sign on the back of
you, maybe you could see it as funny when people reject you instead
of assuming it's a wrongness. You've got to have a little more willingness to be vulnerable. To be vulnerable is to be as the open wound,
which means you don't put up any barriers to anything or anyone.

Last year, after we did a big event with Ricky Williams, there
were some horrible newspaper articles written about me. One said
that I was the charismatic, rich, evil creator of a cult that was about
giving men and women full body orgasms. I said, "That wouldn't be
of interest to you for what reason?" I was being nationally vilified
in the press. The only bad news about that is every time they did a
judgment of me, I got another $5,000 in my coffers. I figure I should
be up to about half a million dollars right now after the things they

have put in the press so far. That works for me. In order to be successful at anything, you have to be willing to be vilified. You have to be willing to be made minced meat of. You have to be willing to receive judgment.

The whole idea of the press right now is sensationalism. All I ask of the consciousness of the world is for a bell jar to go over them, so if they're only doing sensationalism, their careers will die. When they actually start reporting real news, we might get some real newsmakers in the world.

Salon Participant:

When I meet a guy I like, I instantly tap into what my friends and family will think of me and this person. It happens instantaneously. It's a smack in the face with judgment. How can I stay in question with this?

Gary:

Ask: What energy, space and consciousness can I be, to be the dirty little slut I truly be?

Sluts don't take their boyfriends home to meet their parents or their friends. They just use their boyfriends and lose them. I am not saying this as a judgment. You have to be willing to be the dirty little slut you truly be if you want to have the choice of being present with somebody instead of trying to come to conclusion. If you start running that question, you'll get out of the judgment.

Salon Participant:

What does it look like if both people in copulation are sexual healers and both people are receiving?

Gary:

Way too much fun for you to have.

Salon Participant:

If both people are sexual healers and you are open to receiving it but the other person isn't, what does this look like?

Gary:

It means you're bored and you want to go home. The other person's lack of receiving is a turn-off. When somebody is unwilling to receive, it turns you and your body off. When somebody is truly willing to receive, your body becomes more turned on, not less.

Salon Participant:

If you are with somebody who is not receiving and the possibility is there, what can you ask to get them to be more receiving?

Gary:

Ask: Can I blindfold you? Can I tie you up? Can I tickle you with my feather?

Most men don't know how to receive. They just don't know how to do it. Tying them up and getting them to have no choice but to receive is a great way to do it. Go to the Salvation Army and get some silk ties, a blindfold and a really nice ostrich feather.

Can the Other Person Receive What You're Capable Of?

Salon Participant:

You have said that when you were younger, you would have four women a day. What elements worked really well with women who wanted to just have sex with you and not relationship?

Gary:

First of all, I smoked dope. I smoked two joints before I went to bed with every woman so I couldn't hear what her judgments were or what her needs were. I don't recommend that anymore. But that's what I had to do to not be aware of what their needs were. I wasn't willing to make a commitment, but I was not not committed to them. I wouldn't tell them I *would* become their boyfriend, but I wouldn't tell them I *wouldn't* become their boyfriend. I always had the point of view, "Let's see what happens next," because every time I had committed to someone, something terrible occurred.

One lady moved in with me. The night she moved in, I ran my hand three inches over her body and lightning bolts shot from her body into my hand. She got up the next morning and left and never talked to me again. I had scared her, but I didn't get that. I didn't know that you couldn't do magic with people you loved and cared for. I wasn't willing at the time to be aware of that.

After that, I didn't want to create that universe again. I was always willing to stand back and wait to see who could receive what I was capable of rather than trying to give them what I was capable of. This is one of the things you do if you want to create that kind of relationship. You stand back and wait to see if somebody can receive what you're capable of. Don't try to give them what you're capable of unless they can receive it.

This is difficult for most women. In reality, women are far more aggressive than men, but they don't recognize it. They think they are supposed to be shy and retiring. Women can be quiet, but in reality, "shy and retiring" is not a womanly trait.

"Shy and retiring" is a man's trait. Men try to be shy and retiring because they have the point of view that they're supposed to be tall, dark, handsome and silent. But most of them aren't tall, aren't dark and aren't handsome. They're just shy. Men have less faith in themselves than women do.

The Whispers of Change

Salon Participant:

There is something in the wind that is whispering change I cannot fathom. You have previously mentioned the feather touch of consciousness. What is beyond it that can now be brought into awareness?

Gary:

It is beginning to fall into existence, which is why it is a whisper of change that is happening. It cannot be defined. That which is not definable is also something that cannot confine you. Every definition confines you. Definition is confinement. No definition is no confinement. Keep asking for that rather than looking for the conclusion that will give you a sense of the substance of this reality.

Salon Participant:

Can you speak more about the whispers of the possibilities of the future?

Gary:

The whispers of the future are the energy you feel about what's going to show up in life. You try to solidify that energy and make it solid and real, thinking that if you can make it solid and real, you can actualize it. The thing is—you've already made the choices that created these whispers of futures. You have to follow those whispers and let them show you what they're going to actualize as. If you don't do that, you're in a constant state of judgment of what you're doing, rather than being willing to receive what you have already created.

Salon Participant:

How do I do that?

Gary:

It's not a how. It's a recognition of: What is this thing that's niggling at the outside edges of my awareness and my reality? The only way I can describe these whispers of the future is that they feel like a kiss or a caress of a different possibility.

Salon Participant:

Sometimes I have the sense that I have to do something when I get these whispers.

Gary:

You simply have to go to question: Now or later?

Salon Participant:

To have more clarity about what to do?

Gary:

Clarity is not about what to do. You're obviously creating it already or you wouldn't have the whispers of the future. It's already coming into existence. You are trying to jump to the conclusion that you have to do something to make it happen. You've already done what's going to make it happen. You just don't know what it is you've done. You have to be willing to be in the unforgiveable place of no conclusion. You'd rather come to conclusion because if you come to conclusion, you can stop it, rather than going into question and continuing to create the possibilities. Questions create possibility. Choice creates potential. When a potential intersects a possibility, a new reality can be created. That's what the whispers of the future are—those places where potential and possibility intersect in the universe. You then get to create what occurs.

Salon Participant:

Many times I am aware of the whispers of the future. Then I go into "It didn't show up right now."

Gary:

You go into conclusion, which is why I gave you that conclusion process. You have the idea that once you come to conclusion, x, y or z should occur. Conclusion is no longer question. If you come out of question, the whispers of the future die, disintegrate and go away.

That's the reason you have to use the four elements of choice, question, possibility and contribution.

What energy, space, and consciousness can I be to be out of control, out of definition, out of limitation, out of form, structure and significance, out of linearities and out of concentricities for all eternity, especially with regard to sex, copulation and relationship? Everything that doesn't allow that to show up times a godzillion, will you destroy and uncreate it all? Right and Wrong, Good and Bad, POD and POC, All Nine, Shorts, Boys and Beyonds.

Is it a contribution to your life to come to conclusion? No. It destroys every possibility, choice and question. If you come to conclusion, you stop everything you're trying to create as a future. You have to go into choice and possibility at all times.

If you want to create a future, you have to choose something different. Difference creates space. Change creates conclusion and contraction.

All right, ladies, that's it for tonight. Talk to you next time!

4

Creating a Relationahip That Works for You

You have to move beyond this reality's view of what a relationship is in order to create something that actually works for you.

Gary:

Hello ladies.

Probability Structures vs. Possibility Systems

Salon Participant:

When I know a man is lying to me, I want to call him on it. I get the energy he is lying and I look for him to own up to it. I know this is control.

Gary:

No. This is bitchy-dom. Now, you have the right to be a bitch if you want to be, and if you wish to drive a man away, that's the way to do it. If you know he's lying, you can catch him in a big lie that steps over the line and you can destroy him, stomp him into dust and kill him if you wish. But if you want to keep the man, don't acknowledge the lying except to yourself. Never acknowledge to his face that you know he is lying to you. Look at him sweetly, smile at him, and say, "Oh, honey."

When you do that, he will feel guiltier than you can possibly imagine and you'll get a present within three days. Do this when you are looking for a present—because men are not the brightest creatures on the planet. All you have to do is say, "Look! Isn't that beautiful? I'd so like to have that. I wish I could afford it. Oh well." And then walk away.

When you are trying to figure out what to do with men, you are trying to figure out what the probability structures are. If you have the idea that there is a probability he is lying, then you're living in judgment, not in possibility.

Probabilities are what we do to avoid, eliminate or stop risk. The probabilities are that you are going to lose. That's the idea that there is always a risk, there is always a danger and there is always something that is going to turn out badly. So, we spend our lives trying to avoid risks of different sorts, and in the process, we eliminate possibility and choice. A lot of the questions that have been asked during these calls are about the probability of losing or the probability of having a problem. I've come up with this process for you:

> What stupidity are you using to create the probability struc-tures of losing in relationship, rather than creating the possibility systems that would allow it to work for you are you choosing? Everything that is times a godzillion, will you destroy and uncre-ate it all? Right and Wrong, Good and Bad, POD and POC, All Nine, Shorts, Boys and Beyonds.

It also works for money. We try to hold onto what we've got for fear we're going to lose, we're not going to have anything else, and we're not going to have any other choices. All of those have nothing to do with true choice, true possibility or true question. We need to be in a place where it's true possibility and choice and we're asking, "What else is possible?" instead of, "What are the chances I'm going to lose here?"

The Probability of Losing

Salon Participant:

About a year into my current relationship, I went into an insecure energy about life betrayal issues from a male. Since then, I've had a constant energy of doubt. What is this?

Gary:

This is the probability of losing. We go into the idea that the probability is a relationship will work or the probability is the relationship won't work. That's the weighing and measuring of things that people do.

You have to move beyond this reality's view of what a relationship is in order to create something that actually works for you. Right now, people are creating more relationships that do not work than relationships that *do* work. Why is that? Because they are looking for the probability that there is going to be a problem, the probability that there is going to be a loss, the probability that it's going to turn out badly, the probability that there is going to be a lie or a betrayal. We create structures for probability because we buy the idea that you can weigh and measure everything, and that if you weigh and measure accurately enough, you will not lose.

That's the reason most people, once they get into a relationship, get married, so they can live happily ever after, as though the purpose of relationship is to live happily ever after.

What is the real purpose of relationship? To increase your level of comfort and possibility. That's what it should be. But most people see it as increasing their survivability. Stop looking at relationship from the point of view of survival and move into *thrival*. Ask:

- What else is possible now that we have this relationship?
- What could we actually create that we haven't yet created?

When you do that, you create a whole different possibility and a whole different universe.

What stupidity are you using to create the probability structures of relationship so that you don't lose rather than the possibility systems that would allow you to choose, are you choosing? Everything that is times a godzillion, will you destroy and uncreate it all? Right and Wrong, Good and Bad, POD and POC, All Nine, Shorts, Boys and Beyonds.

Salon Participant:

Can you say some more about what you mean by losing?

Gary:

Losing is when you're looking for what is wrong with people or what they are doing wrong. Or you are looking for how they are going to lie to you. Everybody lies. People lie to themselves more than they lie to anybody else; they tend to lie less to other people than to themselves. Is somebody going to lie? Sure. Because people have ideas about themselves that aren't necessarily true.

I had a friend who thought he was always clean and tidy. Actually, he was a slob, but by his standards of clean and tidy, he was clean and tidy. He saw himself as clean and tidy because he would make everything neat and organized. But his house was filthy. Neat and organized was clean to him. Different reality.

I once got fired by my maids because I didn't pick up all the toys after my kids. They said, "Your house is too dirty for us to clean, so we quit."

I asked, "What do you mean it's dirty? I just vacuumed the day before you came."

They said, "But it's dirty."

"What's dirty about it?"

"All the toys on the floor."

That was messy. It wasn't dirty. People have their own standards of what they call messy or dirty or what they call good or bad or what they think is appropriate in a relationship or not appropriate in a relationship, and they are not capable of seeing anything different. So, when you go to live with somebody, it's imperative that you function from the place of, "What can I create and generate today?" not "What do I want to change about this person I am with?" Only by what you create and generate can you alter how you live with someone. You can't make anyone change.

"I Can Fix Him Up"

I've known lots of women who have chosen men and said, "Oh well. He's got some good stuff. I figure I can fix him up." What? Why would you want to buy a fixer-upper? You're going to move into an old house that needs all kind of work? People do this crazy thing where they think they are going to fix other people up and turn them into somebody good.

My ex-wife always used to say, "When I met Gary, he dressed like a used car." I always wondered what that meant. Basically she was saying that I didn't dress well. The truth is that when I met her, I didn't have any money. I was out of a relationship, working my arse off to make money, and I was doing everything I could to take care of my kid and meet my obligations. I wasn't spending any money on clothes. I hadn't bought clothes in eight years. So, I was behind the times as far as style went.

From her point of view, if you weren't in style, there was no reason to be alive. So, as we made money, she started upgrading my wardrobe. She upgraded hers three times faster than she upgraded mine, but nonetheless, I was being upgraded. She would buy me things so I wouldn't embarrass her because I was such a fixer-upper.

If you treat your man as a fixer-upper, at some point he is going to rebel against that, because no man wants to be constantly told in front of others that he was less-than when you got him. Too many women do that. Those are the women who don't actually like men.

Would you like him to upgrade the way he dresses? Sure. Are you going to succeed? Probably not. Be willing to be with the person you're with, not try to turn him into what you think he ought to be. If you're not happy with the person you find, if he doesn't dress well enough for you, dump him and get another one instead of trying to fix that one up.

Guys don't have the illusion they can fix a woman up. They already know they are dead meat in that regard. No matter how good their taste is, they are never going to get a woman who is going to choose to step up to their level. You have to get the difference in the way men and women function.

What stupidity are you using to create the probability structures of relationship to avoid losing rather than the possibility systems that would allow you to be choosing? Everything that is times a godzillion, will you destroy and uncreate it? Right and Wrong, Good and Bad, POD and POC, All Nine, Shorts, Boys and Beyonds.

The Possibility of Success

Salon Participant:

Could you please talk about the elements of success?

Gary:

This is another place where you try to go into the probability structures. Basically, you have the idea of the *probability* of success rather than the *possibility* of success. When you come from the possibility of success, you always remain in question.

If you remain constantly in a state of question with your relationship, you can change the way things work. You will never be able to come to conclusion about whether something is working or not working. You'll be asking: What can I do or be different today that would allow this to change right away?

When you start to function from that place of question instead of conclusion, you'll get to the point where you are on the creative edge of possibility and you are capable of creating something that has never existed here before.

What you have as a reference point for relationship is everything you've seen everybody else do. Is it working? No. But that's your only reference point. You have to be willing to create a relationship that does not fit this reality. Here is a process you need to put on a loop:

> What physical actualization of a relationship beyond this reality are you now capable of generating, creating and instituting? Everything that is times a godzillion, will you destroy and uncreate it all? Right and Wrong, Good and Bad, POD and POC, All Nine, Shorts, Boys and Beyonds.

Let this run for at least ten days and see what starts to show up. You have to get to the place where you begin to recognize that there are different possibilities.

> What stupidity are you using to create the probability structures of relationship to avoid losing rather than the possibility systems that would allow you to be choosing? Everything that is times a godzillion, will you destroy and uncreate it? Right and Wrong, Good and Bad, POD and POC, All Nine, Shorts, Boys and Beyonds.

Living in Ten-Second Increments

With every relationship, you have ten seconds to live. If you live your life in ten-second increments, then you won't be coming to conclusion or judgment because every ten seconds will create something new. You need to live in that ten seconds rather than trying to come to conclusion, which is based on the probability structures that you can balance things out, and that if it's a good relationship, in the end, it will be better rather than worse. That doesn't deal with the structure of your relationship in the first place because it is not about creating possibilities. It's about creating a structure in which you have the conclusion that in the long run it will work out or in the end it will be best. These are things that we keep coming to conclusion about, none of which give us true choice.

Salon Participant:

How do I clear my distress around men and women? It started as a teenager when my parents decided what my career life was going to be. All of this was done without my consent. This call has been rocking the foundation of who I really am. Now I don't think any of my choices are truly mine.

Gary:

You have to get that everything you have ever decided was true or real is a lie or an implant. So, if everything is a lie or an implant, where do you begin? You begin with:

- What would I like today?
- In this ten seconds, what would I choose?

This is the place you have to start to function from, to learn to trust you. The reason you distrust men and the reason you distrust women is because you don't trust you. If you trusted you, you could know that they were not trustworthy or that they were trustworthy, and you'd have a different possibility.

Receiving What You Desire in a Relationship

Salon Participant:

You have talked about how ninety percent of women hate men and ninety percent of men hate women, yet they all would like to own one. Do you sense the possibility that this could change with these calls?

Gary:

Yes. That's the reason I'm doing these calls. I'd like to see this constant state of anger, rage, fury and hate that people function from go away so you learn to have a reference point for being what you desire in a relationship and receiving what you desire in a relationship.

Salon Participant:

Is this learned? Or is it fundamental to beings and their preferences?

Gary:

Everything about relationship is learned. And it's all learned badly. You have been educated by stupid people about stupid relationships so your relationship will be as stupid as theirs are, which validates the idea that their relationships aren't stupid. People teach you and entrain you to bad relationships like theirs because if you get a relationship as bad as theirs, it proves that theirs is as good as it's going to get. The probability is if your relationship is bad too, that their relationship is not as bad as the one they thought they were going to get.

Salon Participant:

I am not in a relationship. It seems like it's more trouble than it's worth because I am very happy on my own. I am not excluding relationship but I'm also not including it.

Gary:

What you're describing is the moment at which you're actually willing to receive a relationship that would work for you. You are perfectly happy not to be in a relationship. At this point, if a relationship walked in that worked for you, would you know it? That's the question to ask. When you're independent, when you have enough money and things are going well, you're out of the needy universe and into the place of "What else is possible?" You're in the questioning universe that can create a relationship that might work for you, that might be fun for you, that might expand your agenda, your reality and your possibilities. You're not going to get into it from lust. You're going to drift into it by accident. You're going to find somebody who enjoys hanging out with you and appreciates who you are. Unfortunately, if you are like most women, you'll say, "He's just a friend." No, he is a possibility, not a friend.

Most women, as soon as they find a guy who likes to talk to them and hang out with them, say, "If he wants to hang out with me, he is a frigging loser." What? Do you like to hang out with you? That would be the question. If you like hanging out with you, you have the place where you can choose different.

Limiting Choices

Salon Participant:

I am baffled by the limiting choices I make, which take away from my potency.

Gary:

Once again, this is probability structures. You take away from what's really potent about you and your choices, and you create limiting choices as a way of functioning within the probability structures to make sure you don't lose.

What stupidity are you using to create the probability structures of relationship to avoid losing rather than the possibility systems that would allow you to be choosing? Everything that is times a godzillion, will you destroy and uncreate it? Right and Wrong, Good and Bad, POD and POC, All Nine, Shorts, Boys and Beyonds.

Salon Participant:

I was in a park some days ago and a guy was looking at me. I sensed that he was going to try to approach me, and my body and my being felt he was creepy. I started to POC and POD that he would approach, and he didn't. What pragmatic tool can we use to let down a guy that is too insistent?

Gary:

POCing and PODing was the perfect thing. You were aware and you knew exactly what was needed.

I was talking with a lady who wanted to get married. I asked her, "What kind of men are you finding?"

She said, "All I find are creeps who go to bars."

I asked, "What are you going to a bar for if you want to get married?"

"Well, how am I going to find a man if I don't go to bars?"

I said, "Go for afternoon tea at the fanciest hotel in your area and sit with a book. Wear a nice dress, one that shows a little cleavage, and a great pair of high heels. Cross your legs, and as you're sitting there, let your foot bob up and down a little bit.

That will intrigue the guy. When he comes over and asks you what you're reading, say, "Oh, I am just reading this interesting book." Have a book with you that you like, something that interests you, but not a romance novel. If you have a romance novel, you're going to turn the guy off because he's going to think you're looking for a relationship.

Do not read *Fifty Shades of Grey* and think you're going to get a man out of it. *Joy of Business* might get you a really rich man. He'll say, "You're reading about business?" And you'll reply, "Yes, I just love business. I find business people so sexy." Don't be afraid to use the word *sexy* if you're interested.

If you're not interested in him, be polite, talk to him and when he asks, "Would you like to go out for a drink some time?" say, "Oh thank you so much, dear, but I don't date. I go directly to marriage and I require a $500,000 surety bond up-front." Before you know it, his car will be screeching down the roadway. One lady told me, "You need to teach CPR if you are going to tell people to do that." She said it to some guy who almost passed out. So, the guy might have a heart attack. But if he's old enough to have a heart attack, he's old enough to take you home and…never mind. That's what you do.

There's Nothing to Fight

Salon Participant:

I have much more peace and ease in my life since I have become more aware of the fight with men and keep choosing to let it go. My barriers are down. I am much kinder. But I am still a little confused. Would you please help me? Some time ago I mentioned to you that there were a few men at work who were being bullies. I felt like I was in Amazon mode and had weapons on my body. I was turning them to dust.

I think you said something like, "Why would you make yourself wrong for that? That's exactly what you needed to create at that moment. Why did you stop? Isn't that sexy?" Can you explain that further in light of what we're talking about? Is it kinder for us to not be warriors?

Gary:

That's an assumption—that it's kinder to not be a warrior. Sometimes being a warrior is exactly what is needed in the moment. You have to be willing to be, do, have, create and generate anything or everything as needed in order to have total choice.

What stupidity are you using to create never being, doing, having, creating, generating and instituting anything and everything as needed are you choosing? Everything that is times a godzillion, will you destroy and uncreate it all? Right and Wrong, Good and Bad, POD and POC, All Nine, Shorts, Boys and Beyonds.

Salon Participant:

You also mentioned that when I do not fight, it is the same as fighting, because I am assuming superiority.

Gary:

I don't think that's what I said. I think I asked you a question: Do you feel superior when you do that? Is that how you make yourself superior enough not to be less-than? If you're trying to prove you're not less-than, you will do superiority rather than choice. Choice means you can pull out your sword and cut off their heads if you want to, or not, as you wish, as kindly as you choose to do it. Sometimes a quick slash to the throat is a very good, kind thing to do. Some people deserve it.

Salon Participant:

When I do interesting point of view, there is nothing to fight.

Gary:

That's the point. There's nothing to fight. So, if you're not fighting, what other choices do you have?

Participant:

You have also said I am not willing to kill, that I'm sexy when I'm evil, and that I keep doing pathetic, and that you hate it when I do pathetic.

Gary:

When you're doing the superior person, when you're doing the person who is not going to take it anymore, when you're doing "Don't mess with me," that's sexier than "Boo-hoo, pitiful me. Nobody loves me; everybody hates me. I'd better go eat worms." That is not much of a turn-on. When you do pathetic, it's the one time you're never being you.

Functioning from Total Choice

Salon Participant:

What does kind or evil look like?

Gary:

You are kind or evil according to the moment, according to the need, according to the desire, according to the requirement of the people you are with. You are however you choose to be because you are functioning from total choice.

What stupidity are you using to create never being, doing, having, creating, generating and instituting anything and everything at will are you choosing? Everything that is times a godzillion, will you destroy and uncreate it all? Right and Wrong, Good and Bad, POD and POC, All Nine, Shorts, Boys and Beyonds.

Salon Participant:

Is this where we find the tiniest scrap of kindness in a man and bring that out?

Gary:

Not really. Start looking at both the evil and the good in people and recognize that you're going to get whatever you get when you get it, and not try to only bring out the good or the kindness. You have to be willing to have the person you're with. Otherwise, don't bother.

Does Your Relationship Create More Comfort?

Salon Participant:

I asked, "Truth, would I like a relationship in my life?" It was a *yes*. Then, when I asked, "Truth, would a relationship expand my agenda?" I got a *no*.

Gary:

Relationships are not necessarily about expanding agendas. In this reality, everybody tells you a relationship is going to expand your agenda. Unfortunately, most people do relationship from a very contracted place and it actually confines them and limits everything they're choosing.

Salon Participant:

You have talked about how a relationship can be great if it creates more comfort. Can you talk about what that looks like?

Gary:

Most people get into a relationship with the idea that they're going to get something from it. They think it's going to provide something they desire or do something for their life. Or they're going to be in love forever or they're going to live happily ever after.

If you go into a relationship because it is comfortable, a whole different universe can open up.

Years ago when I lived with roommates, people would come to interview to be a roommate. I'd tell them what the rent was and I'd say, "Tell me about you."

They'd say, "I'm really clean and tidy, I'm glad to share my food with people, and I take care of things."

I noticed that the people who said those things were not clean and tidy, did not take care of things, ate all my food, and got pissed if I ate theirs.

What happened was when they got to my house to be interviewed, they would look around to see what they had to be. They saw my house was clean and neat, so they said, "I'm very clean and tidy." This is what happens in relationships. People look around to see what they have to be to make it okay for you to have them in your life.

What you should do, if you really want to find out what you're going to have in a relationship, is go to the person's house and see how they live. If you can walk in there and live with everything they've got and be comfortable with it, you have a really good chance of creating a relationship.

If you hate the way they decorate, if you hate the way they keep their house, if you hate the way they have food, if you hate the way they keep their cupboards, if you hate any of that, then you're not going to be comfortable in the relationship.

Most of us don't do any research to find out what's going to work for us. Have you ever lived with somebody and noticed the things that begin to irritate you were things he did all the time that you thought you would be just fine with because you loved him so much? Ever notice that? These were things you didn't consider that bad when you got together, but at the same time, they weren't things you would have felt comfortable actually living with. That's why you need to start asking: If I'm doing a relationship, who would be comfortable for me to live with?

Salon Participant:

How does allowance play into this?

Gary:

When you are living with somebody, you want comfort more than you want allowance. If you have comfort, you will always have allowance. If you're uncomfortable, you will never have allowance.

You can't use allowance as the way to overcome what you don't like. That's not what allowance is. Allowance is "interesting point of view". If you get that the way a person lives is something you can live with, then it's not going to ever be an issue.

Dain and I share a house. We don't "live together" because we're not a couple, although lots of people think we are. At our Christmas party, a neighbor asked, "Are you guys married?"

I said, "No, we're just two straight guys who share a house and a business and do most things together."

Dain has his room and he decorates it any way he chooses. I seem to decorate the rest of the house. Not for any reason other than that's easier for him. He is comfortable with the things I choose to keep in the house. Occasionally, he will say, "That thing is kind of ugly," and I will say, "Okay," and I get rid of it. Why? Because he is comfortable to live with. He has eight million machines that do all kinds of things. We have a margarita machine, an espresso machine and a Vitamix mixer. All I have to do is figure out what cupboard I can get them into.

He is comfortable to live with because he likes things to be clean and organized, at least on the outside. If it looks like trash inside the drawer or in the closet, that's okay with him. That's okay with me too. As long as the visual effect is good, what's in the closet doesn't bother me because I don't think about it.

When I first met Dain, he had his own apartment. I went to his house and I was comfortable there. What is being comfortable about something? It's the energy people create in their life, which is spelled out in their furniture and things. They use the things around them to create a sense of peace in their life. If you have comfort with the person you're with, you're more likely to have a great relationship.

When Does Allowance Come into Play?

You want to see the kindness and caring in the person. You want to know what they're interested in and what they're not interested in. Allowance comes into play when you see that they like some things you don't. For instance, Dain got into archery and we set up our garage as a shooting gallery. We put critters around the yard for him to shoot at. It was very funny to me because he was enjoying the hell out of himself. I had no interest in archery, but I was glad he was enjoying himself. That's where the allowance for differences comes in. You recognize the things the other person likes to do that are not necessarily what you like to do, and you're glad for them. You have the generosity of spirit to be happy that they have something that is of such value and interest to them.

Salon Participant:

Today I realized true kindness is total allowance.

Gary:

Yes. True kindness is total allowance. But it's even more than that. True kindness is also the willingness to be more, to have more. It's the recognition that you have to be kind to yourself—not to others. If you get up in the morning, look in the mirror and judge yourself or your body, are you being kind? No, but most people do that. They say things like, "I'm getting so old. I am so saggy, so draggy." What does that have to do with creating? You have to ask, "Ah! What would it take to change this?"

I've discovered there are times when I look like I'm forty and ten minutes later, I'll look seventy. How the hell does that happen? Does this mean that we have something to do with the creation of how our bodies look? Yeah, we do!

Humanoid Woman Want to Conquer the World

Salon Participant:

Would you please speak about the feminine humanoid body and how to truly enjoy it and use it to our advantage?

Gary:

First of all, as a humanoid woman, you want to conquer the world. So, your body will be designed in such a way that you can conquer anybody—if you are willing to allow yourself to have the feminine humanoid body. Ask: Who can I conquer with this body? Then look around to see who is willing to give himself up for you. There are always men who will give themselves up for you if you're willing to conquer them.

Salon Participant:

What do you mean by *conquer*?

Gary:

To be a conqueror is to control without controlling, to invite to a different possibility without demanding, and to create beyond the limitations of the conquered. That's the reason you want to know who you can conquer today. Asking the question, "Who can I conquer with this body?" will start to show you the kind of person who would be willing to be part of your life. It may not mean that's the person you want. It may mean that's the kind of person you would most likely succeed with.

Conquering means that you have the dominant space, but you don't have to dominate the person's choices. A conqueror will come in and allow you to be what you are but will change the underpinnings of how everything works.

Humanoid women want to conquer the world. They want to rule the world. That's what you, as humanoid women, wish to do. Humanoid women are not weak, pathetic piles of debris who want to stand back and do nothing. If you are willing to conquer, you can create something greater.

Human women, on the other hand, want to control the roost, but they don't want to conquer. They want to emasculate men.

Have you ever had a man or a woman in your life who you totally dominated? Did you like it? No, because they were acquiescing. They acquiesced or gave up. That's not conquering.

Please recognize that you have a commanding capacity—but someone who is a true leader does not command. People who command make demands. They require others to acquiesce to them. To acquiesce is to give up, to surrender, to put up the white flag. You, as a humanoid woman, will always get pissed when people acquiesce because you don't like people who give in to you. You don't like people who fight you either, but you don't want folks who will give in, because if they give in too easily, they are of no value. Their willingness to not give in makes them valuable.

Salon Participant:

If human women want to emasculate men, what do human men do with women?

Gary:

Human men deal with women by disregarding and invalidating them. They create women as polar opposites; it's the way they create attraction to the opposite sex. Human reality is about judging the other sex. Human men say, "Women—you can't live with them and you can't live without them."

Salon Participant:

On of my biggest challenges is cognitively verbalizing the knowing I have without coming off as superior. What will it take to strengthen this capacity?

Gary:

Silence. You have to be willing to not tell people or cognitively verbalize what you're aware of. You have to have the awareness for you and not for anybody else. Just for me, just for fun, never tell anyone.

How to Approach a Man

Salon Participant:

If you want to discuss something with a man, how to do you approach it?

Gary:

If you want to discuss something with a man, you say, "Honey, I've been thinking…."

Never approach a man with, "We have to have a talk" or "I'd like to talk to you," because that scares every man to death. "Honey, we must have a chat" means "You're about to have your testicles cut off. You're wrong and you're going to pay for it."

If you start with, "I've been thinking about this. What do you think?" you can create a discussion, and that's what you have to do. You have to create the discussion.

Don't give the man the early warning shot, which is, "We must have a chat." Men have different signals than women. For a man, that is the signal that the fight is about to begin, so get out the white flag. You're going to have to surrender because you're the man and you're wrong. That's the way it functions in a man's world. You have to know this if you want to create something that works for you with a man that you truly wish to be with.

Dain is my man. We both do, "I was thinking…." so the other person doesn't think he has to grab his white flag. Don't go at your man with a comment like, "We've got to talk." Instead, come around to the back door. Sneak in with, "Honey, I was thinking about this. What do you think? How do you feel about this?"

Another good ploy is, "I was thinking about this, but I feel like I'm missing something. Can you see anything I'm not looking at here?" That way, you engage the man in looking at something instead of confronting him with it. Most people try to confront in relationships, thinking that confronting is the way you get somebody to be honest. You never get honesty from confrontation. You get fight. Dialogue is brought about by, "I think…. What do you think?" If you create a confrontation, the poor guy has got to fight you and there is no two ways about it.

The Dreams, Nightmares, Requirements, Desirements and Necessities of Your Life

Salon Participant:

I have a quickie sex life with my live-in lover. He says I am too demanding and that I require too much time and caressing to have an external orgasm. Now I am almost avoiding sex. What can I do to change this and have orgasmic sex again?

Gary:

Get rid of him. He's an idiot. Get a new lover. You want a man who wishes to nurture your body and your soul.

Salon Participant:

What can I do to have an orgasm just from penetration?

Gary:

That is not terribly likely. Women's bodies are not designed to have orgasm from penetration. Most orgasm occurs from the clitoris, not from inside the vagina, which isn't terribly sensitive. There are a couple of spots in the vagina that are sensitive, but those are not the whole of it. Your body is designed that way so you can withstand childbirth and squeeze a bowling ball out of your vagina.

Find a man who knows how to treat a woman well. There are not a lot of men who study women's bodies. Ask him questions before you get into bed. Ask, "What's your favorite part of sex?" If he doesn't say, "Going down on you," chances are he will never be a great lover because his basic way of doing sex is, "I'll stick it in and she'll be happy." And that's not usually going to make any woman happy.

Salon Participant:

He works fourteen hours a day. I work twelve hours a day and I have kids and a house to nurture. He wants me to stop what I'm doing and go to bed when he does, which I choose not to do. My body is not enjoying his touch. It's not nurturing.

Gary:

Your body is not enjoying his touch because he is judgmental. He is judging that you're not doing it right—and he is. When you get in a relationship with people who are judgmental, the tendency is for your body to withdraw from them and not wish to touch them.

Find somebody else in your life. This man is not going to deliver. If he is not interested in nurturing your body and he wants you to go to bed when he goes to bed, then all he is doing is being a controlling femme fatale.

What physical actualization of a lover, a friend and a life mate are you now capable of generating, creating and instituting? Everything that doesn't allow that to show up times a godzillion, will you destroy and uncreate it all? Right and Wrong, Good and Bad, POD and POC, All Nine, Shorts, Boys and Beyonds.

What stupidity are you using to create the dreams, the nightmares, the requirements, the desirements and the necessities of your life are you choosing? Everything that is times a godzillion, will you destroy and uncreate it all? Right and Wrong, Good and Bad, POD and POC, All Nine, Shorts, Boys and Beyonds.

You have your dreams about what something should be. You have your nightmares about how things show up. You have your requirements, and you think, "Once I fulfill this, everything will be good." You have things you desire of people, which they seldom actually do. Then you have the necessities. Those are all the things you think you have to do that you don't really want to do, but you figure you have to do them because you were told you have to.

Salon Participant:

Is it just about asking, "What do I have to be here?"

Gary:

This is where the need becomes a necessity. That's where things don't show up the way you would like them to. That's where you're creating a dream, a nightmare, a requirement, a desirement or a necessity. Those are all things we do in our lives as though they're all going to work out.

My daughter Grace came home to visit with her baby, and I was thinking, "This is so much work. She's not cleaning anything up. She's not doing anything."

Then I took care of the kid for five hours. I saw that the fact that the girl gets out of bed is a miracle. Having a baby... the fact that you ladies do that is amazing to me. I don't know how she does it. She doesn't have anybody who takes care of her and she is always taking care of the kid. All of a sudden, all the things I thought I was upset about went away, because I got clarity about what it was. You might want to run: What energy, space and consciousness can I be that would give me total clarity and ease with this for all eternity?

Salon Participant:

It's like the other person's reality is imposed on yours. But if you ask what they require, does it become easier?

Gary:

I became aware of what she required when I did her job for a little bit. I became aware of what was driving her need to have a sense that somebody was willing to take care of her. Since then I've been willing to take care of her better. I have also been willing to be there for her in ways that she needed that she didn't even know.

If you ask, "What energy, space and consciousness can I be that would give me total clarity and ease with this for all eternity?" it will start to unwind some of the places where you are confused. There is a disparity between what we receive and what we think and between what we feel and what actually goes on. We have strange places where we try to make what is disparate equal something so that we can come to conclusion rather than realizing that the disparity is the difference between being us and not being us.

How many disparities do you have between what you would be and what you think is required of you and what is being demanded of you that you don't understand? Everything that is times a godzillion, will you destroy and uncreate it all? Right and Wrong, Good and Bad, POD and POC, All Nine, Shorts, Boys and Beyonds.

What stupidity are you using to create the dreams, the nightmares, the requirements, the desirements and the necessities of life are you choosing? Everything that is times a godzillion, will you destroy and uncreate it all? Right and Wrong, Good and Bad, POD and POC, All Nine, Shorts, Boys and Beyonds.

What Is Possible Here That I Haven't Considered?

Salon Participant:

Are you talking about an operative state of functioning?

Gary:

You want to be everything you are and to function within the structures of this reality without being the effect of the structures. This has more to do with the probability structures than anything else.

If you are trying to avoid a fight, you are looking at the probability structures of a fight and trying to avoid those rather than asking: What else is possible here I haven't even considered? If you really want to change something, ask that question. It's about what you haven't looked at. That's what I did with Grace.

When I took care of the kid, I realized that she is taking care of him 24/7 with no help. No one is being there for her, and she needs to feel that she is being taken care of. She needs to feel nurtured; she needs to feel that she can have some time free from having to constantly be "on." So, I have been doing as much as I can to take care of the kid. I will continue to do that because I get how necessary that is for her.

What stupidity are you using to create the dreams, the nightmares, the requirements, the desirements and the necessities of life are you choosing? Everything that is times a godzillion, will you destroy and uncreate it all? Right and Wrong, Good and Bad, POD and POC, All Nine, Shorts, Boys and Beyonds.

Salon Participant:

Will that process also clear the fantasy that a man will take care of you?

Gary:

I am hoping so. Somewhere there is a place where women think, "Someday my prince will come." I have watched them do this forever. I don't find that anybody is going to really take care of us. We need to take care of whatever needs to be taken care of ourselves.

Two friends of mine are getting married. He has always had the point of view that somebody will take care of him. She has the point of view that somebody will take care of her. I don't know how that relationship is going to work out if both of them are looking for somebody to take care of them. It will be interesting to see what occurs.

What Is It You Really Want?

Salon Participant:

In my adult life, I've always taken care of myself. I've never needed anybody to do that for me. Now I'm at a point where that's something I would like to invite into my life. It would be nice to have somebody help me in the garden and do the dishes when I don't want to.

Gary:

That's called a maid and a gardener. You can hire those. What is it that you really want?

Salon Participant:

A partner.

Gary:

Do you really want a partner? I understand that's what you *think* you want.

Salon Participant:

How do you figure out what you want?

Gary:

That's where you have to ask:

- If I was with someone, what would my life look like?
- What would I like my life to look like in five years?
- In ten years?
- What would I like my life to be like?
- What would I like my life to be like in five years?
- In ten years?
- What would I like my life to look like?

It's not the *image* of what it is going to be. It's an *awareness of the energy* it's going to be.

Look around and find somebody who has what you would like to have with another person. Have you ever seen a relationship that you would like to have? No. Then you're going to have to create one yourself. Start with: What would I like my life to look like with a partner?

You're earning enough money. You could afford to hire a partner. Are you willing to pay for a boy toy? You've already come to the conclusion that it wouldn't be that much fun instead of asking: What would I like to create and generate here?

This is probably the most insane area on planet Earth. This is why we are doing these calls.

What stupidity are you using to create the total unawareness of the awareness of what you could be choosing, that you would like to choose, that if you chose it would create a relationship that would be of your choosing? Everything that is times a godzillion, will you destroy and uncreate it all? Right and Wrong, Good and Bad, POD and POC, All Nine, Shorts, Boys and Beyonds.

I've looked around at relationships that I thought would be something I'd like to have. I've seen some people who have great relationships that work for them, but their relationships are not relationships I would want. We don't look from the point of view of: What would be a great relationship for me?

I finally realized I'd have to have somebody in my life that would be willing to let me travel all over the world and have no point of view about whether I came back or not. How many people would be willing to do that? Probably none. It would have to be somebody who would allow me to have total freedom to be and do anything I wanted. Unfortunately the only person who fits that bill is Dain, but he doesn't fit the bill sexually, because he just won't do that.

Salon Participant:

When you look at it that way, how do you avoid going into the conclusion that you're never going to find a relationship?

Gary:

Why do you care? If you come to the conclusion that you're never going to have a relationship, that's exactly what's going to show up. You're never going to have a relationship. Does it matter?

We keep trying to make things matter that may not matter at all. For a relationship to work, it has to be something that allows each person to totally be himself or herself and create different possibilities. You have to know what you'd like to create as your life. Are you clear about what you'd like your life to be in five years? Start with:

- What would I like my life to be like in five years?
- Ten years?
- Twenty years?
- Would I really like to have somebody there with me on that journey?

I discovered that I didn't really care whether there was anybody there with me for that journey. I realized I was going to go whether anybody else went along or not. So, I now have people who want to do things with me in different times and different areas. That sort of fulfills the sense of need of relationship because I have a relationship in those ten seconds. That is a way in which you can incorporate relationship with others without feeling like you need a relationship. Also, you have the opportunity to create something different.

Ask: If I were going to have a relationship, what would I like it to be? I've seen very few relationships that I thought were really great. I have friends who have a great relationship in every way except that they never have sex. I have friends who have a great sexual relationship and fight all the time. I have friends who have everything they would like to have, but they are not happy with their life. It's not exciting. They have everything figured out. Life is predictable. A lot of people think predictability is the relationship they would like to have. Changeability would be closer to what I would want as a relationship—where a constant state of change is possible.

My second wife was changeable, but she was not willing to have a financial reality that included *having* money. She was only willing to have a financial reality that *spent* money. That was the killer of the relationship because I couldn't live with no money and no choice but to go to work. There was a necessity of always having to work because every time I turned around, we were out of money. I didn't like living on that edge. She doesn't mind. It's okay with her.

So, start to look at:

- What would I like my life to be like in five years, ten years, twenty years?
- What would I like to have going on in my life?
- Is there someone in the world who would be fun to do that with or be that with?

Don't even include the idea of relationship. Ask what you'd like your life to look like. If what you're asking to create as your future would include a relationship, then you will get one. If it can't include a relationship, then you won't get one. The relationship is going to create what you'd like to have. Another person is not going to come in and take care of you or anything else. It's about you creating what you would really like to have. When you do that, a whole different reality can start to show up for you.

Then ask: What would I have to be or do today to create that reality right away?

The thing I know about you, H, is you would like to have something that's comfortable and easy, something that provides sufficient money for you to do whatever you want. You've pretty much got that now. So, if you were going to have a relationship, it would have to be somebody who is on the same wavelength with you on that, someone who would not expect you to give that to him. If he expects you to give it to him, you'll be resentful. You don't want to have to provide everything. You have to be clear with yourself about what will and won't work for you. It's not about good or bad. It's just about the way you want to create your life and your relationships. If you start to get clear about that, everything will start to work more easily.

Remember, you're looking for comfort, you're looking for ease and you're looking for whatever makes your life work. Start by asking:

- What would I like my life to be like in five years?
- In ten years?
- In twenty years?

If you start to look from there and you get the energy of what that would be like, you'll get the elements of what you wish to create. If the elements also include a relationship, you'll be able to create it.

Thank you all for being on this call.

5

Pragmatic Choice

*You've got to look at the pragmatic choice you have at each moment.
If you start to look at the pragmatic choice,
a different possibility can show up.*

Gary:

Hello ladies. Let's begin with some questions.

Looking for Comfort and Reassurance Outside of You

Salon Participant:

I find being held by a man very comforting and reassuring. My current boyfriend does not hold me enough. I oscillate between telling myself it's my own silly need and I shouldn't impose on him to fulfill it and feeling that being held provides me with a nurturing energy. What is going on here and what energy am I really after?

Gary:

What you're really after is the first thing you said, "I find it comforting and reassuring."

What stupidity are you using to create the comfort and reassuring you are choosing? Everything that is times a godzillion, will you destroy and uncreate it all? Right and Wrong, Good and Bad, POD and POC, All Nine, Shorts, Boys and Beyonds.

If you are totally present as you and you totally have you, the comfort and the reassuring you get by being held is not a necessity.

Unfortunately, that means you'll get a man who wants to hold you all the time, which will be really annoying.

There are people who use food as comfort. There are people who use sex as comfort. There are people who use alcohol as comfort. There are people who use shopping as comfort. There is a lot of comfort and reassuring that goes in many different directions. That's the reason I picked up this particular issue.

Salon Participant:

Are support and caring similar to comfort and reassuring?

Gary:

Support and caring are part of comfort and reassuring. Women comfort and reassure one another by sharing, by going to the bathroom together and by shopping together. There are about twenty-five other things they have to do together. That sense of togetherness is what people look to as comfort and reassurance. If you are truly willing to have you, the being, in totality, you need nothing outside of you to comfort or reassure you. You're comforted and reassured just by being. That's the whole idea.

How do we get to the point where we have comfort and reassurance based on being, not based on what we have to do or any of the other crazy stuff that people think is necessary?

Salon Participant:

What is support?

Gary:

Support is a job title and a choice. You can be a support person. That means you either get to be a jock strap or you get to be a bra. What part of the body do you want to hold up with your support?

Or do you want to look for how you can empower instead? Support is a reference for not embracing the possibilities of empowerment; instead you're being a support for somebody.

You use the past for comfort and reassurance. You use reference points, you use your family, you use your kids. There are a thousand things you use. People say, "It's so comforting to have my family around." Not exactly. It takes a lot more work.

You use work as comfort. There are people who are comforted by having too much to do. There are people who are comforted by their drugs. There are people who are comforted by the kind of clothes they put on. They have comfort clothes. It's like looking for something that will take the place of what Mom or Dad should have been for you that they might not have been. Or if they were comforting people, it's a place where you are reassured or comforted by the way you were by them.

Salon Participant:

It feels like rather than being me, I'm always looking outside of myself for something.

Gary:

Exactly. When you are looking for comfort and reassurance outside of you, you never actually get to be present enough to ask yourself:

- Do I really want this?
- Is this really necessary?
- Do I really care?
- Is that really what I need?

You have places where you have created comfort and reassurance as though that equals security. People look for security. It is the idea that you have a solid place on which to stand rather than a solidity of being, which allows you to stand anywhere and everywhere without a sense that you cannot be or cannot hold your position.

Everybody is trying to create a position. This is a positional world. We are always trying to find where we belong, what we belong to, and who we belong to. What is the appropriate thing to have? What is the appropriate thing to do? Who is the right person to talk to? Who is the right person to be with? All of these things are the positional hierarchy we create to determine a fixed point of view that gives us the comfort and reassurance of having a solid and secure reality. Comfort and reassurance are part of the certainty universe for creating a sense that you have a place in which you can be instead of being the space you are, which is where you are always you and you are never in need of changing.

I was talking with someone the other day and he said, "This woman is so amazing. It's like she is one person when she's with kids, she's another person when she's with parents, she's another person when she's in class. She's another person when she's with me and another when she does processing."

I said, "Yeah. Welcome to the world."

He asked, "What do you mean?"

I said, "She has to continuously adjust herself because from her point of view, being who she is, is not enough."

Salon Participant:

You've talked about the stupidity of where we bring things back from the past. Is that related to the comfort zone?

Gary:

Yes, you're always trying to bring back the sense of comfort you had at some earlier point. People ask, "What about my past? What about my story?" Those are things that recur in people's universes. The validity of the story. The right thing to do. The necessity of getting back their sense of self. The necessity of getting back their sense of me.

What stupidity are you using to create the comfort and reassuring you are choosing? Everything that is times a godzillion, will you destroy and uncreate it all? Right and Wrong, Good and Bad, POD and POC, All Nine, Shorts, Boys and Beyonds.

Salon Participant:

Are comfort and reassurance energies—or are they just ways of thinking?

Gary:

They are mostly ways of thinking, because we've been taught that life is supposed to be about comfort and nurturance. If you ask the question, "Can this person provide the comfort, nurturance or reassurance that I desire?" you'll get a *no*. He cannot provide what you desire. He can only provide what he desires. That's all he can see.

You guys say, "I want to be held, and it will be so wonderful." But if you have a man who gets what holding is from your point of view, he's probably going to be a mangina, a man who is so sensitive he cries every time you have sex. You're going to be saying, "This is so boring. I want out of here."

"That Was Really Nice, Darling"

You are the only one who can see what is comforting and reassuring to you. You're the only one. No one else can see it. You have to find out whether the person you're asking to provide it can give it to you the way you desire it. If he doesn't provide it the way you desire it, there will be a tendency to go into judgment of the guy. The moment you go into judgment, you're killing the relationship.

However, when he gives you five minutes of what you'd like, if you say, "That was really nice, darling. That made me feel so good. Thank you. I'm so grateful," the next time you might get six minutes.

And after those six minutes, if you say, "That felt so wonderful. I love it when you hold me," you might get seven minutes the next time.

But if you go to, "You just don't hold me enough!" you're going to get three minutes from then on. You have to learn how to create a situation that *encourages* the guy rather than the complaint that *kills* the guy. If you want a stallion in the bedroom, you'd better not be a nag in the kitchen.

If you start nagging the boy, you're going to have a gelding. You're cutting off his testicles every time you nag him. Nagging does not help men become erect! If you want a man to be erect, you're going to have to curb your tongue.

Men Suppress Their Sensitivity

Salon Participant:

Have men always been much more sensitive than women? Is it actually the opposite of what it seems?

Gary:

Yes. Men have always been much more sensitive because they've had to suppress their sensitivity from day one. Women have been allowed to express theirs by screaming, yelling, crying, stomping their feet or doing something else. Men always have to depress their sensitivity. That doesn't make them any less sensitive. They get their feelings hurt just like women do. The difference is, a woman will say, "You hurt my feelings." A man will go silent and withdraw.

Salon Participant:

How does it work with women who suppress stuff?

Gary:

They end up becoming like men. They have the sensitivity but they cannot express it, they cannot live with it and they cannot do anything with it. So, they tend to withdraw. If you're somebody who is sensitive and has not been allowed to be sensitive, you will withdraw every chance you get because you think that's the way to protect yourself or others.

You have to have allowance for you. What percentage of allowance do you have for you? Less than ten percent? What percentage of allowance do you have for others? More than fifty percent? You have more than fifty percent of allowance for others and less than ten percent for you. That's not your best choice, yet that's where all of us function from. If we don't have allowance for us, how can we expect *others* to have allowance for us? How can we expect to get anything in life the way we would actually like to have it?

What stupidity are you using to create the degrees of allowance you are choosing? Everything that is times a godzillion, will you destroy and uncreate it all? Right and Wrong, Good and Bad, POD and POC, All Nine, Shorts, Boys and Beyonds.

Sharing is something you do with women because you find it comforting and reassuring to be able to talk things out. Men are not comforted or reassured by talking things out. They are traumatized by it. I would love to tell you that there are men out there who can talk to you about this. There aren't. That's not the way they are trained from the beginning.

Salon Participant:

Are you saying that men function completely from looking for encouragement and that any comment that looks like it's not gratitude makes them withdraw?

Gary:

Yeah, they withdraw and go away. This is something that is created in men from the time they are little boys. When I was a kid, I was told, "You have to stand strong, you have to be quiet, and you have to not cry." Not crying was considered the most important thing about being a man. It was about not showing emotion and not being emotionally involved in anything. It has not changed that much.

Men are far more delicate in their space of the energetics of living than women are, because women have someone to share with—another woman. Women share their "feelings." Women share what's going on for them. Women talk about things. Men never do. They don't say things like, "My wife hurt my feelings last night." They never mention those things. They suck it up. What they learn to do in life, for the most part, is withdraw. That's what they're taught as little boys.

Sometimes women say things like, "You should just tell that man what to do." That's not going to get you what you want. When people tell you that, are they your friend—or your enemy? This is hard for women. Men assume everybody is an enemy until they prove they are a friend. Women assume everybody is a friend until they prove they're an enemy. Even then, they can't believe it.

Most men are taught that they are not allowed to have any sensitivity, and if they have any sensitivity, they must withdraw. However, there are some men who have been taught that they need to be sensitive New Age guys. Most of them cry on command in order to manipulate a result, just like women do. Women have learned that if you cry at the right moment, men will do what you want. So, that's what they do. That's not a bad thing or a good thing. That's just the way it works. I would like you to get the pragmatics of how it works, and not try to get the perfect relationship. There is no perfect relationship. There are relationships that work and relationships that don't work. There are relationships that will get better and relationships that won't. Be willing to look at how you can use things to get what you want.

It's not about being positive. It's about being present without judgment. It is manipulation. What's wrong with that? Isn't it sad they didn't teach you this when you were twelve? Wouldn't that have made your life easier?

Confrontation doesn't work. All it does is require the other person to fight or surrender. When people surrender and become the servant or the slave, they go into resentment and you lose your relationship and your connection. If they go into fight, they have to fight for the rightness of their point of view no matter what. That accomplishes little to nothing in life. What would you like to accomplish in your life with respect to relationship?

Please try this stuff. It works.

Copulation without Judgment

Salon Participant:

What does copulation without judgment look like? Do our bodies know how to be no judgment on their own? Or does our body's consciousness judge our partners too?

Gary:

No. Your body does not judge. You, the being, are the one who determines what is appropriate sex play, based on judgment.

What stupidity are you using to create the sex play you are choosing? Everything that is times a godzillion, will you destroy and uncreate it all? Right and Wrong, Good and Bad, POD and POC, All Nine, Shorts, Boys and Beyonds.

Most of us do not do sex as sex play. Women tend to do sex in order to create relationship. Men tend to do relationship in order to create sex. But nobody does sex for the play in it. If we did it for the play in it and had it as a joyful, playful thing, different possibilities could show up.

Do any of you think sex is about romance, rose petals and candles? Sex play can be just the fun of enjoying somebody's body. There is a great pleasure in finding a place on a person's body that is so sensitive that it becomes more and more pre-orgasmic every time you touch it in a way that it demands, requires and desires. You have probably never exposed yourself to recognizing your body's ability to speak to other people's bodies and to ask them:

- Body, what would you like to experience?
- What would you like to have done that would create the most enjoyable, orgasmic sexual possibility you ever had?

When I ask such a question, all of a sudden, a thought goes off in some part of the other person's body, and I start to touch that.

Should sexual excitement be from a *place*? Or should it be a *space*? When it's from a space, you start to do what people's bodies desire and you have no judgment. When you have no judgment, the *place* disintegrates and the *space* begins. Unfortunately, it doesn't work this way with a lot of people. What I would like to create with this call is more opportunities and possibilities for you and everybody you come into contact with.

What stupidity are you using to create the sex play you are choosing? Everything that is times a godzillion, will you destroy and uncreate it all? Right and Wrong, Good and Bad, POD and POC, All Nine, Shorts, Boys and Beyonds.

"Hey, Do You Want to Have Sex?"

Salon Participant:

I sometimes find myself averting my eyes when a man meets my gaze. Can we change this?

Gary:

Yes. You can become a gay man. A gay man will always intensely look at a man he wants to have sex with. He will never drop his gaze, which means, "Hey, do you want to have sex?"

Men who don't wish to do gay sex look at a man until they realize that he wants to have sex with them and then they drop their gaze.

When you don't drop your gaze and you look at a man directly in the eyes, his point of view is that you're saying you want to have sex.

What stupidity are you using to avoid creating a future beyond this reality are you choosing? Everything that is times a godzillion, will you destroy and uncreate it all? Right and Wrong, Good and Bad, POD and POC, All Nine, Shorts, Boys and Beyonds.

What energy, space and consciousness can you and your body be that would allow you to have a relationship that's greater than any reality? Everything that doesn't allow that to show up times a godzillion, will you destroy and uncreate it all? Right and Wrong, Good and Bad, POD and POC, All Nine, Shorts, Boys and Beyonds.

What stupidity are you using to create the men you are choosing? Everything that is times a godzillion, will you destroy and uncreate it all? Right and Wrong, Good and Bad, POD and POC, All Nine, Shorts, Boys and Beyonds.

Sexual Harassment

Salon Participant:

Can you speak about sexual harassment and catcalls?

Gary:

Sexual harassment and catcalls is men trying to do sexual intimidation. As a woman, you can out-intimidate any man. Just look at him condescendingly and say, "I am sorry that piece of shit ain't big enough," and walk away. You have spent your whole life trying to avoid being a slut.

What stupidity am I using to invent the lack of being a slut I am choosing? Everything that is times a godzillion, will you destroy and uncreate it all? Right and Wrong, Good and Bad, POD and POC, All Nine, Shorts, Boys and Beyonds.

Is it just in America where you feel wrong for being a woman? No, it's everywhere in the world that men stare you down and prey on you and judge you. You have to be sexually intimidating, and that's one thing you are not willing to be.

What physical actualization of being the physically intimidating bitch of possibility are you now capable of generating, creating and instituting? Everything that is times a godzillion, will you destroy and uncreate it all? Right and Wrong, Good and Bad, POD and POC, All Nine, Shorts, Boys and Beyonds.

If you have big boobs, you are more of a sexual target. But it doesn't matter whether you have big boobs or little boobs, men are idiots. They are always trying to prove that they have a desire for sex—and ninety percent of them don't. They are afraid of it. Look at them and say, "If you don't drop it, my point of view is that you have a tiny dick." All you have to do is be willing to be more intimidating than they are willing to be and they will stop harassing you.

Being Pragmatic about the Choices You Have

Salon Participant:

I have a question about a past lover. He does things to create relationship with my son and me, and at the end of the day, he doesn't want sex. He just wants to go home. Yet I know that he does want sex. I'd like to have sex and not make it significant.

Gary:

This guy is trying to create a relationship and a family, not sex.

Salon Participant:

Exactly. I don't get that.

Gary:

He is a woman. He wants a relationship.

Salon Participant:

I know. It's weird. He doesn't want sex. What is going on?

Gary:

He is trying to create a family situation. He doesn't have sex included in his picture of family and relationship. That's where he's functioning from. That's the thing about the pragmatic choices you have. Every person comes from his or her own point of view. If you're pragmatic about the choices you have, you can ask: Is this really where I want to go?

Salon Participant:

So, I would make no attempt to get him out of functioning from that because it's his choice and that's what he's after? Should I just be in allowance of it?

Gary:

You could be in allowance of it and realize he isn't the man you want.

Salon Participant:

I have other men that I sleep with because it doesn't work with this one.

Gary:

That's a great justification, "because it doesn't work with this one."

Salon Participant:

I've made it clear that I want sex. He doesn't.

Gary:

Does your son need him?

Salon Participant:

Yes, my son needs him. They are super close, and I don't want to cut that off. But I can't turn off my sexual desires. We spend the whole day together, he buys dinner, he buys lunch, he pays for every-thing and then he just wants to go home. It's weird.

Gary:

That's when you call up your boy toy and say, "Hey, you want to come over? I'm hot and bothered."

Salon Participant:

That's what I do.

Gary:

What's wrong with that? Why are you making that wrong? You can have anything you want. It's called a pragmatic choice.

Salon Participant:

I get that he wants sex. He's just scared to go there.

Gary:

Well, you could ask him, "So, what kind of commitment would I have to make to you for you to be able to have sex with me?"

Salon Participant:

That's a weird place to go.

Gary:

If you want to have sex with this guy, that's what you're going to have to choose. That's the pragmatic solution. Find out what the other person wants. What you want is fine and great and wonderful, and it means nothing to the other person. I am being blunt. I'm sorry.

The other person has an idea of what he wants. If you provide any part of that, he says, "Good. I'm getting what I want." He doesn't even see what you want. He can't. He can't read your mind. He can't be aware of what you are, even though you've been taught by every woman you've ever known that men are supposed to be able to read your mind. They are not able to. They were taught that if they did, they were wrong, and if they didn't, they were wrong. So they just get confused instead.

Fixing Things with an Ex

Salon Participant:

I would still like to fix things with my ex-husband.

Gary:

You couldn't fix things while you were with him. Why fix them when you're not? There is a difference between fixing and being aware that you care about somebody. I care for my ex-wives. I know I cannot fix things with them. I know I cannot make their lives better. I know I can never have a relationship with them again. So I do not try. Why? Because it is not pragmatically capable of being accomplished.

What stupidity are you using to create the fixing of men you are choosing? Everything that is times a godzillion, will you destroy and uncreate it all? Right and Wrong, Good and Bad, POD and POC, All Nine, Shorts, Boys and Beyonds.

This is a common flaw in the female of the species—the idea they can fix a man and then he will be fine. You don't pick a man for his fixability. You pick him for what he can fix for you.

That's the job he's been given his whole life "Mommy will love you if you fix this for me." This is how he has been entrained to this reality.

Don't look at how you can take a man and fix him. And find a man who can fix *things* for you—not *fix* you. There is nothing broken about you. Unfortunately, I see women who tend not to choose fix-it men. They choose a man who will fix them, and then they get pissed at him. If you pick a humanoid male and decide he needs fixing, he's going to do whatever he needs to do to prove to you that he doesn't. And you're going to do whatever you need to do to prove to you that he does.

What stupidity are you using to create the fixable man you are choosing? Everything that is times a godzillion, will you destroy and uncreate it all? Right and Wrong, Good and Bad, POD and POC, All Nine, Shorts, Boys and Beyonds.

Allowance

Salon Participant:

In my current relationship, I'm not hearing "thank you" or sensing appreciation from my partner for little things I do for him, such as buying a small gift or doing everyday chores to help our household run more smoothly. It is beginning to irritate me. Am I just not in a state of allowance?

Gary:

The state of allowance. I think that's next to Arkansas, isn't it?

Salon Participant:

How can I have less irritation around this?

Gary:

By recognizing what allowance really is.

What stupidity are you using to create the degrees of allowance you are choosing? Everything that is times a godzillion, will you destroy and uncreate it all? Right and Wrong, Good and Bad, POD and POC, All Nine, Shorts, Boys and Beyonds.

Salon Participant:

In a relationship, how can I tell when I am divorcing parts of me versus when I am in resistance to what a man says or what he is asking of me?

Gary:

Whenever you're in resistance and reaction or alignment and agreement, you are divorcing you because you're not in question. You give up your awareness in favor of conclusion. You need to ask:

- Do I really want to do this?
- Is this fun?
- Is this what I would like to have?
- What would actually create the greatest effect and the most fun in my life?
- What would I like more than anything else in life?

Those are the places you want to go.

"Marriage Scares Me"

Salon Participant:

I have noticed a pattern. I will be in a relationship with a man for one-and-a-half years and then I leave him.

Gary:

That's a long-term relationship.

Salon Participant:

What can I ask that will stop this pattern? I don't like commitment—and marriage scares me.

Gary:

It scares you? It ought to frighten you to death! You're not the
only one.

    What stupidity are you using to create the marriage and the
sacred vows you are choosing? Everything that is times a godzillion, will you destroy and uncreate it all? Right and Wrong, Good
and Bad, POD and POC, All Nine, Shorts, Boys and Beyonds.

Salon Participant:

I have a question about the 1-2-3 rule, where you say that after
the third time you have sex with someone, you are married. What is
the marriage you're talking about?

Gary:

After the first time you have sex, you tend to say, "That was fun.
See you later." After the second time, you say, "Let's do that again."
After the third time, you go into being married. Marriage is a place
in which you've made a commitment. You think that if you sleep
with a man three times, you've made a commitment.

    You don't even know what you're committed to because you
don't ask him, "Exactly what are you going to expect of me? Exactly
what would you like this relationship to look like? What would you
like to have next?"

Salon Participant:

Could that commitment look like anything if you're asking questions?

Gary:

Yes. Ask him, "What would you like next?" You might also ask of yourself, "Does he expect something of me?"

You don't expect anything of him because you are not looking for a normal relationship. You want to be a shagmaster. You've already had the 2.5 kids. You don't want to do that again. But that doesn't mean that the man doesn't have that kind of expectation. There are a lot of men who have the expectation that they have to find the right person for the genetic material for the family they are supposed to have. It is insane.

Relationship with a Man Who Is Bipolar

Salon Participant:

I am in a relationship with a sweet man who is bipolar. He is on meds. I suspect he is a humanoid, as he comes across quite intuitive.

Gary:

It is not intuition that characterizes humanoids. There are many humans who are intuitive. There are many humans who are psychic. There are many humans who are psychic readers. They do tarot, astrology and every other form of metaphysics. But they do it to prove something.

Salon Participant:

I struggle with feeling close to him.

Gary:

You cannot feel close to someone who is bipolar because when they feel close to another person, they feel threatened, and that brings on a bipolar episode, which creates a separation between them and their partner. This prevents you from getting close to them at all. It's a result of how they see the world and the way they'd like it to be.

Salon Participant:

I have a hard time getting where he is coming from. In past relationships, I have been more able to get where my partner is coming from.

Gary:

Coming to conclusion about where someone is coming from and being present with where he is are two different universes.

Salon Participant:

I want to connect with him. I want a working relationship. What do I need to do?

Gary:

That's not possible with someone who is bipolar. People who are bipolar create a positive world that is based on nothing but positive polarity. Then they create a negative world that's based on nothing but negative polarity. They try to avoid one and choose the other, and they can't. Do you really need to be that close—or can you enjoy the parts of him that you enjoy? You can just enjoy the man you're with.

It is hard for individuals who are bipolar or who have Asperger's or autism to have a sense of ease in connecting with other people and being close to them. They create a separation because it's the only way they can maintain the space they're in without worrying about it being shattered by somebody else's needs, requires or desires. That's just where they function from.

Being a Parent

Salon Participant:

I am getting that being a parent is part of this security thing where I'm looking outside of myself for the security I would like to have.

Gary:

When you become a parent, you are committed to your children for their entire lifetime. They are not committed to you. They will never commit to you if you're lucky. But they want you to be committed to them because that's your job. It is also about comfort and reassurance.

What stupidity are you using to create the security you are choosing? Everything that is times a godzillion, will you destroy and uncreate it all? Right and Wrong, Good and Bad, POD and POC, All Nine, Shorts, Boys and Beyonds.

Salon Participant:

I have a child who has special needs. I've been told that certain types of things will be helpful to him. Do I go for doing some of those things rather than just trying to be the energy of what he needs?

Gary:

You have to be willing to do whatever it takes for your kid. That's your job. Once you become a parent, you have decided to give up your life temporarily for theirs. In order to secure their life, you will give up part of yours. That's the pragmatic thing. What choices do you have here? Do you really have a choice to not take care of your kid? No. You made a choice. You had a child. Now it's:

- How is this going to be fun?
- How do I create my life while taking care of him?

Once you have children, you have made a commitment. You have to be willing to do that job and do it gladly, not because you have to, but because it was what you chose. The problem is most women get to a place where they become a parent, and then they lose their lives.

What stupidity are you using to create the life of motherhood you are choosing? Everything that is times a godzillion, will you

destroy and uncreate it all? Right and Wrong, Good and Bad,
POD and POC, All Nine, Shorts, Boys and Beyonds.

And when you choose not to be a mother, you judge yourself
for not having chosen it. You're damned if you do and damned if
you don't.

Salon Participant:

Is the job of taking care of kids different for men and women?

Gary:

Men have been taught that their job is to go out and earn money
and pay for the kids. Women have been taught that their job is to
nurture the kids, take care of them, change their diapers and do all
the work.

Is that anything you ever really wanted to do? No. As a humanoid woman, you would rather go out and conquer the world. You
ended up being the breadwinner and teaching your kids to take care
of themselves.

Salon Participant:

Their father is refusing to take care of them or be the breadwinner.

Gary:

He is never going to do that. You chose him for the fact that he
was going to go away. And your kids chose you and him because he
was going to go away. The girls wanted to know that they didn't have
to have a man if they didn't want to. Then they found out how to
take care of themselves whether you have a man or not. You taught
them that.

What's Wrong with Giving Your Mom What She Desires?

Salon Participant:

What occurs when you have a parent who requires nurturing and if she doesn't get it from you, she drives you nuts?

Gary:

What's wrong with giving it? What would it look like if you did give it? What is it she's requiring of you? Is it that big of a deal? You have to be in the question, "Mom, what can I do for you that lets you know how much I care about you?" Ninety percent of the time when parents say they need nurturance or caring, they just want you to tell them that you love them. Parents like to know they're being loved.

Salon Participant:

It seems like she wants me to fight with her.

Gary:

Some people consider that comforting. But if you fight with her, fight with no point of view, then you won't walk away upset. You'll say, "Wow. That was funny." My sister likes to fight. So, when I want her to know that I care for her and love her, I call her and I say, "Those damn tea-baggers!" My sister hates them. So, I rev her up for twenty or thirty minutes and she says, "Gosh, it was so much fun talking to you."

I say, "Cool! Thanks, sis!" I don't give a damn about them, but it's amusing to me to call them tea-baggers because she doesn't know what tea-bagging is. For you ladies who don't know either, tea-bagging is putting the man's testicles in your mouth and sucking on them lightly and gently.

Salon Participant:

What are the basic, commonly shared characteristics that we humanoid women seek in a relationship?

The Attitude of Gratitude

Salon Participant:

I have immense gratitude for nature and animals; however, I struggle in being grateful for the people who care most for me, including my family and my boyfriend. What is so different about having gratitude in a relationship with people than with nature and animals? Does it have to do with animals and nature not judging? What is possible regarding having more gratitude for my own human species?

Gary:

Don't bother. It's okay not to have gratitude for them. You might want a relationship with a lot of people. That doesn't mean it's going to work. That doesn't mean it's going to be easy. That doesn't mean it's going to be what you truly desire. It just means you want a relationship. If you don't do judgment, you'll have no problem.

Salon Participant:

I grew up hearing constantly from my mother that I should be grateful for everything. I should be grateful for the peas on my plate even though I hated them. I was always told that I had to have an attitude of gratitude. It's not that I'm not grateful, but how can I increase my capacity for gratitude?

Gary:

Your mother forced you into the attitude of gratitude rather than the joy of the possibilities of gratitude. She didn't educate you. She enforced it. "You will be grateful. Eat those damn peas and be grateful for them." That creates a place for you where you have resistance as your only choice. Unfortunately, she was saying, "Do what I tell you." She was putting her spin on it with, "You should be grateful," which is an underlying judgment that you're not grateful rather than a recognition of what you actually were, which was a kid who didn't like peas.

Your mother learned from her mother how to make her children wrong. Isn't that cool? She wasn't really talking about gratitude. She was talking about, "You should appreciate the fact that I've given you this." It wasn't about gratitude at all. You've misapplied and misidentified that gratitude is obligation. It will make things easier if you recognize what is gratitude and what is obligation.

Okay, ladies. That's it until next time. What I want you to get is that you need to have a sense of comfort with a man. You need to have pragmatic choice. You have to ask: What's the pragmatic choice I have here that will create greater, more expansive and more joyful ease in my life? Your life—not theirs! A lot of women are taught that they're supposed to do for the man, do for the man, do for the man and be happy. Most of the men I know have been taught that they are supposed to do for the woman, do for the woman and be happy. Except nobody is ever happy. Why? Because everybody is doing and nobody is enjoying. Nobody is actually receiving the doing the other person is doing. You've got to look at the pragmatic choice you have at each moment. If you start to look at the pragmatic choice, a diferent possibility can show up.

Thank you, all. Please use these tools. I would like you to have greater freedom in this area where you can create and generate relationship and sex in a way that works for you. You are all such powerful and amazing women. You should not have problems in this or any area, but you create yourself as less-than in order to have problems. I will do my best to get you to the place where you don't have a problem to overcome and instead you create a possibility as a new choice, which creates a new possibility, a new choice, a new question and a new contribution that you can be or receive. This is where we are heading.

6

You Are a Creator of the Future

If you don't acknowledge that you're a creator of the future,
if you don't acknowledge that you foresee the future and you can
alter and change it,
you will never be everything you are.

Gary:

Hello ladies. Are there any questions?

Women Are the Source for Creating a Different Reality

Salon Participant:

Can you talk about rape, war, the sex trade and child molestation? I hear about women being stolen and sexually assaulted. What can we do about it? Can we change it? How do we change it?

Gary:

As a female, you created the possibility of you being the source for creating a different reality for men. That's why you became a woman instead of a man.

This is the thing that you women don't get about yourselves. You look at how men force you to do things, how there is rape, how it's terrible and how it shouldn't occur. But in order for any of that to occur, there is some awareness that has to be turned off. The reality is that you, as a woman, have the capacity to change all of mankind. That's what you came here to do and that's what you're not doing.

What stupidity are you using to avoid the awareness of being the catalyst for changing all mankind are you choosing? Everything that is times a godzillion, will you destroy and uncreate it all? Right and Wrong, Good and Bad, POD and POC, All Nine, Shorts, Boys and Beyonds.

Men Are Here to Maintain the Status Quo

Salon Participant:

Would you say that about men as well?

Gary:

Men have come here to maintain the status quo. They don't realize it. The status quo is men go to war and die and women create the future. The difficulty is that women are not creating the future, which is what they came here to do.

What physical actualization of being the creator of a totally different reality, of a future that's beyond this reality, are you now capable of generating, creating and instituting? Everything that doesn't allow that to show up times a godzillion, will you destroy and uncreate it all? Right and Wrong, Good and Bad, POD and POC, All Nine, Shorts, Boys and Beyonds.

The best way I can describe it is this: There are people who are healers and who don't acknowledge it. They don't allow themselves to move into their abilities and their capacities. They keep trying to function as though they're not really healers. They lock stuff into their body and they hurt their body with it. It's the same with you as a creator of the future. If you don't acknowledge that you're a creator of the future, if you don't acknowledge that you foresee the future and you can alter and change it, you will never be everything you are.

Everything that does not allow you to perceive, know, be and receive everything you actually are, will you destroy and uncreate it all? Right and Wrong, Good and Bad, POD and POC, All Nine, Shorts, Boys and Beyonds.

Salon Participant:

Is this underlying the battle of the sexes?

Gary:

That is what has been done to us to create the separation of us from infinite being. Make men the purveyors of the status quo and make women the creators of the future and then tell them that the only way they can create the future is by having children—not that they have the ability to create the future. So, they keep thinking having children is creating the future when it's not.

Salon Participant:

If men are maintaining the status quo, and we have so many men who are "leaders," is that a way to get them to not look at the future? It's all backwards.

Gary:

This whole reality is backwards. We have men as the leaders. But how does that work? It doesn't. With men as leaders, our political system is about, "We need to make things change without changing. We need to make things better without changing them or by changing them as little as possible. We need to make things better, but we'll do it the way we've always done it. We won't do it totally different."

If you women don't acknowledge the fact that you have the capacity to create a future that has never existed on the planet, you are not being the strength you are. Humanoid women want to go out, do battle and conquer the world. That's what you want to do—because you know there is a future that's possible that has not existed on this planet.

Everything you have done to deny, not know, not see, not be, not perceive and not receive everything you're capable of changing and how you are capable of changing it and creating a different reality on this planet, will you destroy and uncreate it all? Right and Wrong, Good and Bad, POD and POC, All Nine, Shorts, Boys and Beyonds.

If you were willing to be 990% of who you are, you would be willing to see how you can change things. You'd be willing to see how you can create a different possibility. Apparently, I'm a woman in a man's body, because I am always willing to see how things can be changed and how the future can be different. I'm willing to see a possibility that's different from anything we have ever perceived, known, been or received. It's imperative to realize that the reason you came to planet Earth is to create a reality that has never existed before.

The way you create the human version of perceiving, knowing, being and receiving is by doing petty, backstabbing stuff. If you were competitive about creating a reality that has never existed and you were more willing to compete about creating something greater than what currently exists, would that change what happens in your life? Would that change the way you function with one another? Would that change what you're trying to create and generate?

A Future We Haven't Stepped Into

Salon Participant:

Are you talking about a future in which people are aware that they can heal themselves?

Gary:

I don't know what the future is that I am talking about. I just know there is a future available to us that we haven't stepped into.

What generative capacity for the instant solidification of the elementals into reality by request of the quantum entanglements fulfilled as perceiving, knowing, being and receiving a future that will create a future beyond the future that is currently being created are you now capable of generating, creating and instituting? Everything that doesn't allow that to show up times a godzillion, will you destroy and uncreate it all? Right and Wrong, Good and Bad, POD and POC, All Nine, Shorts, Boys and Beyonds.

You're not willing to create the future. You don't want to be responsible for what the future creates. If you were responsible for what got created in the future, you'd have to be responsible when half the people on the planet had to die based on the future you created. Would that be easy for you or hard for you? What are you not willing to do and be? Most of this has occurred because you are not willing to do and be something.

What are you not willing to be and do, that if you were willing to be and do it, would create a future that mankind could never deny? Everything that is times a godzillion, will you destroy and uncreate it all? Right and Wrong, Good and Bad, POD and POC, All Nine, Shorts, Boys and Beyonds.

A future that has never been is not definable. Creation in this reality is about creating what everybody else understands—what they already have, or should have or ought to have. I'm not talking about that. I'm asking: What do you want to create?

Salon Participant:

What if I don't have a definition for the future? I know there is a lightness and a space. It's out there, but I don't have a definition for it. It's not, "I want to create a hundred million dollars."

Gary:

Creating a hundred million dollars is a definition of future based on this reality. What if the future you could create would give you ten billion dollars? Could you define that? You keep trying to define what creating the future is rather than being aware that creation of future is the creation of an undefined reality based on possibilities—not conclusion. An undefined reality is realizing, "What I would like is something different. What I can create is something different. I have no idea what that is. If I have no idea what I can create, what can I create?"

Salon Participant:

Does it matter what the future is? Isn't it more that if everyone is aware of what they choose, then they can choose it or not choose it? There is no need for any of these issues.

Gary:

Yes, but you would rather deal with the issues because you would rather have a problem to solve or something concrete to do than live from a future that has no solidity.

"I Get So Bored"

Salon Participant:

I get so bored running MTVSS. Can you help me with that?

Gary:

You haven't been claiming that you can create a future that hasn't existed. When you don't claim that, you make yourself bored with what you're not willing to be and do.

What stupidity are you using to create the boredom and the diminishment of you that you are choosing? Everything that is times a godzillion, will you destroy and uncreate it all? Right and Wrong, Good and Bad, POD and POC, All Nine, Shorts, Boys and Beyonds.

The things we do in Access Consciousness are not about giving you an answer. They're about opening the door to what you're capable of that you have not yet acknowledged, perceived, known or been. Access is about giving you the possibility of creating and choosing that.

Get clear on what you are capable of. You keep trying to pretend that you're somehow stymied by this reality, stopped by this reality, controlled by this reality and limited by what other people will not choose.

As a woman, you can choose what other people cannot choose. How many of you have spent your life creating as though there is no future? Yet you are the source of future, and you are giving men the source of future. That's why I have so many women working for me.

What stupidity are you using to create the no future you are choosing? Everything that is times a godzillion, will you destroy and uncreate it all? Right and Wrong, Good and Bad, POD and POC, All Nine, Shorts, Boys and Beyonds.

If you had to acknowledge the fact that you are the creator of the future, would you want to acknowledge that—or would you try to find a reason why there was no future so you wouldn't have to create?

I'm not asking you to create a future based on the past. I'm asking you to create a future that has never existed here. Do you notice that when I ask that, there is a lightness in your universe you cannot define? That's because this whole area of what is definable isn't definable.

All of you who are trying not to create so you won't have to create a future and be responsible for the future that gets created because you think the past sucks, will you destroy and uncreate it all? Right and Wrong, Good and Bad, POD and POC, All Nine, Shorts, Boys and Beyonds.

Salon Participant:

You've talked about creating a future that has never existed as well as a future beyond this reality. Is there a difference between the two?

Gary:

Not really. If you create a future beyond this reality, it has to be something that has never existed here. The only futures that have been created here are the predictability of the future based on the past—the probability structures of this reality.

The Ultimate in Credentials

Salon Participant:

I have been giving the Bars to people without charging them anything, hoping that will change someone's universe. But then people say I don't have any qualifications as a life coach.

Gary:

You've been hoping and praying—but you haven't been imposing what is actually possible. Tell people you have a "CFMW" degree. Just state that. They won't ask what it is. They will assume they should know what it is.

You are looking for the justification that what you are doing is right instead of being willing to be the awareness of how you can create a different future.

People are saying you don't have credentials because you're not charging them for what you do. The ultimate in credentials on planet Earth is the willingness to charge. The more you charge, the better people think you are. If you're trying to give something away, it's worth exactly what people are paying you. Nothing. You have to charge people if you want them to value what you give. You are trying to create a future. You're not willing to charge what will create them being willing to have that kind of future.

Salon Participant:

When I think of money, it feels elusive.

Gary:

You are choosing not to have it, which is why you keep trying to give Access Consciousness away by running people's Bars for free. You keep trying to make Access a religious experience instead of a creative experience. Access Consciousness is not religious. It's not something you have to worship. It's not something you have to do. It's not something you have to see as greater than you. It's something you have to see as the possibility of a different possibility that has never been a possibility in this reality.

Salon Participant:

Access Consciousness speaks to an energy that I always knew was possible.

Gary:

Yes, I know that. You keep trying to define it by this reality, which is why you keep trying to give it away instead of charging enough to make people value it. People value nothing that they get for free. Stop trying to share it. Women try to share. Go beyond being that. You can see what would change things for people—but you have to wait and listen for what people request of you.

"Do They Desire What I Have to Offer?"

Salon Participant:

I would love to bring more awareness to everyone I am around.

Gary:

You haven't asked whether they want that. You're not functioning from the question, "Do they desire what I have to offer?" You're like the Southern mother who cooks grits and says, "Eat these. These are good for you." Whether the person like grits is irrelevant. The fact that they were made means he or she has to eat them.

Salon Participant:

I don't get it.

Gary:

What is your ethnic background?

Salon Participant:

I am Cambodian.

Gary:

What is the primary sauce in Cambodia?

Salon Participant:

Fermented fish sauce.

Gary:

You create fermented fish sauce and you say to someone, "Here's some fermented fish sauce for you. I put it on everything you are going to eat. Now enjoy it." You're trying to say, "This consciousness is the perfect fermented fish sauce. Eat it."

The other person is saying, "But I don't like fermented fish sauce."

You're saying, "That's all right. It's good for you. Eat it."

That's the conclusion it's good. You keep trying to come to conclusion about what you're supposed to deliver instead of asking the question: What can these people hear? That's being aware of what they can hear and not hear—and not having a point of view about it.

The future is an undefined reality—but you are trying to define it. You're saying, "As long as it has fish sauce on it, it'll be fine," rather than, "I can have a reality in which fish sauce exists or fish sauce doesn't exist. I'm going to create a future which will work in a different way than everybody here thinks is real because that's what works for me."

You don't know what the future is going to be, but you keep trying to create a future based on what you've decided is appropriate as a future rather than asking: What could exist as a future that we haven't even considered?

Your Capacity to Change Reality

Salon Participant:

What can women be or do to invite more men to Access Consciousness?

Gary:

There are more women in Access than men because men are trying to maintain the status quo. That's what they've been taught to do. They've been taught from day one, "You have to fix this, not change it."

Women have been taught they've got to change their clothes because that's changing. Of course, that's just changing the image. What if you didn't change the image but you changed you?

What physical actualization of the eternal capacity to change reality are you now capable of generating, creating and instituting? Everything that doesn't allow that to show up times a godzillion, will you destroy and uncreate it all? Right and Wrong, Good and Bad, POD and POC, All Nine, Shorts, Boys and Beyonds.

I am going to talk about your capacity to change reality over the next few calls. The willingness to do this and to be this requires a commitment on your part to give up everything you defined as real and good in this reality, whether that's being in a family, living by other people's needs, having a perfect relationship or creating someone in your life. There is a point at which you have to be willing to create a future that has never existed, which will alter the way everything shows up in your life.

Look at what you'd like your life to be and create from that, so if having a man in your life works, then you have it. If it doesn't, you don't. It's not about creating your life based on, "How do I get the relationship I need?" but "How do I get the life I'd like to have?"

Now I am going to ask you to go a step further. Ask: What would I like as a future that I have never even considered possible? Have you considered a hundred million dollars? Yes. No problem. But you won't let that happen because of what? The reality is you have no idea.

Everything you have done to eliminate the hundred million dollars you could have in your life because _____, will you destroy and uncreate it all? Right and Wrong, Good and Bad, POD and POC, All Nine, Shorts, Boys and Beyonds.

You've defined the kind of future having a hundred million dollars would create for you. You've decided, "Having a hundred million dollars means I do this, this and this. I have this, this and this." What if your definition of you is part of the limitation you're functioning from? The only reason you don't have a hundred million dollars is that you've defined yourself as not having a hundred million dollars.

What stupidity are you using to create the definition of you that you are choosing? Everything that is times a godzillion, will you destroy and uncreate it all? Right and Wrong, Good and Bad, POD and POC, All Nine, Shorts, Boys and Beyonds.

You Have to Look at How Men Function

Salon Participant:

My husband and I have been together since we were fifteen and seventeen years old. We have been through amazing changes in our relationship. When we are both vulnerable and connected we have a relationship that really works. However, there is a problem. It seems that when things are really wonderful, my husband will go into trauma and drama about something I do. I don't get upset about it, but it seems the more I don't get upset, the more he gets mad. He withdraws and puts walls up.

Gary:

That's because he has to maintain the status quo.

Salon Participant:

The last time this happened, he pulled his energy back so strongly that he literally disappeared in front of my eyes. He disconnected from me for several days or a week. Eventually he wanted to reconnect like it never happened. Can you provide some clarity on this?

Gary:

Try asking: What energy, space and consciousness can I be to create a different reality in totality? It may not happen immediately. It takes the universe a little while to rearrange things.

Salon Participant:

I try to talk to him about it, but that doesn't work.

Gary:

You have to look at how men function. Men function from, "If we have to discuss it, it means there's something wrong, and I've got to fix it." If you really want to discuss something, you have to say, "Honey, I've been thinking about this. What do you think?" Then leave him alone for two to three days. He'll come to some conclusion, which will give you clarity about what you have to handle and what you have to change to make it different.

Never say, "Tell me what you want." He has no idea. A man has to sit down, watch TV for twenty-seven hours, and come to a conclusion. He cannot come to an instant conclusion about it. He doesn't know how to share. He has never been taught to share. He has no idea what sharing means. You women keep asking, "Will you share your feelings with me?" He can't share his feelings because he has been taught that the one thing he needs to do when he feels something is withdraw from it. If you try to get him to share, you're punching him directly in the testicles. That's not the way you want to create a relationship.

You keep choosing the same kind of man over and over again instead of choosing a relationship that will work. Part of the problem is that you have standards or ideals about what you think a man should be. The men who don't meet those standards are the men who would give you what you say you want, not what you're getting.

I'd like you to get that you don't have to hate men. You don't have to push men away. You don't have to choose men. You just have to be willing to allow men to be exactly who they are and have no point of view about it. Interesting point of view will create a different reality.

The joy of being a feminine humanoid is that you have the ability to create the future. That's one of the things most of you have not been willing to acknowledge.

What stupidity are you using to create totally avoiding creating the future you know is possible are you choosing? Everything that is times a godzillion, will you destroy and uncreate it all? Right and Wrong, Good and Bad, POD and POC, All Nine, Shorts, Boys and Beyonds.

It is about creating a reality beyond this reality. It is not about creating beyond what you know. You know that a different reality is possible, and you've been trying to figure out what it is forever. Haven't you noticed? You have not been willing to see what you're capable of that others are not capable of.

What stupidity are you using to create the lack of generative capacity and awareness of future are you choosing? Everything that is times a godzillion, will you destroy and uncreate it all? Right and Wrong, Good and Bad, POD and POC, All Nine, Shorts, Boys and Beyonds.

Being Out of Context

Salon Participant:

It seems like choosing our generative capacity and awareness of future would require getting out of any kind of context. Is that correct?

Gary:

If you define yourself as a woman, is that a context? Yes, it is. It creates the parameters of how you relate to everything and everyone. How much of what you have learned about being a woman indicates that you're supposed to be a major support, the backbone of a reality, not the creator of a reality? Is that true? Or is that what you've been buying as true that's limiting you?

Everything you've bought as true about being a woman, a feminist and a feminine person that isn't true, will you return it to sender with consciousness attached? Right and Wrong, Good and Bad, POD and POC, All Nine, Shorts, Boys and Beyonds.

By the Choices You Make, You Create a Different Future

Salon Participant:

Recently I was watching *Jane Eyre* and I began crying at the end. I realized it wasn't that I was waiting for Mr. Rothschild. It was more like any time I've gone into a relationship, my requirement has been to have intimacy with that person, with all things and with all people. I saw how much intimacy I've been looking for. Is going with that energy looking to create a different future?

Gary:

Yeah. This reality is not based on an intimacy of possibility. This reality is based on the distance we can create between us to make sure that we are never close enough to actually create and generate something that will dynamically change everything around us.

Salon Participant:

Would following the energy of the places I have been looking for intimacy create a different future?

Gary:

Yes, it would. By the choices you make, you create a different future. This is what you can do. This is the way you can create a future that doesn't exist here.

What stupidity are you using to avoid the future you could be creating and choosing are you choosing? Everything that is times a godzillion, will you destroy and uncreate it all? Right and Wrong, Good and Bad, POD and POC, All Nine, Shorts, Boys and Beyonds.

You can create a different future by the choices you make. This is easier for women than men because men have been taught they are supposed to maintain what is. They are supposed to work and fix everything; they're not supposed to change things. You were taught that at the very least, you should change your dress. That's a very different place to function from.

When something doesn't turn out the way you thought, you go to the judgment of it. But if you're willing to create the future, you cannot predict how anything is going to turn out. It's not a probability structure. It's a possibility system. We try to avoid losing by creating probabilities of what will win or lose. Does that create? No. It just maintains. That's what men have been taught to do—maintain, based on the probability: "If I don't speak, women won't hate me. If I don't make a mistake, women won't be angry with me. If I don't do this wrong, women will be happy with me." Men function from a level of probability structure that is demented and cemented into their reality with such intensity that seldom do they actually get true choice. But when they chose it, like you, they can create a different possibility.

It's One Choice, Then Another

Salon Participant:

Are you saying I don't have to create the whole thing today? It's one choice, then another and another?

Gary:

Yes, it's one choice. It's choosing to hear when you don't want to hear. Choosing that one thing that gnaws at you until you choose it. Being aware of what you're aware of, even though you don't want to be aware of how aware you are. You know you have to do it. You know you can. You know something is possible. What other choice do you have?

What physical actualization of a totally different reality and a totally different future are you now capable of generating, creating and instituting? Everything that doesn't allow that to show up times a godzillion, will you destroy and uncreate it all? Right and Wrong, Good and Bad, POD and POC, All Nine, Shorts, Boys and Beyonds.

You Can Have a Different Reality

Salon Participant:

I've been waking up with the question, "What if today was different?"

Gary:

What if today can be different than I've ever imagined? Choose to create something that actually is a future. That will create something different from what has been here before. Everything right now is designed to destroy the Earth.

Salon Participant:

Since I was a child, each time I have tried to create a different reality, I have been called stupid.

Gary:

Do you get that you are one of the people who could create a different future if you would choose it? You can create a different future for the people in your life by the choices you make when you are with them. Every choice you make can create a different future than you think you are creating. Come out of this reality and start realizing that you can have a different reality, one that is yours, regardless of what anyone thinks. There is always some kind of judgment. There is always someone who thinks you are stupid. But regardless of what anyone thinks, there is a different future.

Definition Is the Destroyer

Salon Participant:

You're talking about creating a future that's undefinable and you're asking us to be undefinable. Anywhere there is definition, is that where the destroyer would come into the creation to undo it?

Gary:

Yes. Wherever you try to define what creation of future is, you destroy future in favor of a different version of present.

If you couldn't define what you thought was a good thing for the future, would you have to create what would create a future that was greater than what you knew possible? What if the choice you had available in the creation of the future was not what you thought it was, but was greater than what it could be? If you define that creating a great future reality is creating a hundred million dollars, then you've defined that as a great future. What if that's a limited future, not a great future? What if that's the thing that blocks you, not the thing that creates for you?

What's My Target Here on Planet Earth?

I created Access Consciousness beyond what anybody in this reality said was possible. From the very beginning, everybody told me I was wrong. Everything I did was wrong. The way I created it was wrong. The structure of it was wrong. The system I was choosing was wrong. I wasn't doing the things that would create it as the perfect cult. I wasn't creating it in a way that would make everybody come and stay. But that wasn't my target.

You have to start looking at:

- What's my target here on planet Earth?
- Do I want to have a relationship and a family and live happily ever after, according to somebody else's reality of "happily ever after"?
- Or do I want to create something different?
- What would actually work for me that wouldn't necessarily work for anybody else?

You have available to you the capacity to create a future that nobody else can see, nobody else can be, nobody else can choose and nobody else will ever consider as valuable—but it will always be valuable to you. A different possibility exists here. But you have to choose it.

You have to see your capacity as the woman you are. You have the capacity to create a future that has never existed. That's what you came here to do. That's what you're here for. That's what you know is possible. That's what you have not yet chosen to be or do. You've tried to choose it according to this reality's version of what's right.

What if that was the least of you, not the best of you? You keep trying to look at the best of you as though the least of you is the best of you. It isn't. You have so much more of you available. I'm sorry I can't give it all to you on this call.

Salon Participant:

Could you talk about the difference between *valuable* and *significant*?

Gary:

You make things *valuable* according to other people's realities because what other people define as *significant* is what you think you're supposed to deliver. That which is least significant to you is what is most valuable about you.

Future based on propagation of the species is not creating reality beyond this reality. It's creating this reality over and over again as though you're going to get a different result. Are your children going to get better than you are? From personal experience, I'd say *no*. Your kids will be who they are. You can't expect them to be better than you. You can only expect them to be who they are. If they turn out to be better than you, it's amazing.

Salon Participant:

But I see my kids as better than me.

No. You *judge* them as better than you. That's different. You try to see them as better than you rather than seeing the gift you've given them—the ability to choose something that might be possible. That doesn't make them better than you. It makes them different than you, because you weren't taught that. You accumulated that on your own.

What would it be like if you were the gift that made their life better instead of thinking they are the gift that makes yours better?

What kind of future are you trying to create?

Thank you, ladies. I look forward to talking with you next week.

7

Giving Others the Realm of Possibility

True caring is not doing everything for others.
It is giving others the realm of possibility.

Gary:

Hello ladies. I'd like to begin with some questions.

What Will Allow Everything to Be Handled with Ease?

Salon Participant:

My twelve-year-old adopted son has fetal alcohol syndrome, ADHD and emotional challenges. I have struggled with him and experienced a lot of stress being a single mom. Recently he was kicked out of his after-school program. This provided a reason for him to live with his dad. I thought maybe he needed a different type of discipline than I was providing, and he had stated on several occasions that he wanted to live with his dad. Yet after this decision was made, he felt I had abandoned him.

Gary:

That's called manipulation, darling, it's not reality.

Salon Participant:

For the most part, he seems to be fine living with his dad. He is only fifteen minutes away, and I see him regularly. After all this occurred, I took some Access Consciousness classes, and at times I feel guilty, as I am learning tools that are helpful with him but I now have less access to him. The feeling of guilt has lessened over the past six months, but things still occur to make me aware of it. For instance, recently I heard from my fifteen-year-old daughter that her dad was telling people I had abandoned our son.

Gary:

You have not abandoned your son. That's the dad's way of making himself look good and you look bad. He is trying to make himself better than you; he is trying to compete with you to prove he is a good parent and you are a bad parent. That will not work out well for him in the long run, but it will work out for you if you don't buy it.

Salon Participant:

I know what he's saying is not true, but it bothers me. I am hanging onto guilt or feeling like I am not doing enough even though I remain active in my son's life and pursue things I think will benefit him. I have a lot of new awareness of the capacities he possesses. I ask myself, "What energetic synthesis of communion can I be, to be the parent my kids need me to be?"

Gary:

No, no, no. You need to ask: What energetic synthesis of communion can I be to allow all of this to happen with total ease? Don't take the point of view that you are trying to fill your kids' needs. If you take that point of view, you have already come to conclusion, decision and judgment of whom? You!

You never want to ask what your kids need you to be because kids are always asking for somebody who will do everything they want without their having to provide a single ounce of awareness. Don't ask what you can be for your kids. Ask: What will allow everything to be handled with ease?

True Caring vs. Taking Care Of

Salon Participant:

Thank you. I would say I have created a better reality with my daughter the way things are going now. She is a much happier and more engaged teen than she was a year ago.

Gary:

Yeah, because your son is not around taking up all the energy.

Salon Participant:

I am told that my son is not doing poorly and he is in the best school in the district for kids with special needs. His dad works there as well. So, what stupidity keeps me feeling guilty and susceptible to the emotional jabs his father makes about me giving up on him?

Gary:

You haven't given up on him, sweet thing. You haven't given up. You are still there for him. You haven't given up on anything. You are someone who cares.

How many of you women do not want to recognize how much you care? Everything you have done to deny your caring, will you destroy and uncreate it all? Right and Wrong, Good and Bad, POD and POC, All Nine, Shorts, Boys and Beyonds.

Recognize that *true caring* is part of you; it's not *taking care of*. If you recognize you are the creator of the future and you are willing to do it from a sense of the caring of possibilities of the future, the choices of future, you won't get caught in, "I have to take care of," "I have to do-do-do," "I have to give myself up to men," "I have to undo myself." None of that will occur.

Taking care of is an invention that says if you do something for others, you are caring. This is the invention of caring. It says that what you do for others equals you care. Caring in this reality is, "I take care of them; therefore, that proves I am caring." You do everything for someone to prove you are caring rather than recognizing what caring actually is.

True caring can be, "You do that again and I will kill you." Sometimes caring is cutting people off and not supporting them regardless of the situation. At one point, my younger son was drinking a lot, and when he drank, he became really obnoxious. Caring for him was saying, "Don't come around me when you drink because I don't like you."

As a result, he toned down his drinking. He has given it up for the most part and he is more in control of his life. My caring was to tell him, "You are not okay when you are drinking because you become an asshole. Don't drink when you are around me."

He asked, "Dad, where is your allowance?"

I said, "That is allowance, as a) I haven't reported you to police, b) I haven't killed you, and c) I have put up with your crap for long enough. Now that I am over that, you have to change." Sometimes asking somebody to change is caring. We have all signs, seals, emblems and significances of what caring is, none of which are true caring.

> What stupidity are you using to create the signs, seals, emblems and significances of caring as the wrongness, doubt, stupidity and insanity you are choosing? Everything that is times a godzillion, will you destroy and uncreate it all? Right and Wrong, Good and Bad, POD and POC, All Nine, Shorts, Boys and Beyonds.

True caring is not doing everything for others. It is giving others the realm of possibility. You have been taught that doing everything for someone proves you care. But why would you need to prove you care? We don't look at caring as giving others the realm of possibility because we are taught that in order to prove we care, we need to do x, y or z, none of which has anything to do with true choice or true possibility.

You Have to Recognize What Is

Salon Participant:

Can the same be said for love, as in, "If you love me, you will do this"?

Gary:

That's just manipulation. A woman in Access Consciousness once said to me, "I would love to have a relationship with you, but I couldn't have a relationship with Dain because he would hurt me." I told Dain she had that point of view.

After that, they got together. She started doing mean and ugly things to him, and he couldn't do anything back because he was bent on proving he wouldn't hurt her. She almost killed him!

Salon Participant:

So, in taking on the point of view, "I can't hurt her," he did everything he could do not to hurt her, including killing himself?

Gary:

Yeah, and that's not going to create possibility. You have to recognize what is rather than seeing what you *think* is.

The realm of possibility is a place in which you recognize what is actually possible, which is the whole idea of creating future. I talked about this in our last call. Women think that creating children or being a mother is creating future. That's not it. Creating future is recognizing that the choices people make are the only thing that create possibility.

Salon Participant:

I have been taught that future is what it is and I can't change it.

Gary:

It's not about changing future; it's about creating it.

Salon Participant:

That's a block for me. I have never been told the future is a creation. I have been taught it is what it is.

Creation and Invention

Gary:

Part of the problem is that we are taught to create a visual reality of something, and we get stuck with the idea that creation and
invention are the same thing.

Salon Participant:

What's the difference?

Gary:

The best way I can describe it is this: I was in Latin America
once, and I was watching television. Everything was in Spanish, and
I didn't fully understand it. They were talking about seduction and
passion, and to represent passion, they showed a pair of panties falling to somebody's ankles. The person, who had big feet, was wearing
tennis shoes and low tennis socks. It could have been a man's thong
falling down or it could have been a woman's, but whatever it was,
there was no passion in it. It was supposed to be a visual reality of
passion. It was an invention.

Salon Participant:

Could you talk more about the visual realities we invent?

Gary:

How many times do you say, "I have to see what this is going to
look like" or "I have to see how this is going to work"? It's as though
you think that if you can get the visual aspect of how something is
going to work out, you can bring it into existence.

Salon Participant:

You know where I went, Gary? I went to the visual. I see my couch. I make this couch so solid that I invent it. If I didn't use that visual, I could change the energy of this couch as I sit on it right now.

Gary:

That's probably true. When you try to do something from the visual aspect, you can only see it the way it *looks*—not the way it *is*.

Salon Participant:

That's how I see this whole reality. I use the visual. I come from that place, and I would like something different to show up.

Gary:

So, how much of this reality have you invented as real that actually isn't?

Salon Participant:

All of it.

Gary:

I have spoken about thoughts, feelings, emotions and sex or no sex being the lower harmonics of perceiving, knowing, being and receiving. We are taught to invent emotions around things that are not real. What would it be like if you weren't trying to invent these things?

What stupidity are you using to invent the signs, seals, emblems and significances of caring that you are choosing? Everything that is times a godzillion, will you destroy and uncreate it all? Right and Wrong, Good and Bad, POD and POC, All Nine, Shorts, Boys and Beyonds.

You invent thoughts, feelings, emotions and sex or no sex in order to fit in this reality. I just spoke to a woman who felt guilty

about not being a good mother to her son. Are you actually a mother? Or are you an infinite being who has invented that these kids
are related to you? Every relationship is an invention, not a creation.
When you go from invention to creation, you open the door to possibility. Invention, on the other hand, creates conclusion.

What stupidity are you using to invent the mother, the father,
the son, the Holy Ghost, the daughter and every relationship are
you choosing? Everything that is times a godzillion, will you
destroy and uncreate it all? Right and Wrong, Good and Bad,
POD and POC, All Nine, Shorts, Boys and Beyonds.

Salon Participant:

That immediately takes away a lot of judgments on ourselves.

Gary:

Yes, because every invention is designed to conclude something.
And what do you mostly have to conclude? How you are wrong.
How you are judge-able. How you made a mistake.

Salon Participant:

Yes, how I'm not good enough.

Gary:

So, how much of what you are trying to make wrong is totally
an invention? All of it, some of it, or totally all of it?

Salon Participant:

All of it.

Gary:

Everything that is times a godzillion, will you destroy and
uncreate it all? Right and Wrong, Good and Bad, POD and
POC, All Nine, Shorts, Boys and Beyonds.

Salon Participant:

Is that where we got "Necessity is the mother of invention"?

Gary:

Yeah. Because we are always trying to invent how we fit.

Salon Participant:

We make ourselves necessary.

Gary:

Yeah. If you weren't necessary, what would you actually do or be that you haven't been willing to do or be?

Salon Participant:

So, the way to get out of the invention of motherhood or parenthood is to be totally present and just be there with what's going on?

Gary:

If you were actually being there, could you be aware of possibility and what choices might be available to create possibility? Would that be a greater thing than you are currently choosing?

Salon Participant:

Much greater.

Gary:

That's why you want to go there.

You Have to Be the Energy That Shows the Possibilities

Salon Participant:

What about the children and people around you who cannot see what you see and who are trapping themselves in judgments?

Gary:

They can only trap themselves in judgments if you are not willing to create future. You have to be the energy that shows the possibilities that will give them the choices that can create and generate
the possibilities. Then a different reality shows up.

Everything that is times a godzillion, will you destroy and
uncreate it all? Right and Wrong, Good and Bad, POD and
POC, All Nine, Shorts, Boys and Beyonds.

How much of what you see as relationship with your parents is
based on a visual reality that is totally invented?

Salon Participant:

All of it.

Gary:

Everything that is times a godzillion, will you destroy and
uncreate it all? Right and Wrong, Good and Bad, POD and
POC, All Nine, Shorts, Boys and Beyonds.

How much of sex and copulation is based on visual inventions?

Salon Participant:

Oh my God, all of it!

Gary:

Everything that is times a godzillion, will you destroy and
uncreate it all? Right and Wrong, Good and Bad, POD and
POC, All Nine, Shorts, Boys and Beyonds.

Which Are You Living By—The Reality or the Illusion?

I was watching a program on TV where a woman with a glass
of champagne was sitting on a bed with rose petals spread on it. Her
lover came in with a gun in his pocket. He was angry at her for

something and was ready to blow her away. This is an example of the invention of relationships, sex, feelings and romance in your life. They invent the illusion of your life, not the reality of it. Which are you living by? The reality or the illusion?

How much of the illusion of your life have you invented that actually isn't working? Everything that is times a godzillion, will you destroy and uncreate it all? Right and Wrong, Good and Bad, POD and POC, All Nine, Shorts, Boys and Beyonds.

Salon Participant:

Can I use this visual reality to my advantage?

Gary:

All you have to do is ask:

- How much of this is real?
- How much of this is invention?

Look at the relationships you currently have. Look at your relationship with your son. How much of that relationship is real and how much is invention?

Salon Participant:

None of it is real. It's all invented.

Gary:

Everything you have done to invent the relationship, will you destroy and uncreate all of that? Right and Wrong, Good and Bad, POD and POC, All Nine, Shorts, Boys and Beyonds.

If you are inventing your relationships, is true caring actually available?

Salon Participant:

No.

Gary:

Why?

Salon Participant:

Because there is no awareness and no choice. There is nothing real there.

Gary:

Yes, true caring is based on awareness. It's not based on visual invention.

What Would You Like to Create as a Future?

Salon Participant:

Wow! How do we get there, Gary?

Gary:

That's what I am trying to get you to do. First step, you have to realize you are the creator of your future—and that's not done by having a baby. What would it be like if you were willing to perceive, know, be and receive what it would be like to create the future?

What physical actualization of creator of the future am I now capable of generating, creating and instituting? Everything that doesn't allow that times a godzillion, I destroy and uncreate it all. Right and Wrong, Good and Bad, POD and POC, All Nine, Shorts, Boys and Beyonds.

Please put this on a loop and listen to it non-stop, ladies. This is where you need to go if you really want to create a different world:

Salon Participant:

Thank you, Gary. This is so liberating. I realize I have been looking at what people are doing and asking questions like, "What is this person doing for work? How do these people survive what they are doing in their life?" I see that I have to create my own reality.

Gary:

Most people in the world are inventing their lives. How much of the life you have lived up until today has been an invention—and not a creation?

Everything you have done to create the invention, will you destroy and uncreate it all? Right and Wrong, Good and Bad, POD and POC, All Nine, Shorts, Boys and Beyonds.

How do you actually create? You start with the energy of what you'd like your life to *be*. *To be*. Not what you would like to *do*. What you would like it to *be*. Then you start to create it by bringing into physical actualization the energy you have been able to perceive that is actually possible to choose. That's where possibility and choice start to come into the computation.

Salon Participant:

I am starting to see or be that energy. Now I want to ask about phase two, bringing it into physical actualization.

Gary:

I want to talk some more about how you, as women, are the creators of the future. Men are the nesters and creators of the now. Men try to solve all the problems so everything can be easy. They want to create a situation in which there is a sense of a nest of possibility. That is the sense of peace they want to create.

Salon Participant:

Earlier you asked, "What would it take for you to have the joy of embodiment as a woman?" I said, "I don't even know what it means to help women realize that."

Gary:

That's what I am trying to do. You can't have the joy of embodiment if you don't realize that you are the creator of future. This is what you, as women, took on as a job when you came here, to be the creator of the future, and then you diminished that to the lower harmonic of having a baby.

You have to ask:

- What would I like to create as a future?
- What possibilities and choices will come into existence as the physical actualization based on future I am willing to create and generate?

Salon Participant:

You often say, "creating future" and I say, "creating the future."

Gary:

When you say, "the future," you are trying to define the future, which is not possible. Future is a multiplicity of possibilities and choices that can create and generate something greater than what we know.

Salon Participant:

So, as soon as I say, "the future," I know I am sticking it with something?

Gary:

When you say, "the future," it is as though there is only one.

Salon Participant:

It's as though it is defined.

Gary:

That's part of what has been impelled on us to believe—that there is one future for each of us, as though we have only one destiny and everything is predetermined. Is that a reality or an invention?

Salon Participant:

It's an invention.

Gary:

How much of your destiny has been invented—not created? Everything that is times a godzillion, will you destroy and uncreate it all? Right and Wrong, Good and Bad, POD and POC, All Nine, Shorts, Boys and Beyonds.

Choice Is the Dominant Source of Creation

Salon Participant:

If we choose to create beyond the illusion of invention and beyond this reality, does that take care of all our oaths and vows from the past?

Gary:

Yes. Choice is the dominant source of creation here, but we have not acknowledged that. We keep trying to look at what we have to do right to have the sense that the choices we are making are the best choices and the right choices and the choices that should be, will be or ought to be, rather than what are we creating by the choice we make today.

When you are making a choice, ask: What reality am I going to create by making this choice?

I always function from that. Lots of times when I have no clue what something is, I ask:

Do I choose this? Yes. Do I know why I am choosing it? No. Do I know my choice is going to create something? Yes. Do I know what it is going to create? No.

I am willing to be the creator of the future as well as creator of the present that creates ease. I am willing to be the man and the woman; I'm not willing to be just one or the other. I hope some of you would be willing to embrace that possibility as well.

Salon Participant:

When people take or steal from you, are you are still moving in your reality and creating your future?

Gary:

Can people actually steal from you or do they simply stop their future possibility? When people steal from you, all they are doing is stealing their future possibility. They are ending everything that could have been created and generated because of and with you.

Money is valuable based on what? Why don't you look at what people are creating? I look at how people are trying to create their lives, and I ask:

- How is this valuable?
- How is this going to work?
- What's going to happen here?

Salon Participant:

Gary, that's the way you say you function, but you exist in another reality.

Gary:

My reality is about creating future, choices, possibilities, ease and comfort in this reality. My reality encompasses all that. What if you were willing to be the creator of the future and ask: By this choice, what future am I going to create?

Future may not end up looking like you thought it would. You have to take money and other things out of computation. You have to ask:

- What is this choice going to create as a future possibility?
- What choices are going to be available to me and everybody else as a result of my choice?

I never see what I choose as a completion of anything. I make a choice, and it opens doors to other possibilities for all kinds of people.

Are you guys beginning to get how caring and future are related?

Salon Participant:

I am not quite there.

Gary:

Tell me the parts you understand.

Salon Participant:

I understand that my choices create a future whether I know what the future is or not.

Gary:

You have to ask: What future am I going to create by the choice I am making today? You cannot *not* do that.

"I Want This Now"

Salon Participant:

I have been very frustrated the past few weeks.

Gary:

What is frustration? Frustration is you decided you needed a particular result and your choices are not creating that. When you decide you need a specific result, you're inventing a timeline on it.

"I want this now. I want this next week." You are putting time into the computation of what your choice is going to create—and you can't do that.

You stop the energy that is going to create the choice and possibility. You stop the future in favor of the now that you think has to occur. *Now* is not just today; *now* is also next week or next month. You have to be willing to create a future that goes beyond your lifetime. *That's* the future you have to be willing to create.

Salon Participant:

I don't find a lot of significance in this, so I don't know what the future is.

Gary:

Have you ever heard the commandment, "No form, no structure, no significance"?

Salon Participant:

Yes, I feel like I literally walk around, disappearing into the wind.

Gary:

And that would be wrong based on what?

Salon Participant:

That I am not here, living an easy, luxurious life or somehow creating a life.

Gary:

That's a conclusion; it's not a question. You have already decided that future looks like x, y, z, which means it's an invention. You are trying to see what it looks like, which is all invention.

Everything you have done to invent all of that, will you destroy and uncreate it all? Right and Wrong, Good and Bad, POD and POC, All Nine, Shorts, Boys and Beyonds.

Why would you worry about this reality? Are you trying to invent you working in this reality, you fitting into this reality, and you functioning in this reality?

Salon Participant:

Yeah.

Gary:

Everything that is times a godzillion, will you destroy and uncreate it all? Right and Wrong, Good and Bad, POD and POC, All Nine, Shorts, Boys and Beyonds.

How much of your dysfunction with your family and your husband is totally an invention?

Salon Participant:

All of it. But where do I go from here?

Gary:

Don't go into the *but* routine! Every time you say *but* you are sticking your head back up your arse.

Everything that is times a godzillion, will you destroy and uncreate it all? Right and Wrong, Good and Bad, POD and POC, All Nine, Shorts, Boys and Beyonds.

You think, "Where do I go from here?" is a question. It is not a question; it's a conclusion that you don't know where to go. You conclude you have no clue where you are going—but you don't create a future based on a knowing of where you are going, a perceiving of where you are going or a concluding of where you are going. You create a future based on receiving whatever shows up in your life and recognizing the choices you make, the possibilities you create, the questions that manifest, and the contribution that will exist if you don't come to conclusion.

The Problem with Living in the Present

Salon Participant:

Is it a trap for me to have the idea that living in the present is all there is? I have been focused on living in the present and asking questions that would seem to assist me in the immediate future, but I am not looking beyond the immediate.

Gary:

Yeah. Is that what you have been taught and impelled to have as a point of view in this reality?

Salon Participant:

Yes.

Gary:

Is that true and real—or is it an invention?

Salon Participant:

Invention.

Gary:

All the invention you created with that, will you destroy and uncreate it all? Right and Wrong, Good and Bad, POD and POC, All Nine, Shorts, Boys and Beyonds.

Salon Participant:

Are many of us caught up in that? I have been taught that.

Gary:

Has that worked?

Salon Participant:

I guess it has been working until now, but now that you are talking about this, it is shattering that.

Gary:

Living in the present and being focused on the now has worked to a degree—but a degree of working is not about creating a future reality. You have bought the point of view that creating the now is the only thing worth having. Living in the now is the place in which everything is designed to give you the sense that you have to get your results now. Living in the present is, "This is going to give me the result I want tomorrow." It's not a question of, "What will this create in the long run?" It's "What will this create and generate in the future?"

I have always looked at all my choices based on the creation and generation of the future. Interestingly, a number of years ago, I got into Costa Rican horses. I started buying them and breeding them, and then I had way too many of them. I thought, "I have to sell them, I have do something with them," and then with a little luck, I realized, "Wow, I have these Costa Rican horses in United States and all kinds of people are coming down to Costa Rica in the next couple of years to have horse adventures with Costa Rican horses. After they've ridden them, they will want Costa Rican horses in the USA, and I will have them." I did not start out with the point of view of, "This is how I am going to create a future," but I see that I got the Costa Rican horses as a creation of future. I had no idea how I was creating a future. It's only now that I see how this is going to work.

Trusting You as the Creator of Your Future

Salon Participant:

That requires trust on your part, is that correct? Trust of the universe or trust of the energy?

Gary:

No, it's trusting you as the creator of your future. If you don't see you as the creator of the future then you become the flotsam and jetsam in the stream of everybody else's reality.

Salon Participant:

I guess that's the hang-up for me.

Gary:

How many of you have invented that you cannot trust you?
Everything that is times a godzillion, will you destroy and uncre-
ate it all? Right and Wrong, Good and Bad, POD and POC, All
Nine, Shorts, Boys and Beyonds.

There are people who say, "I am going to create this, and it's
going to be great." Is that creation, generation or invention?

Salon Participant:

It's more invention. For it to be creation, you have to keep your
awareness as well.

Gary:

I met with the architect who is designing the resort we are trying
to create in Costa Rica. I said, "Creating this from a modern point
of view is great, but ten years from now, it will be obsolete. I want
to create something that is classic and traditional enough that in 100
years people will still see it as valuable."

The architect said, "What!"

I said, "I am not creating this so it will fall apart tomorrow. I am
creating this to be here in a 100 years, and people will see the value
of it."

The architect said, "Oh!" It was a totally different reality, because
today people do not build for the future. They build for something
that will give them money right away. It's for the now. It's all about
living in the now and not about what will create a sustainable possibility.

It's interesting that everyone is saying they have sustainable proj-
ects and buildings. They have all this so-called green stuff, and ninety

percent of it is not green. It's not sustainable and it will not be here 100 years from now.

Trusting the Awareness You Truly Be

Salon Participant:

You mentioned trust. What is trust? For me, trust is like a judgment or a limitation.

Gary:

Trust is not blind faith. Trust is knowing that people will do exactly what they are going to do. They will do it if they choose to do it.

Salon Participant:

So, trust is knowing? It's being?

Gary:

Trust is about knowing and receiving.

Salon Participant:

That's lighter than just trust in me.

Gary:

Why would you trust in you? All you have ever done is screw yourself over as often as possible. Instead, what if you were willing to trust the awareness you truly be? What if you were willing to trust in your capacity to perceive, know, be and receive?

Everything that doesn't allow that to show up times a godzillion, will you destroy and uncreate it all? Right and Wrong, Good and Bad, POD and POC, All Nine, Shorts, Boys and Beyonds.

Put this one on a loop:

What physical actualization of total awareness of perceiving, knowing, being and receiving in totality as the trust of the awareness that I truly be, am I now capable of generating, creating and instituting? Everything that doesn't allow for that to show up times a godzillion, will you destroy and uncreate it all? Right and Wrong, Good and Bad, POD and POC, All Nine, Shorts, Boys and Beyonds.

True Wealth

Salon Participant:

Gary, what do I have to give up about money?

Gary:

You have to give up the idea that you can control it. If you recognize that you are capable of creating the future, truth, would you create a future in which you had no money?

Salon Participant:

(Laughing)

Gary:

That would be a *no!* You would not create a world without money. That is not a reality for you. You are going to create a world with enough money to do what you need to do, when you need to do it, where you want to do it.

Here is an example from my own life. I am making around five million dollars a year with all the things I am doing. And I have been walking around, saying, "I don't have any money. Why are these people using me and taking stuff?"

My friend, Claudia, said, "But, Gary, you are rich."

I said, "No, I am not rich!"

She said, "Yes, you are."

I said, "No, I am not. I don't have any cash."

She asked, "And how much stuff do you have that is worth money?"

I said, "That doesn't matter. I don't have cash!"

She said, "Dude, you are rich."

I said, "That can't be true. I am just an ordinary guy."

When I finally had a look at it, I said, "Yeah, I am rich." I saw that I had the point of view that if I was not rich, people would not take advantage of me, which meant I bought myself out of having cash so I couldn't be rich. I wasn't thinking in terms of stuff as wealth, and the end result was that I wasn't looking at the fact that I could be rich or that I was rich. I had been trying to make myself poor.

As a being, I am richer than anybody I know based on the awareness, the caring, the kindness and the gift I receive from everybody every day. And the gift that the universe is to me all the time.

So what stupidity are you using to invent the lack of richness you are choosing? Everything that is times a godzillion, will you destroy and uncreate it all? Right and Wrong, Good and Bad, POD and POC, All Nine, Shorts, Boys and Beyonds.

True wealth in the world is the ability to have possibility and choice. That's the true wealth—not what you can spend. The idea that wealth is something you can spend is like dropping your panties to prove you are passionate. It's the visual invention.

How much of the money you don't have in your life is based on the visual invention of the wealth you cannot imagine being? Everything that is times a godzillion, will you destroy and uncreate it all? Right and Wrong, Good and Bad, POD and POC, All Nine, Shorts, Boys and Beyonds.

Confidence

Salon Participant:

I'd like to talk about a slightly different topic. Confidence or lack of confidence. Is that an energy? Is that a mindset? I have been accused of not being confident, and I wonder if I agree with that.

Gary:

People only accuse you of what they themselves are doing. Have you heard that?

Salon Participant:

Yes, I have heard that, and I think I am in agreement with it.

Gary:

No, you are inventing that you must be in agreement with it. You are inventing that because you think that if someone says it, it must be true.

Everything that is times a godzillion, will you destroy and uncreate it all? Right and Wrong, Good and Bad, POD and POC, All Nine, Shorts, Boys and Beyonds.

Salon Participant:

So, what is confidence, then? Is that just belief in yourself? If it is just a belief, then it is nonsense. Beliefs are nonsense.

Gary:

Why do you care about the person who told you that?

Salon Participant:

It is somebody I have decided I am close to.

Gary:

Oh good. In other words, because you like the person, you let her abuse you.

Salon Participant:

Ah, okay. So, do I just let it go and say, "That has no significance to me"?

Gary:

Yes. First of all, is it real—or are you trying to invent it as real because you like this person?

Salon Participant:

I was trying to see her point of view.

Gary:

My point of view is just because I like you doesn't mean you aren't an asshole. When you are being an asshole, you are being an asshole. That's all there is.

> Everything that is times a godzillion, will you destroy and uncreate it all? Right and Wrong, Good and Bad, POD and POC, All Nine, Shorts, Boys and Beyonds.

Salon Participant:

I love seeing shows with stars because I love seeing them express their talent. Have I misidentified and misapplied that because they have confidence, they are expressing their talent? Or what is it that I am aware of when I watch them, if it's not confidence?

Gary:

Marilyn Monroe expressed her talent. Did she have confidence?

Salon Participant:

No is lighter.

Gary:

That's correct. She didn't have confidence. She thought that if she kept putting up what she was putting up, that somebody would finally love her. That's not confidence. Are you inventing these people telling you that you are wrong as love?

Salon Participant:

Yes is lighter.

Gary:

Everything that is times a godzillion, will you destroy and uncreate it all? Right and Wrong, Good and Bad, POD and POC, All Nine, Shorts, Boys and Beyonds.

Salon Participant:

In this reality, when you have vulnerability in your voice or presence, people might assume that is lack of confidence.

Gary:

Is that really a lack of confidence—or is that a place where you have invented that you can't trust you?

Salon Participant:

So you're saying we create little traps for ourselves like, "I am not going to trust me because I don't have confidence" and all the other streams of ideas that we have.

Gary:

Here is a process you can put on a loop:

What stupidity am I using to create the lack of trust of me I am choosing? Everything that is times a godzillion, will you destroy and uncreate it all? Right and Wrong, Good and Bad, POD and POC, All Nine, Shorts, Boys and Beyonds.

The only one who knows what's right for you is you. Everybody else can tell you anything under the sun, but you cannot believe them. I believe no one. Why? They can only see from their limited point of view.

Nobody Can See You Except You

Salon Participant:

At what point, Gary, when nothing is shifting along the way, will there be a big shift, where I can get away from the significance of what others say and what I think of it?

Gary:

Why does thinking of their words seem valuable to you?

Salon Participant:

I wonder if they are right.

Gary:

You mean you would rather doubt you than believe in you?

Salon Participant:

Wow, yeah.

Gary:

It ain't your brightest moment, darling.

Everything that is times a godzillion, will you destroy and uncreate it all? Right and Wrong, Good and Bad, POD and POC, All Nine, Shorts, Boys and Beyonds.

The first thing you have to recognize is nobody can see you except you. No one! You are the only one who has all the pieces of your reality. You are the only one who has all the pieces of awareness. You are the only one who can see every aspect of what you are. If you keep trying to believe others can see some part of you, you might as well put a gun in your mouth and shoot yourself. That's what you are doing every time you take somebody else's point of view about you. You're putting a gun to your head. The one thing I know is that what people can see is a piece of me that matches a piece in them that they want to believe is reality.

Salon Participant:

Okay, that makes sense.

Gary:

That's all there is for them. So, can you trust them?

Salon Participant:

No.

Gary:

So, why do you keep trusting them instead of you? It's about trusting you.

Salon Participant:

Okay, I get that.

Gary:

Everything you have done to invent that you can trust others instead of you, who can see all of you, times a godzillion, will you destroy and uncreate it all? Right and Wrong, Good and Bad, POD and POC, All Nine, Shorts, Boys and Beyonds.

Salon Participant:

Thank you, Gary!

Gary:

Thank you, all, for being as amazing as you are. Take care. 'Bye.

8

Creating Peace instead of War

*Things don't change in this reality because we are battling against what is
as though that is going to create peace.
I want you to understand that the way it currently is on
our planet creates a problem.
As long as we keep men's and women's roles reversed,
we keep conflict in existence.*

Gary:

Hello ladies.

The Reversal of Men's and Women's Roles

I'm going to talk about the fact that on this planet, women
are supposed to be the peacemakers and men are supposed to be
the warriors, when really, it's the other way around. The roles are
reversed. Actually, women are the warriors and men are the peacemakers.

Men have been taught that they are supposed to be the aggres-
sors, they are supposed to go to work, and they are supposed to die
in front of the cannon. Things are screwed up on this planet because
we have men trying to battle for peace. Through our entire history,
we have done war to create peace.

If we wished to create peace instead of war and we had women
battling for future, we would be in a much better place. If you are
inventing a womanly reality, would you destroy things to create the
future—or would you create something different? You would create
something different! You would not battle *against* something; you
would battle *for* the future.

Things don't change in this reality because we are battling against what is, as though that is going to create peace. I want you to understand that the way it currently is on our planet creates a problem. As long as we keep men's and women's roles reversed, we keep conflict in existence. You have to start to look from a different place.

What stupidity are you using to create the invention of the womanly reality you are choosing? Everything that is times a godzillion, will you destroy and uncreate it all? Right and Wrong, Good and Bad, POD and POC, All Nine, Shorts, Boys and Beyonds.

What stupidity are you using to create the invention of the manly reality you are choosing? Everything that is times a godzillion, will you destroy and uncreate it all? Right and Wrong, Good and Bad, POD and POC, All Nine, Shorts, Boys and Beyonds.

The reversal of manly and womanly roles puts you in a constant state of conflict with what is actually true for you, which means you have to look for approval from somebody else. You have to *invent* who or what you are instead of *being* who or what you are. You have to pay attention to whether other people see you, because if *they* see you, maybe *you* can see you. Except that doesn't really work. Seeing anything is an invention.

What stupidity are you using to create the invention of the womanly reality you are choosing? Everything that is times a godzillion, will you destroy and uncreate it all? Right and Wrong, Good and Bad, POD and POC, All Nine, Shorts, Boys and Beyonds.

What stupidity are you using to create the invention of the manly reality you are choosing? Everything that is times a godzillion, will you destroy and uncreate it all? Right and Wrong, Good and Bad, POD and POC, All Nine, Shorts, Boys and Beyonds.

Salon Participant:

While I was growing up, I had a sense of who men were. They were the professor. They had a future in terms of being a professor and giving papers. The women had almost no identity. They were just professors' wives and they didn't have a future.

Your Battle Is for Creating a Future

Gary:

Well, the women did have futures, but their future was predicated on their husbands. You probably didn't notice at the time, but I noticed later in my life that women did have a job, and they would go to battle against *other people* rather than going to battle to create *a future.* Unfortunately, that's the way people function. It's not the best choice, but currently that's what they are choosing.

If you ladies would recognize that your battle is for creating a future—not battling against anyone—you might stop battling against each other. That's been one of the hardest things, people battling against each other. Wait a minute, this woman is not your enemy, but you have made her your enemy. Is that because she is a bitch, and you are not?

Salon Participant:

Exactly.

Gary:

Let's get real here. We are all bitches, we are all bastards, we are all assholes. Why don't you look at what *is* rather than what *someone says has to be.* That's the place that has to change. If you ladies start battling to create the future instead of battling against what is, this world can change. You have the ability to do that.

Salon Participant:

Can you help me with this? What will creating a future look like? In Australia, I often experience the bloke-y thing, the man's world thing, where there's harshness and an inability to allow gentleness and kindness. I think women act like shielders and take on a beingness to match it. I think when we allow softness and kindness and gentleness, it scares people and threatens them.

Gary:

Does that scare them or does it threaten their reality?

Becoming the Warrior Woman

If you are trying to be gentle, you threaten their reality. If you started to battle for creating a future, you would be willing to battle for what would actually be the future, which would mean that instead of becoming the shielder, you would become the warrior woman. You'd say things like, "Say that again, asshole, and I will cut those testicles right off."

Salon Participant:

Is that what you do?

Gary:

Yes, that's what you do if you are willing to battle for creating a different reality. Why don't you be you instead of being the sensitive being you are trying to be? It's saying what is instead of fighting against.

I talked with a lady who said, "I want to tell people *what is* upfront."

That's not what you need to do. You don't want to tell people *what is* upfront. Warriors wait for the right moment to insert the knife that will create an opening for a different possibility as the future. You think you have to be aggressive or do something that isn't a necessity. Battling *for* something is different than battling *against* something.

Right now most of you are trying to battle against the animosity that exists between men and women—because there are few men who appreciate women and few women who appreciate men. Does that make what's happening right or wrong—or does that create an opening for different possibility?

Salon Participant:

Gary, explain what you mean when you say, "That will create an opening for different possibility." What would that look like? How would you do that?

Gary:

If you were to appreciate your lazy son for being the lazy bum he is, you would just sit down and have a quiet nap. Would that change your relationship with him?

Salon Participant:

Absolutely. That would change everything.

Gary:

That's the place where you wait for the opening that allows you to insert something to create a different future. You can't get people to do things the way you want them to. Trust me. I have tried and I failed miserably—repeatedly. I know how to fail really well.

Salon Participant:

Brilliant! What questions can we ask to have an awareness at the moment of when to do that?

Gary:

What if you ran: What energy space and consciousness can I be, to be the warrior I truly be?

A warrior knows how to do this stuff. A warrior is willing to do the battle at the right time. She waits for an opening to deliver the blow that is going to create a different scene, a different element of the battle. If you try to fight all the time, you are screaming violently to no avail. How's that working?

Salon Participant:

Not!

Battling For *vs.* Battling Against

Gary:

If you start to invite the peace in a man to come out instead of trying to create him as the person you have to battle with, a different possibility can show up.

You can battle *against* or battle *for.* Most women, when they have kids, will battle to protect their kids. Is that battle for or battle against?

Salon Participant:

It's a battle against.

Gary:

Yeah. If you were battling for them, you would try to figure out what you could do or say or be that would give them everything that they require.

Salon Participant:

Where does ease come into that?

Gary:

Ease is when you are willing to do that kind of battle.

Possibilities and Choices

Salon Participant:

What's beyond battle?

Gary:

The choice. If you are battling for something, you are battling to create a future. You are willing to look at every choice that is available to you in any moment. The difficulty is we have been trained to believe there are only two choices—and that's not really true.

You have been told that if you make the right choice, you will get the result you want. But that's not what it's about. You have to see the possibilities of the choices and how those can create and generate something different. It's very different than trying to create a two-choice option or the three-choice option.

Think about this right now: You want to create a future, where in three years, your life is better and more expansive than you ever knew was possible. Now, how many choices and possibilities did you just create by thinking that? Hundreds, thousands, millions?

Salon Participant:

Yeah, thousands, many.

Gary:

Many, many, many. You just created 100,000 choices right there—and each one of them can be chosen to create a slight variation in the future that you will create. When you start to battle for creating a future, you look at how every choice you make creates a future. You say, "Oh, I am going to take this one instead of that one because that one is creating less future than this one is," and you begin to see the future and what is going to be created. You have to learn to begin this process. It is something you have to learn. It doesn't just automatically happen.

If we function from possibility instead of other things, a whole new era opens up for us.

Salon Participant:

How do we do that?

Gary:

It's not a *how*. You start with: My job is to be a warrior and to battle for the creation of future. When you start to function from that, you will stop thinking about whether somebody insulted you. You'll say, "Sorry, the insult doesn't mean a thing; I just have to kill you. Okay, 'bye!'"

Salon Participant:

Can you speak about how *battle* and *choice* play together and how that looks pragmatically?

Gary:

Let's say you have $500,000. You have a choice to battle to create the future, so what would you like that future to be? If you try to protect that money and not lose it, are you battling for the future or battling against the future?

Salon Participant:

Against.

Gary:

You have to ask: What choices do I have here that will generate and create the future I'd really like to have? Then you start to see how you can bring that future into existence.

Salon Participant:

Okay, that's where the ease comes into it.

Conquering

Salon Participant:

Would you please speak about how to conquer in more detail and give some pragmatic examples of how it works?

Gary:

The first beginning of conquering is to recognize the place where you are the warrior who goes to battle for the creation of a future. If you go to battle for the creation of a future, you will be willing to conquer the man if he is somebody you want as part of the future or someone who will create the future for you.

I talked with a young lady recently. She is very young and very good looking. She was introduced to a slightly older man who is a little paunchy and not perfectly good looking. She said, "Oh, I don't know whether I want to go out with him."

I said, "Well, you know what? Have you been asking for someone who idolizes you?"

She said, "Yes, but he isn't pretty."

I said, "A pretty man will never idolize you; he will only want to be idolized."

She said, "What?"

I said, "Every pretty man in the world wants to be idolized because he thinks that's his due. You want somebody who will idolize you and love you totally. This man is just old enough, he's not pretty enough, not ugly, and he will adore you totally. Consider that as a possibility."

She said, "Okay."

I said, "You don't have to marry him and have babies with him. All you have to do is recognize he is a step in the direction you want of having somebody who adores you. He may introduce you to somebody else who adores you more. Who knows? You have to be willing to look at this in terms of creating a future."

Or say you are with a man who is trying to fix you up. Men who are trying to fix you up have decided that once they fix you up, you will be the right person for them. If that's what is happening in your life, you might want to say, "Thank you so much for what you are willing to do for me. Let's go shopping." Keep him shopping for six hours, and that will be the last time he ever tries to do anything for you. Six hours of pain and suffering for you in order to create six hours of pain and suffering to get rid of him. That's conquering the situation—it's knowing what you have to do.

"I Would Like to Have a Man Seduce Me for Once in My Life!"

Salon Participant:

Things have definitely shifted for me since I did Levels Two and Three and several teleclasses with you. I've gone from having no libido to being turned on all the time. I am constantly thinking about having sex, especially with Gary and Dain and other men who know how to play with a woman in a sexual-sensual way. I am married and do not desire to have sex with my husband since he is the forceful and fast kind of man you see in porn. I would like to have a man seduce me for once in my life!

Gary:

Run this:

What energy, space and consciousness can my body and I be to allow us to be seduced and saturated with sex in totality for all eternity? Everything that doesn't allow for that to show up times a godzillion, will you destroy and uncreate it all? Right and Wrong, Good and Bad, POD and POC, All Nine, Shorts, Boys and Beyonds.

Salon Participant:

How do I teach my husband to be slow, sensual, nurturing and all that good stuff? It has been a challenge for me to ask for what I would like.

Gary:

You could get the book, *Sex Is Not a Four Letter Word,* put it in the bathroom, and pretend you are reading it. That way, when he goes to the bathroom, he will pick it up and start to look at it. If he starts spending more and more time in the bathroom, you will soon get what you want.

Living for Other People

Salon Participant:

From the time I was growing up until recently, I have been a parent emotionally to my parents. I have tried to protect them and care for them.

Gary:

Until recently? You are still going to do it. It's the reason your parents had you. They wanted somebody who could take care of them to make their life real and good. A lot of you don't realize that your parents had you to know that somebody cared about them. They chose you to have someone who would care about them while they were not caring enough about themselves. You were supposed to do it all for them. They couldn't care for you, as they were trying to get you to care for them.

Everywhere you have been unwilling to perceive, know, be and receive that, will you destroy and uncreate it? Right and Wrong, Good and Bad, POD and POC, All Nine, Shorts, Boys and Beyonds.

Here is a process a bunch of you need to run. It is a result of reading the questions you have sent to me. I want you to run this:

What stupidity am I using to create the invention of the requisite and requirement of living from and for and of other people am I choosing? Everything that is times a godzillion, will you destroy and uncreate it all? Right and Wrong, Good and Bad, POD and POC, All Nine, Shorts, Boys and Beyonds.

Salon Participant:

Does this have to do with requiring approval?

Gary:

No. You think it has to do with requiring approval. If you look for approval, you're not willing to recognize you. It's the recognition of being the warrior who battles for the creation of the future. If you start to function from that, you will have a greater sense of yourself than you ever had before. The reversal of manly and womanly roles puts you in a constant state of conflict with what is actually true for you, which means you have to look for approval from somebody else. You have to see whether they see you, because if they see you, maybe you can see you. Except that doesn't really work. Seeing anything is an invention.

Everything that is times a godzillion, will you destroy and uncreate it all? Right and Wrong, Good and Bad, POD and POC, All Nine, Shorts, Boys and Beyonds.

Visual Representations and Inventions

Salon Participant:

Can you please explain more about how seeing is invention?

Gary:

In our last call, I talked about a time I was watching television. The visual for passion was someone's panties falling to the floor. That was supposed to represent passion. That was not passion; that was panties falling to the floor. We have the point of view that the visual representation of the world is the truth of the world.

> What stupidity are you using to create the invention of the visual reality as the true reality of this reality are you choosing? Everything that is times a godzillion, will you destroy and uncreate it all? Right and Wrong, Good and Bad, POD and POC, All Nine, Shorts, Boys and Beyonds.

You try to see things the way other people visually represent them. Take somebody who is an intellectual in New York City. He will talk voluminously about what one line in a book means. He will make all kinds of assumptions about what the author's point of view was. If you look at the line he is talking about, it will be clear ninety percent of the time that what the intellectual came up with was what he was trying to see. It was an invention, not a reality. That's what we do in our world too. We try to invent something that is not.

Salon Participant:

As a child, I had so much trouble seeing that.

Gary:

It's because you knew it was an invention, but people kept telling you it was reality. People create inventions as realities. Have you ever noticed that when people talk, it sometimes feels like they are reciting lines out of a movie? They phrase their lines in a way that is so not who they are. You know that it is an invented reality for them. It is a visual representation of what they think they are supposed to be, not an awareness of what they are.

> What stupidity are you using to create the invention of the visual reality as the truth of this reality as the only reality you can choose are you choosing? Everything that is times a godzillion, will you destroy and uncreate it all? Right and Wrong, Good and Bad, POD and POC, All Nine, Shorts, Boys and Beyonds.

I recommend that you get smart and recognize the place where you lock into points of view about what you are supposed to do that are inventions, not creations. If you are going to be a warrior to battle for creation of future, you have to get rid of invention. How much of what you are doing in your life right now with your relationships are inventions? A lot, a little or megatons?

Salon Participant:

Megatons.

Gary:

Everything that is times a godzillion, will you destroy and uncreate it all? Right and Wrong, Good and Bad, POD and POC, All Nine, Shorts, Boys and Beyonds.

How much of what you see as problems in these questions are actually inventions?

Everything you have done to invent that times a godzillion, will you destroy and uncreate it all? Right and Wrong, Good and Bad, POD and POC, All Nine, Shorts, Boys and Beyonds.

You have to be willing to see how much of your relationship you have invented as a problem. Are you like the woman who said she has a challenge asking for what she wants in bed? Are you not willing to lose your husband? If you were willing to lose your husband, would that create a different possibility for you, so you could actually ask him for what you want? Apparently this applies to everyone on the call.

Everything that is times a godzillion, will you destroy and uncreate it all? Right and Wrong, Good and Bad, POD and POC, All Nine, Shorts, Boys and Beyonds.

Salon Participant:

What is an invention?

Gary:

Invention is this: Look at TV and watch two people kissing. It is supposed to be about how they care about each other, how they want each other. Is it true or an invention? All thoughts, feelings, emotions, sex and no sex are inventions.

Salon Participant:

I see everything as an invention.

Gary:

A whole lot of it is, except when you are actually creating a future. So much of what you have done in your life is an invention. You try to invent who you are. You try to invent your money situation. You try to invent your relationships and how everything is supposed to appear to everybody else. It is about what everything appears to be, not what it is. Everything is the opposite of what it appears to be and nothing is the opposite of what it appears to be. It's all invention.

> Everything that is times a godzillion, will you destroy and uncreate it all? Right and Wrong, Good and Bad, POD and POC, All Nine, Shorts, Boys and Beyonds.

Salon Participant:

Thank you for this call, Gary. This part of my reality is like a stale energy, yet there is a lot going on here, and a new possibility is opening up.

Gary:

That's the reason I am trying to get you to recognize you are inventing this stuff rather than creating. If you decide you are in love with somebody, is that a truth, a creation or an invention?

Salon Participant:

Invention.

Gary:

Yes, because it's a thought, a feeling, an emotion.

Creating From Choice, Possibility, Question and Contribution

Salon Participant:

What would it look like to create, then? I don't get it.

Gary:

You have been creating through invention. You haven't been creating from choice, possibility, question and contribution.

Salon Participant:

Is it like a generative energy?

Gary:

When you function from energy, it is generative and creative. Start to generate and create from being a warrior who battles for the creation of future. Literally feel the solidity in the energy of, "I am a warrior battling for the creation of future." There is no doubt in your universe when you say that. All of a sudden, the doubt goes away and you know what to do. It becomes very pragmatic and institutive. As long as I am heading in this direction, I know where I am going.

Salon Participant:

How do we be the warrior, healer and conqueror without and beyond abuse?

Gary:

You keep looking at what's happening on the planet in the way the males have been creating. That's a problem, because they have to go against their desire for peace to create war, and in order to do that, they create anger, rage, fury and hate (all of which are distractor implants) as real in order to carry out the mission of being the con-querors and destroyers of the world that they think they have to be.

If you are creating from a different place, a place of, "How do I expand this and create a future?" you will not be doing destruction, anger, rage, fury and hate to get there. You will be doing question, choice, possibility and contribution.

Salon Participant:

Wow, this is cool. Thank you.

Don't Exclude Anger

Salon Participant:

I was listening to a CD where you talk about no exclusion—and about not excluding anger. You say anger is a distractor implant. Can you talk about this more, please?

Gary:

Yes, anger is a distractor implant. The one time that anger is real and not a distractor implant is when somebody lies to you.

You have to include anger as part of the gig. It's not that you have to include the distractor implant, but you need to be willing to include the anger to the degree that you realize somebody is using it as a distractor implant. If you try to eliminate or exclude the distrac-tor implants, you are trying to see how they are not present instead of seeing when they are present.

Salon Participant:

I have the point of view that I hate getting angry. I get mad that I am feeling angry, and I am not sure where to go with that.

Gary:

If you include anger, then anger can be something that flashes—and then you can get over it. Or when it flashes, you can ask, "Did this person lie to me?" If you get a yes, the anger goes away. When you suppress anger, it explodes, and that hurts you. It hurts your body and makes you upset for having it. From your description, it sounds like you are trying to suppress your anger and not let it happen, so, when it does happen, it is a giant explosion, which is not helpful. And it hurts.

Salon Participant:

I am scared of what is going to happen with the anger toward my son if I don't suppress it.

Gary:

You have to include your anger towards your son, too, and say, "If you do that again, I will stuff your head in the toilet and flush it." I did that with my kid, today. He calls me all the time and says, "Let's get together for a drink, let's have dinner." He always wants to get together. He loves me unbelievably because I am honest with him. I didn't suppress my anger today; I expressed it, but didn't explode all over him, which is what so many people do.

Salon Participant:

So, how do I that? What do I need to ask before I explode?

Gary:

What energy, space and consciousness can I be that would allow me to include my anger in my reality for all eternity?

"I'm Just a Naïve Little Girl"

Salon Participant:

I have had something going on for quite some time that I have avoided revealing or discussing. I think I have usually chosen to be friendly, joyful, sexually open, encouraging, courageous and much more, thanks to Access Consciousness and you, Gary. It seems like all of this leads men, and sometimes their partners, to misconstrue my intentions, and I perceive the projections, expectations, separations, judgments and rejections. I'm not aware of what is going on.

Gary:

To be unaware is to be naïve. To not receive the projections, expectations, separations, judgments and rejections is a way in which you maintain, "I am just a naïve little girl." That would lead you to do things like laughing or giggling at the wrong times, doing things you don't want to do, and having people in your life you don't know how to say no to.

When you are not being aware of what is going on, ask: What stupidity am I using to create the naiveté I am choosing?

You are going to be a warrior for creation of a future. You are going to have a different point of view show up, and you will not be giggling at stuff to get your way.

Who Does This Belong To? Is This Mine?

Salon Participant:

When I am aware that a man is attracted to me, I get quite uncomfortable. Sometimes I giggle or put up barriers or even flirt back so he will feel bad or uncomfortable.

Gary:

Have you ever asked: Who does this belong to?

Men are the most insecure people on the planet, ladies. If you are feeling insecure, there is a ninety-nine percent chance that it is a man's point of view. Very few men have total security in themselves. Those who do are highly intimidating to everyone. If you are intimidated by people, it's probably because they are comfortable in their own skin, and if you are not feeling comfortable in your skin, it is because you are aware—not because you are having a problem. I love you—and you have to get over this.

Salon Participant:

Somewhere I have bought everyone's projections, expectations, separations, judgments and rejections as real. I have made myself wrong, blamed myself, gotten paralyzed and put up barriers. I would like to get some clarity with all this.

Gary:

Wow, what a nice invention.

How many of you are inventing your ways of dealing with men, women and relationships? Everything that is times a godzillion, will you destroy and uncreate it all? Right and Wrong, Good and Bad, POD and POC, All Nine, Shorts, Boys and Beyonds.

You have to get clear on that fact that 99,000% of this stuff doesn't belong to you. You have to start asking the question: Is this mine? When you do, you are going to find that none of it is yours. The insecurity and all that stuff don't belong to you. Not wanting to be rejected doesn't belong to you. Please get that this is not yours, sweet thing. You don't have those points of view.

Exclusive Relationships

Salon Participant:

Thank you for these calls. I get that it's really okay just to have a lover. He doesn't have to fulfill everything—and now I have a really amazing life going on.

Gary:

Yeah, you have to get the awareness that you don't need to have one person to fulfill everything you desire. Would an infinite being only have one person in their life? The whole idea of exclusive relationships is to exclude everybody except the one, and when you do that, "everybody" includes you more often than not. You start down the trail of excluding you instead of recognizing, "Okay, I'm including me in this." You don't ask:

- What would I really like to have?
- What would it take to make my life fun?

You don't say: Just for me just for fun, never tell anyone!

Being vs. Doing

Salon Participant:

I need some clarification about *being* vs. *doing.* I think I am trying to be successful by doing stuff, but I am feeling inadequate, unsuccessful and attached to an outcome. What's going on? Can you help me with a clearing I can run?

Gary:

What stupidity am I using to create invention by the doing I am choosing? Everything that is times a godzillion, will you destroy and uncreate it all? Right and Wrong, Good and Bad, POD and POC, All Nine, Shorts, Boys and Beyonds.

Did you get that? You are inventing by doing, as though if you *do,* you are actually going to *create,* which isn't so.

Do We Come Back to Work Things Out?

Salon Participant:

I have heard that we often reincarnate again and again to be with certain people. What is your awareness around this idea? Would we be doing this out of a preference as well as taking an opportunity to let go of limitations we have around another person?

Gary:

No, usually you pick somebody you have a limitation around so that you can kill them this lifetime. If you are highly attracted to somebody or if you have a sense of passion with somebody, usually that passion is based on the idea that in this lifetime, you get to kill them or they get to kill you.

So, do we come back to work things out? Apparently not! When I was in my metaphysical phase, they told me you choose people so you can let go of your limitations, but I have not found that to be true so far. When you have a volatile relationship with somebody, it's because you have been killing each other back and forth for centuries, and you are looking for whose turn it is this time.

Love at First Sight

Salon Participant:

Does love at first sight truly exist?

Gary:

Yes, because you have so many oaths, vows, fealties, comealties and commitments from other lifetimes that when you run into somebody that you committed to in another lifetime, you suddenly recall all of that. It is not the person's physical form that creates that response; it is their energetic form. You suddenly become enamored of the person.

All the oaths, vows, fealties, comealties, commitments and swearings you have to anyone across any lifetime, from any lifetime that still exists, will you destroy and uncreate all of them? Right and Wrong, Good and Bad, POD and POC, All Nine, Shorts, Boys and Beyonds.

The good news is you guys have been doing a lot of that stuff. The bad news is you have been doing a lot of that stuff!

Labels Limit Possibilities

Salon Participant:

I did an experiment once where for one day, I decided not to think of my boyfriend as my boyfriend but just as a good friend. On that day, I noticed my behavior toward him was different. The inter-action between us was less controlling and more playful. I suspect that has to something to do with the meaning of the word *boyfriend*. Can you speak to that? Are the meanings of words and labels really that powerful?

Gary:

Yeah. Every time you put a label on what someone is to you, you cannot open the door to possibilities greater than the label. You limit the possibilities with every label you put on someone. That's why I ask people to call the person they like their *insignificant other* not their *significant other*. If that person is your insignificant other, there are more possibilities. If he or she is your significant other, you have to make it important, significant, controlling—and not fun at all.

Everything you have done to invent those as really important things, will you destroy and uncreate it all? Right and Wrong, Good and Bad, POD and POC, All Nine, Shorts, Boys and Beyonds.

Can You Actually Control Anything?

Salon Participant:

Can you speak about the idea of control? Is it an energy or a mental idea? I get that I am stuck in both polarities, controlling and not controlling, and I'm struggling to know when to control and when to let go. I am making the idea of control more potent than me.

Gary:

Control is mostly an invention. Would a conscious relationship have any control in it? No. Can you actually control anything? No. Try to control the energy in the room. Can you? No. Why? Because energy is not controllable. Is your partner energy? Yes. If you try to make him controllable, how much contraction of his reality do you have to put into existence? How much contraction of his whole life, living and body do you have to do to him to control those things? A lot, a little or too much? Too much!

Everything that is times a godzillion, will you destroy and uncreate it all? Right and Wrong, Good and Bad, POD and POC, All Nine, Shorts, Boys and Beyonds.

Love Itself Is an Invention

Salon Participant:

What is beyond the invention of being in love?

Gary:

Love itself is an invention. This is probably one of the hardest things for people to get. People say, "That person loves you." Does he or she love you? Or does he or she *desire* something from you? Or what? Your parents love you. Do your father and mother love you the same? No, it's totally different. Is one or the other love—or are all they inventions of what love is?

Salon Participant:

Inventions.

Gary:

Yes, love is invention. Do you have more gratitude for your mom or dad?

Salon Participant:

For my mom, for giving birth to me—and for my dad because I get along with him better.

Gary:

You have gratitude for your dad and you tolerate your mother.

Salon Participant:

Exactly, thank you.

Gary:

You have to call it like it is, folks. If you are tolerating your mother, that's fine. If you are in gratitude for somebody, that is different. Gratitude has no judgment; love does. That's the reason I say love is an invention. If it was true loving, it would not have judgment. True loving is an ongoing expression of possibility. Do you get the difference?

Salon Participant:

Is it advantageous to creating a different future if we have a conscious relationship with all beings?

Gary:

If you are willing to create your reality, you will have a different relationship with every person you come in contact with. You will be more open to greater possibilities than other people. Does that mean they will receive what you have to say? No. Will they receive you? No. Does that mean we are going to change the human/humanoid race on the planet? With a little bit of luck, yeah. Just keep liking yourself because you are the one who will create possibilities.

Every Relationship Is an Invention

Salon Participant:

Aren't relationships just another invention?

Gary:

Yes, every relationship is an invention. Relationship as created here is an invention.

Salon Participant:

Everywhere I function from being in-synch with a relationship seems to be an invention. I don't get how to function outside of that, and I end up choosing not to go there at all because I have an awareness that it is stupid.

Gary:

Is that awareness or conclusion?

Salon Participant:

I don't know. I don't have that clarity.

Gary:

It is pretty much a conclusion. What if you asked a question:

- Would this one work out?
- Would this be fun or interesting to me?
- Would this be something that would create and generate more in my life?

If you start to function from the place of being a warrior who is going to battle for creating future, you will see, "Oh! I am not choosing to be with this person because that would not be creating a future that has any contribution to me or where I can be the contribution I want to be." Do you get the difference?

Salon Participant:

I do. Do I need to do some processing there to clear the struggle I have around relationships?

Gary:

Truth, do you really want a relationship?

Salon Participant:

No.

Gary:

So, no problem!

Salon Participant:

But during these calls, all everybody talks about is relationships. Not about anything else. That's what everybody does.

Gary:

Not everything. Haven't I been telling you that your real job is creating a future?

Salon Participant:

Yeah, that's cool.

Gary:

I am trying to get you to the awareness of what you really came here to do, and what is really possible for you. If you want a relationship, I will do what I can to help you get that too. But I also want all of you who don't desire, need or want a relationship to know that you don't have to do relationship. It is just a choice. That's really the way all of us have to function.

A Warrior Is Willing
to Do Whatever It Takes to Win the Battle

Salon Participant:

I have a question about being a warrior. I think of warriors as beings who do it all on their own. When I look at creating and generating a future that would work for me, more and more I seem to be collaborating with other people. It's like our futures overlap. What is that about? Can you talk about being a warrior and collaborating?

Gary:

A warrior is willing to do whatever it takes to win the battle. If it means standing back-to-back with somebody against unbelievable odds, you will do that. If it means charging ahead, you will do that. When you are really being a warrior, you will plow the ground if that's going to create the future you need. You will use your sword to plant. You will use your weapons to create barricades against invaders. You will do whatever it takes. A warrior doesn't just chop, bend, kill and mutilate. A warrior is one who can do whatever it takes to get where she is going.

That's why I keep trying to get you ladies to recognize you are warriors—because you will do what it takes to get going. You don't hesitate to do that unless you go into projection, expectation, rejection, separation, judgment or a place where you feel you are wrong. You come out of that and realize, "I am a warrior who is going to battle to create for future."

Interesting Point of View

When you have an awareness of self, you stand like a rock in the stream. Polarity comes at you and goes around you, and you are interesting point of view. When you are willing to recognize where you stand in the stream of things, you are a warrior battling for the creation of future.

There is a solidity in that, but there is no stagnation. Most solidity becomes stagnation. If you say, "I am a fighter," it becomes a stagnant position and you must fight everyone all the time to prove you are right. Is that a place you want to live?

When you are interesting point of view, all the polarity, craziness and invention swirl around you yet have no effect on you because you know where you are going. From this space, you can battle for the creation of future.

Salon Participant:

Thank you so much for this call, Gary. And thank you to all the amazing women on this call. For the first time, I feel a sense of peace between men and women and my relationship with them in general. There used to be such anger, hatred and mistrust about relationship between people, but now with this call, it doesn't even matter. I can handle it.

Gary:

Yes, that's the reason I did this call. I was looking to create that, to get you to create your reality. It will give you that sense of peace that creates possibility and choices. Thank you, ladies.

9

Creating a Sustainable Future

*Maybe you should stop trying to survive
and start looking at what it would take for you to thrive.*

Gary:

Hello ladies. Let's start with some questions.

Having Children

Salon Participant:

You said that for most women, creating the future is about having children, and that having kids is a lower harmonic of creation of future. Can you be a warrior for creating the future—and also choose to have you and children?

Gary:

Yes, you can. Most people have decided that future is about children and not about creating a long-term effect in the world. That's the reason children are seen as long-term effects in the world—but they're not the only long-term effect. You have to have all choices. All choices should be available to you.

Salon Participant:

I have been choosing to invite children into my universe and this has expanded my living infinitely. What else is possible when I choose this?

Gary:

You have to look at this choice and ask: If I choose to have these kids in my life, is it going to create a greater future or lesser future for me and for them?

Future does not mean just you, it's you and them. Most people do children from the point of view, "Now I will have somebody to care about me" or "I will have somebody who will love me forever." You have to be willing to recognize that when you move into the place of creating future for you and others, a different possibility can occur. You have to create a future that is not based on a solid point of view; you have to create a future with a sustainable reality that is beyond this reality.

Salon Participant:

You said we are conquerors and we battle for future, and when we see an opening, that's where we go through.

Gary:

You will see the place where an opening occurs because of your willingness to create a different future beyond this reality. An opening will come to you and you will say, "Oh! I have to go there!" You know it because you are more willing to function from your knowing than anything else.

It's Not about Getting out of This Reality

Salon Participant:

I am so frustrated with being a stepmom to a stepson who has moved back home again. I don't know how to put it into words. How do I *not* be the kid's stepmother?

Gary:

You are asking, "How do I get out of this reality?" But it's not about getting out of this reality. If that was going to create everything you desired, then getting out would be easy. You want to ask: How do I create a reality beyond this reality that would actually work for me?

Salon Participant:

How do I do that?

Gary:

You say to him, "Now that you are back, you are too old for me to be a mother or stepmother for you. So, how do we create a friendship and a working relationship as roommates?"

Salon Participant:

I did that. He basically told me non-verbally to go f--- myself and continued to do whatever he felt like doing.

Gary:

So, why are you putting up with it?

Salon Participant:

Yeah, why am I putting up with it? I want to run away from home.

Gary:

Why are you not telling him, "You straighten up or you get out"?

Salon Participant:

I would, but I am the stepmom. If I say that, I have turned into the nag I never wanted to be.

Gary:

If your husband isn't backing you up with the kid, then tell him, "You have a choice. It's either me or the kid. One of us has to go". Have you sat down with your husband and said, "We have to chat"?

Salon Participant:

We are going to do that tonight. The humanoid woman I am can't handle this anymore. The warrior is coming up.

Gary:

That's not true. The humanoid woman you are can handle it. You are simply not willing to put up with it any longer.

Salon Participant:

No, I am not.

Gary:

All you have to say to your husband is, "Do you realize your son is treating me like crap? Is this the way you want him to treat me?"

Salon Participant:

Got it.

Gary:

Then you have to say, "Either he changes or I leave. What do you want?"

Salon Participant:

That's exactly where I am.

Gary:

All you do is say it. Not with anger or charge. It's just, "This is what it is. I don't wish to deal with this anymore. I have stuffed my feelings, my awareness, everything. This needs to change or I need to go. Which do you want?" If he is not aware of his son treating you that way, do you really want to deal with that?

Salon Participant:

He is aware. He is just not dealing with it. This is the situation he doesn't want to deal with. He even joined a country club to play golf—and I am at home.

Gary:

That works for him. Is it working for you?

Salon Participant:

It's not working for me. It is putting more on me. I am responsible for changing everything.

Gary:

Stop. "It's making me" is a lie you are telling yourself. Nothing and no one makes you be or do anything, except you.

Salon Participant:

Right, I am making myself responsible. I am doing it.

Gary:

You have a choice. You can either do what works for you—or not.

I talked with a lady who said, "I am so angry at my grandson for not cleaning up after himself. He creates a mess, and it makes me crazy. I tell him he has to clean it up, but doesn't do it. "

I asked, "Who do you clean the house for? You or him?"

She said, "For me. What does that mean?"

I said, "He is not cleaning up the house because he doesn't want to do it for you. He eats cookies and doesn't clean up the crumbs and the mess he makes. So, put the cookies in your room, lock the door and leave. He won't be able to find the cookies." You have to be pragmatic about how you make this stuff work.

Salon Participant:

Thank you very much.

Why Don't You Be You?

Salon Participant:

In the last call, you asked, "Why don't you be you?" It's a question you have asked many times previously. I guess it's about being the warrior fighting for the future who is willing to be every bit of kindness, gentleness, nurturing and healing every moment with total presence and allowance. Is that correct?

Gary:

Absolutely. You have to be brutally honest with yourself about what you would like to create.

Salon Participant:

Sometimes the awareness of what I truly am is so huge that it seems too much to translate into this physical reality.

Gary:

It is. But you are not trying to *translate* it into this physical reality. You are trying to *permeate* it into this physical reality. If you try to translate it, you are trying to make it fit into this universe instead of making it a choice you have available to you.

A Sustainable Reality beyond This Reality

Salon Participant:

What does creating a future with a sustainable reality that is beyond this reality look like?

Gary:

Right now all of you are choosing a better version of this reality. But this reality isn't sustainable the way it is functioning. That's the reason we have to create a sustainable reality beyond this reality. Everything that we are doing right now is moving toward an end to the viability of planet Earth that it currently is. Something has to change. What is it? I don't have a good answer for you, and I don't know pragmatically what it means except that you must live as the difference.

Salon Participant:

Can you say more about sustainable reality beyond this reality? You said that right now, we are only able to create or generate something that is better or a just little different.

Gary:

I am trying desperately to get you guys to see that you have different choices than you ever thought you had, yet you are trying to choose a better version of this reality. "I will make a better life for myself" isn't the same thing as, "I am going to create something so different that nothing like it has ever occurred here before." I can't give you a good example of this other than what I did with Access Consciousness. I knew I had to do something that had never existed here. I had to do something that created a different kind of possibility and a different reality.

Salon Participant:

You've talked about how you often use future without an "a" or a "the" in front of it because you don't wish to define it or limit it, as though it's one thing. I keep making it "the" future or "a" future, which limits it and makes it solid. I have been trying to create the future, and that's what you are trying to dismantle. Is that right?

Gary:

No, I am trying to give you a willingness to create a sustainable future beyond this reality. You have been trying to create a future, but it is contracted because you are looking at a future based on what you already have and how you can make that better.

Salon Participant:

That's correct. I have already decided what the future should be, what it can be and so on.

Gary:

How many things have you decided you have gotten right in your life? Everything that is times a godzillion, will you destroy and uncreate it all? Right and Wrong, Good and Bad, POD and POC, All Nine, Shorts, Boys and Beyonds.

Let's say you had the idea that you needed to have three million dollars to be secure in life. So, you got three million dollars to create a future beyond this reality, and you had no clue what that would be unless it was more money.

Salon Participant:

That's correct. I have created four million dollars. That's it for me. I don't know what's beyond that.

Gary:

You are not trying to create a reality beyond that. You are trying to create a reality that keeps what you have decided is right so you can hold on to it. Everything you are trying to hold on to from the past, you have to be willing to let that go. Are you willing to let go of having four million dollars?

Salon Participant:

Yes.

Gary:

Truth?

Salon Participant:

Yes.

Gary:

You're willing to let go of it? You just lied.

Salon Participant:

I can't see where I am lying.

Gary:

Would you be willing to lose it all?

Salon Participant:

If you are telling me *no,* I will trust you. Please help me see it.

Gary:

You will say yes because your assumption is you will have more instead. What if money was the one thing that was creating a place of non-sustainable future? Would you have to choose something different? What would "different" look like?

Salon Participant:

I go there, I go to a future without money. And by "without money," I don't mean the energy, I mean the paper.

Survival vs. Sustainability

Gary:

Hold on. You're going to future from a place of being where you are. You are going to the idea, "I cannot survive." Survival is not creating a sustainable future. You have to be willing to lose survival.

You have to be willing to lose survival because you have spent your lifetime surviving and only occasionally thriving. Regardless of the condition, you always know you can make it in this reality.

Everything that is times a godzillion, will you destroy and uncreate it all? Right and Wrong, Good and Bad, POD and POC, All Nine, Shorts, Boys and Beyonds.

Salon Participant:

What is survival?

Gary:

Survival is no matter what occurs, you will continue.

Salon Participant:

I believe that. Are you asking me to give that up? Is that it? Why would I give that up?

Gary:

What if true sustainability was not survival?

Salon Participant:

That doesn't make sense.

Gary:

It is not supposed to make sense. You can survive anything. But survival is one thing you have to give up if you want to create sustainability. Survival and sustainability are not the same. Even though plant life is dying, you can adjust to continue on.

Salon Participant:

What would I take with me to contribute to my being sustainable?

Gary:

"What would I take with me?" is not a place from which you can create sustainable reality beyond this reality. That's what is killing you.

Salon Participant:

What *sustainable* means to me is there is more contribution. Where am I not allowing more contribution?

Gary:

What do you mean by *contribution*? What others can give to you, what you can give to others or what you can get in both directions?

Salon Participant:

What other people would be to me and what I would be to them.

Gary:

Why is it that you consider people valuable?

Salon Participant:

Because I think all the things in my life are contributing to me— except the people.

Gary:

What if there were no people? Would you be okay?

Salon Participant:

Yeah!

Gary:

Good. You have to recognize that there is a different possibility.

Salon Participant:

Can you go into what survival and sustainability are, please?

Gary:

Survival is the idea that you can maintain regardless of the circumstances. If you are doing survival, you could manage to continue
to exist regardless of the circumstances. If your target is to continue
to exist regardless of the circumstances, is that creation?

Salon Participant:

No.

Gary:

So, you have to be willing to lose survival as even a vague concept in your world.

Everything you have done to make survival a reality for you,
will you destroy and uncreate it all? Right and Wrong, Good and
Bad, POD and POC, All Nine, Shorts, Boys and Beyonds.

Sustainability means that whatever it is continues to grow and
expand. When you are doing something that is sustainable, it will
continue to grow, expand and take care of itself. When you create a
sustainable reality beyond this reality, you are taking into consider-
ation the question: What would it look like if everything here was
not dying? Right now, if you look around, there is a lot of stuff dying.

Salon Participant:

Have I misapplied sustainability as survival?

Gary:

Yes, you have misidentified and misapplied survival and sustainability.

Everything you have done that creates that, will you destroy
and uncreate it all? Right and Wrong, Good and Bad, POD and
POC, All Nine, Shorts, Boys and Beyonds.

What would it be like to create a sustainable world? I look at
what's going on in the world, and I see that if we continue to go in

the direction we are going, people will survive for another 100 years and then the planet will be used up.

Salon Participant:

People will survive, but there will be no sustainability. There is a big difference in the energy of those two.

Gary:

Yes, that's what I want you to get. If you start looking for survival, if you hold on to the idea of surviving, you are like the lady who was talking about her stepson. She was surviving the situation, but it wasn't a sustainable reality for her. You can survive anything. You don't want to survive these situations; you want to do what will create a sustainable reality. What would it look like if your reality was sustainable?

Salon Participant:

I have a question. When we give up survival, will we just do creation?

Gary:

Survival is the limit of what you can receive. It's as if you have created a limit of what you can receive based on survival. Based on that, you are satisfied. You say, "I only need this much to survive," or "I need these kind of people if I am going to survive." No, you don't!

If you are going to have a sustainable reality, there are people who will have to change and choose and be different for sustainability to be created. Sustainability is creation, and survival is institution to keep in existence what currently exists.

What stupidity are you using to create the invention of survival as the primary choice you are choosing? Everything that is times a godzillion, will you destroy and uncreate it all? Right and Wrong, Good and Bad, POD and POC, All Nine, Shorts, Boys and Beyonds.

Salon Participant:

My husband and I started to have a talk about money, and next thing I knew, I was saying, "This isn't enough for me. This is not working." The survival I have chosen and not chosen doesn't work for me, yet that is what's happening.

Gary:

Did you survive your childhood?

Salon Participant:

Yes, there were moments of living.

Gary:

Did you decide that because you survived, you are a survivor?

Salon Participant:

Yes.

Gary:

Everything you decided with that, and all the decisions, judgments, conclusions and computations creating that, will you destroy and uncreate it all? Right and Wrong, Good and Bad, POD and POC, All Nine, Shorts, Boys and Beyonds.

As a survivor, you tolerate the situation and you do the best you can to live regardless of what occurs. But it is not a place to create a sustainable future.

Salon Participant:

Sustainable or not, it is not worth it.

Gary:

That's a judgment. Why do you go to judgment? Judgment and conclusion are the systems you have in place to create survival. You have to come to conclusion and judgment; you compute and decide to have survival.

All the decisions, judgments, conclusions and computations you are using to create your survival, will you destroy and uncreate it all? Right and Wrong, Good and Bad, POD and POC, All Nine, Shorts, Boys and Beyonds.

It doesn't matter if you have four million dollars; you are going into decisions, judgments, conclusions and computations so you can survive. Those are symbolically, systematically and simplistically the elements required to survive. You are coming to conclusions like, "I can't do this anymore," "I can't survive," "This isn't working ," "This is not enough." Those are judgments.

The awareness is, "I don't want to live like this. Something has to change." Then you go into question.

What physical actualization of the creation of a sustainable future beyond this reality are you now capable of creating, generating and instituting? Everything that doesn't allow that times a godzillion, will you destroy and uncreate it all? Right and Wrong, Good and Bad, POD and POC, All Nine, Shorts, Boys and Beyonds.

Salon Participant:

In the world of addiction, it seems like the Twelve Step Program is survival and the Right Recovery for You program is sustainability. Is that accurate?

Gary:

Yes, *Right Recovery for You* is a set of tools and techniques that allow people to create a future that is sustainable.

Salon Participant:

When we apply Access Consciousness tools to anything, we are creating sustainability?

Gary:

Yes, a question creates a future that has some sustainability. As long as you are not doing decisions, judgments, conclusions and computations, you are in a creative mode.

Creating a Sustainable Monetary Future

Salon Participant:

We require money to survive rather than a sustainable power of living.

Gary:

But you have not created money as a sustainable future for you, have you? You came to a conclusion that you didn't need money or want money or that money wasn't solving problems or money wasn't creating something for you. People have a lot of ideas about what money is and isn't.

Salon Participant:

I got wild and angry around money being the main focus of this reality.

Gary:

Yes, but it doesn't have to be the main focus of your reality. Money is never the focus of my reality. My focus is: How do I change things?

I was talking with my daughter today, and she told me about a friend of hers whose husband informed her, just after she had a hysterectomy, that he had a girlfriend in Mexico. He told his wife he wanted to leave her, but he couldn't because he didn't have enough money. The idea was the wife needed to work more so he could leave her!

I said to my daughter, "I wonder how much money she would need to change things and kick that jerk out of her life. I will give it to her. That guy is mean and deserves to die!" That's not something you tell somebody when they are in the midst of an operation.

Salon Participant:

What would creating money as a sustainable future look like? Would you create money?

Gary:

What I ask everybody to do is put away ten percent of all the money that comes in. When you do that, you are creating a sustainable monetary future. You are telling the universe, "I would like to have enough money coming in so I can put ten percent away."

Salon Participant:

I already do that, so I wanted something more. Please help me with that.

Gary:

Yes, but you didn't like that answer.

Salon Participant:

I didn't like it because I am already doing that.

Gary:

Are you willing to recognize where you create a sustainable future because of what you are choosing?

When you do that, you are starting to create a sustainable future. I created Access Consciousness as a business, and if I die tomorrow, it will continue on. That is a sustainable future. I put as many things in place as I can so that I am replaceable. Have you made you replaceable in the future or have you tried to be indispensable?

Salon Participant:

Mostly I've tried to be indispensable.

Gary:

That's not creating a sustainable future.

Salon Participant:

What about leaving an inheritance?

Gary:

That is not a sustainable future. That is just money you are leaving for other people to throw away because they didn't earn it.

Salon Participant:

What would it take for me to create a sustainable future with the capability that I have and be with money?

Gary:

You haven't looked at that at all. Start looking at it before instituting a future.

What physical actualization of a creation of a sustainable future am I now capable of creating, generating and instituting? Everything that doesn't allow it times a godzillion, will you destroy and uncreate it all? Right and Wrong, Good and Bad, POD and POC, All Nine, Shorts, Boys and Beyonds.

Salon Participant:

Thank you, Gary.

Nobody Can Make Anyone Else Happy

Salon Participant:

My relationship runs in weird circles. My husband and I talk about marriage and divorce a lot. He says things like, "If I didn't have to give you money, I would leave" and "If the kids weren't here, I would leave." I say, "The kids will be fine, and you don't have to give me money," yet he won't leave, and we spend every day not being happy. I would like to change this.

Gary:

He doesn't really want to leave.

Salon Participant:

I get that, but there is so much anger, blame and shame. I am constantly POC and PODing distracter implants. There is no desire for sex. What is this insanity?

Gary:

Are you willing to change and make the relationship work for him?

Salon Participant:

He is asking me to be the housewife and to earn money. I do both, and nothing makes him happy.

Gary:

Nobody can make anybody else happy.

Salon Participant:

Where do I begin to choose my life?

Gary:

You have already chosen your life. What if you started to ask a question: What would it take to create a sustainable future for me, my kids and my husband?

Salon Participant:

I have asked that.

Gary:

No, you haven't. I've never given you this question.

Salon Participant:

I said to him, "Let's change this. What is required? What would you like? What would work for you?" and we have gone through scenarios. It is insane. I've been doing this since day one—choosing this insanity.

Surviving vs. Thriving

Gary:

That is interesting. "I have been doing this since day one." Does that mean that you went into your marriage with those decisions, judgments, conclusions and computations?

Salon Participant:

Yes.

Gary:

When you do decisions, judgments, conclusions and computations, all you can do is survive. You cannot create a sustainable future.

You are coming to *conclusion* about what you are *supposed* to do instead of coming to *awareness* of what you *could* be doing. You have to be clear that for you right now, life is about survival. Maybe you should stop doing survival and look at what it would take for you to thrive.

What stupidity are you using to create the invention of life as survival you are choosing? Everything that is times a godzillion, will you destroy and uncreate it all? Right and Wrong, Good and Bad, POD and POC, All Nine, Shorts, Boys and Beyonds

What if you didn't invent decisions, judgments, conclusions and computations?

Salon Participant:

I love the concept of sustainability. Over the last twelve months, I have spent a huge amount of money creating a garden. I have noticed that any person who comes into the garden changes, even my neighbors. Their horses are winning races. To see the magic that occurs here is awesome. I see where I am creating a sustainable future, but this, by itself, is not enough for me.

Gary:

You haven't been creating a sustainable future financially. When you were working with your ex-husband, you were creating together. Did you consider what you were creating was a sustainable future?

Salon Participant:

Yes.

Gary:

Is he still doing that or is he coming to decisions, judgments, conclusions and computations?

Salon Participant:

He is destroying his future. Oh, so that's where my anger and confusion is! I am not creating in the way that I was with him.

What Can I Create as a Sustainable Future?

Gary:

Right. You have to do that with something else. Find something that would create a sustainable future that you never considered.

Salon Participant:

You always get me to this place, and I can't push through it.

Gary:

You can.

Salon Participant:

But I won't?

Gary:

Yes. Run this:

What physical actualization of the creation of a totally sustainable future am I now capable of creating, generating and instituting? Everything that doesn't allow that times a godzillion, will you destroy and uncreate it all? Right and Wrong, Good and Bad, POD and POC, All Nine, Shorts, Boys and Beyonds.

I am trying to get you to a stage where you have been unwilling to go in the past. I'd like to see all of you start to look at: I am a warrior who is going to battle to create a future that has never been.

Once you do that, you will not fight against anything, because as soon as you are *against* a situation, you stop fighting *for* creating something that has never been. If you go for creating a sustainable future, you will have even greater choices.

Try asking:

- What brings me joy?
- What is joyful for me to do and be?

You have to look at your future from: What can I create as a sustainable future? You have to do this with no indication of what it is supposed to look like. Many of you are trying to decide what it will look like before going on the trip. Go on the trip, folks, and you will find out what it looks like when you get there.

All right, that's it for tonight. Thank you, ladies. It has been awesome.

10

Conscious Relationships

*Instead of being active or conscious when you create relationships,
you look for an unconscious place where you can create relationship called
"I love him and he loves me."
How many of those relationships have worked well for you?*

Gary:

Welcome, ladies. I think, from the tone of your questions, that you're getting the awareness that you have something major to contribute to life—and that's really cool. I'm very happy about that.

The Six Elements of Conscious Relationships

Salon Participant:

Can you talk about the creation of a conscious relationship and what that looks like as a working possibility? What are the pragmatics of it?

Gary:

There are six elements of a conscious relationship:

Number one: The person you choose (Who is choosing? You are!) should be independent while thinking they are screwed up. Why? That means they are just like you.

Salon Participants:

(Laughing)

Gary:

Number two: You want to be acknowledged, never needed.

The other person should want someone to take care of them, while knowing that when they get you to take care of them, they will leave. Why? Don't you always leave when you are not getting what you really want—and you don't want to be needed?

The other person has to believe he wants to be with you. He wants somebody in his life who will take care of him, but at the same time, he is too independent to even think that, as are you. You don't do dependence, do you?

Salon Participant:

Not at all.

Gary:

You are lousy at dependence. You can't even pretend it! "I need someone" is not part of your vaguest reality. Most people are trying to figure out how they can get someone who needs them, while in reality, they would hate it if someone needed them—it would suffocate the hell out of them.

Salon Participant:

I didn't understand that one. You spoke Chinese. I have no idea what you said. If you could go over that, it would be lovely.

Gary:

You always want people to take care of you, don't you?

Salon Participant:

Yes.

Gary:

And every time they do, you dump them.

Salon Participant:

Correct.

Gary:

That's what I am talking about. If you found somebody who wanted to take care of you, how quickly would you get rid of them?

Salon Participant:

I wouldn't even be there in the first place.

Gary:

Yeah, I know. But that's the kind of person you will find truly wonderful to be with. You think the other person wants to be taken care of *and* you recognize they don't really want to be taken care of. They just want you to empower them.

Salon Participant:

Oh! I see! Someone like me.

Gary:

Yeah. Instead of being active and conscious in the way you create relationships, you try to create relationship from an unconscious place called, "I love him and he loves me." How many of those relationships have worked well for you?

Salon Participant:

None.

Gary:

Why?

Salon Participant:

I have walked away from every one of them. It was not nurturing, it was not expansive. It was nothing.

Gary:

That's what I'm saying.

Number three: Everything you do or say must be about empowering them to be everything they are—and never about them choosing you.

Make sure they are never dependent on you. Because if they become dependent on you, they have to screw you over. They have to. So, you have to empower them, no matter what the situation is.

The other day I talked with a young man who was angry at his girlfriend. They had been on vacation with some other people and everything had gone swimmingly till the last night when they both got a little overzealous with the spirits. Another guy started to hit on this guy's girlfriend and tried to create problems between him and her. So she, being a peacemaker, tried to make peace and get her boyfriend to settle down, and he wasn't having any of it. He got mad at her and said, "You've got to do what I want!"

How many of you , when people tell you that you have to do what they want, say, "F--- you, I am out of here"? None of you want to be given orders. Have you ever noticed? That's because you are fiercely independent. You might think you'd like somebody who is willing to take care of you, but you don't really want someone to take care of you because you know you are capable of taking care of yourself. What you are looking for is somebody who will empower you to know what you know and be grateful for you just how you are.

Number four: It's never ever about you.

This is a hard place to come from because you've been taught that you have to ask for what you really want. Does that work?

Salon Participant:

No!

Gary:

Why not try something new that does work? Dain and I have a conscious relationship. We don't have sex. If I wanted to have sex and he didn't, that would limit our relationship and destroy it, so I won't ask for sex because I know it would destroy the relationship from his point of view.

What would it be like if you were willing to look at relationship not from your point of view or the other person's point of view, but from the choice of things. What if you looked at what you would like to create from choice?

Salon Participant:

Can you say more about this, please?

Gary:

Don't assume a point of view; *create* your point of view. I invite Dain to go everywhere I go. I never require him to go anywhere with me. I don't expect him to invite me to go anywhere with him. That's a conscious relationship.

Number five: Be always available but never have an answer. Only a question. When you are available for people any time they have a problem, it's amazing how quickly they are willing to listen to you.

Number six: Let the person lead in sex. If they say, "I want to have sex," then be available. Let them tell you what they want or else you're in trouble. They have to be as controlling as you are sexually or it will never work for you.

Sex Is a Created Reality

Salon Participant:

Something is coming up for me. When we get into bed and my husband rolls over and says, "Hi Honey," I am not really interested. I know I can POC and POD myself into being interested, but....

Gary:

Do you really believe that sex is not a created reality?

Salon Participant:

I believe that it is spontaneous. I need to be in the mood.

Gary:

"I need to be in the mood. Where is the romance? Where is the wine?"

You have to get that sex is a choice, like everything else. If you are willing to be the conscious one in relationship, you can create a phenomenal relationship. You have to do it from the point of view that, "Oh, you want sex? Cool! Let's go."

It's not, "I am not in the mood," "I don't know what your problem is," or "Why do you always want it when I don't want it?"

Salon Participant:

Are you saying that we can change anything?

Gary:

Yeah. You can change anything. You can be anything—but you have to be willing to change and create anything.

Salon Participant:

If sex is a created reality, then we can create anything at that moment?

Gary:

Yeah.

Salon Participant:

So, does my resistance come from not wanting to do what I am told?

Gary:

Yes. You are never good at being told, are you? You often want to kill the person.

Salon Participant:

Yeah, that's not a good place to create sex from.

Gary:

Right. That's not a good place to create sex from! Killing energy in sex definitely kills the mood.

Salon Participant:

How do I change that?

Gary:

Look at:

- What do I really want to create here?
- Do I want to create a place where my husband, lover or significant other is actually happy?

You have a choice: the rightness of your point of view—or happiness.

"Sorry, I am not in the mood. I am not prepared." Do you really have to be prepared?

Salon Participant:

I always thought so.

Gary:

You thought so or you bought so?

How many of you bought that you have to be in the mood before you can have sex? Everything that is times a godzillion, will you destroy and uncreate it all? Right and Wrong, Good and Bad, POD and POC, All Nine, Shorts, Boys and Beyonds.

You guys have bought a whole lot of crap with that.

Salon Participant:

Isn't being prepared carrying a condom in your purse?

Gary:

That's a whole lot closer to being prepared! Let's do a little process:

What stupidity are you using to create the invention and artificial intensity of the demons of need as a source of relationships are you choosing? Everything that is times a godzillion, will you destroy and uncreate it all? Right and Wrong, Good and Bad, POD and POC, All Nine, Shorts, Boys and Beyonds.

Would It Be Fun to Have Sex Now?

The idea that you are not prepared to have sex is, "I need to be in the mood," "I need you to smell right, taste right and everything else." It's not the question, "Would it be fun to have sex now?"

Salon Participant:

I don't think I have ever asked that question, Gary.

Gary:

I guarantee you haven't asked it. We've never been told we have choice whether we have sex or not. It's all about, "I am not in the mood," or "I have a headache." Anything except the willingness to recognize that it is a choice, not a need.

Salon Participant:

We have a choice but we also create it, and we can create whatever we want.

Gary:

Exactly, because you are what?

Salon Participant:

An infinite being.

Gary:

You are women who create future!

What stupidity are you using to create the invention and artificial intensity of the demons of need rather than choice are you choosing? Everything that is times a godzillion, will you destroy and uncreate it all? Right and Wrong, Good and Bad, POD and POC, All Nine, Shorts, Boy and Beyonds.

Salon Participant:

"Would it be fun to have sex now?" I am telling you, that question is great!

Gary:

Yeah, "Would it be fun to have sex now?" instead of, "I am not in the mood and you haven't done all the appropriate foreplay and set up." Which of those is a question? Men are cute. As long as the bed is comfortable, they are ready to have sex. If the bed is hard as rock, they are still ready. For the most part, women have created relationship as an appendage to sex as the source for the creation of their choice and need. They would rather *need* their relationship and *have* sex.

Salon Participant:

Fun came up for me. I would rather have *need* than *fun*.

Gary:

This whole thing that got created about the feminine mystique—the idea that a woman doesn't need sex and a man does. Well, a man doesn't *need* sex; he *likes* it.

How many of you have tried to create a *need* for relationships rather than the *fun* of relationships? Everything that is times a godzillion, will you destroy and uncreate it all? Right and Wrong, Good and Bad, POD and POC, All Nine, Shorts, Boys and Beyonds.

We have these points of view. What makes you think there is love in relationships? You had a relationship with your parents; was that loving? No. You have had friends; have they been loving?

Salon Participant:

No.

Gary:

The purpose of relationships is to have someone who will provide money, someone who will let you do what you want to do when you want to do it, and someone who is good to have sex with.

Salon Participant:

I was okay with the last two, but for the first one about money, I went "Aaahh…."

Gary:

You are so independent that you don't want anybody to take care of you by having more money than you.

Salon Participant:

I would like to change that, please.

Gary:

It's fine if you are willing to buy a boy toy for money. Everything you have done to be the person who always provides money, will you destroy and uncreate it?

Salon Participant:

I am over that now. I am willing to have lots and lots of money.

Gary:

Let me ask you a question. What does, "I am over that" mean?

Salon Participant:

It means, "been there done that."

Gary:

Is there a question in that?

Salon Participant:

No.

Gary:

Is that a conclusion?

Salon Participant:

Absolutely. It is even more than conclusion. It's like I am checking it off a list or something like that.

Gary:

Yeah, you have decided that these are the things worth having. As soon as you have checked them all off, you don't have to create or generate beyond the conclusions you have made. This is how you cut off your creativity.

Salon Participant:

Yeah, it stops everything and doesn't include anyone. It stops all the possibilities around having twenty boy toys.

Gary:

Or having somebody to have sex and fun with and to hang out with. Someone who has as much money as you have and who doesn't need you any more than you need him. Someone who would allow you to have everything you want whenever you wanted it. That would be terrible because then you would have no justification or excuse for being miserable.

> Everything that is times a godzillion, will you destroy and uncreate it all? Right and Wrong, Good and Bad, POD and POC, All Nine, Shorts, Boys and Beyonds.

What if You Never Wanted Another Person to Do Anything?

Here's what is creative about this: You allow him to be himself and to do everything he desires. You invite him into your life and you invite yourself into his life. You don't put him in control or make him responsible for your life and he doesn't have to do anything. You provide everything that works.

Most of you get upset when the other person doesn't provide what you want. What if you never wanted another person to do anything?

> Everything you have put in place to come into the need of what you can need from people, so you can know you are needy enough to get what you want, so freaking needy, will you destroy and uncreate it all? Everything that is times a godzillion, will you destroy and uncreate it all? Right and Wrong, Good and Bad, POD and POC, All Nine, Shorts, Boys and Beyonds.

You are knocking me out here, folks!

What if you never wanted another person to do anything? What you live from now are projections, expectations, separations, judgments and rejections—not from choice, desire, question or fun. You are trying to create a relationship based on whose point of view?

Your mother's, your father's, your friend's, your brother's, your significant other's.

Everything that is times a godzillion, will you destroy and uncreate it all? Right and Wrong, Good and Bad, POD and POC, All Nine, Shorts, Boys and Beyonds.

You ladies keep trying to take care of your man because periodically you want to be mothers to your child. You put the man in the child's position and wonder why he is not good in the bedroom. "You are going to do what I want because I want you to" is most people's definition of caring. You humanoid women don't want to be taken care of—but you pretend you do so you can beat the crap out of the man who takes care of you.

From this reality's point of view, *taking care of* means controlling someone. For me, *taking care of* is empowering somebody. Ask the person questions. Don't try to solve their problems. Women have been entrained to believe they have to solve problems. So you try to solve the problem by talking about it terminally.

Deal and Deliver

Relationship is a business deal, so you have to do "deal and deliver," just as you would in any business deal. Ask these questions when you go into relationships:

- What is the deal?
- What are you going to deliver?
- What do you expect me to deliver?
- Exactly what is this going to look like and how is that going to work?
- What am I going to have to be for you?

Here's the rest of "deal and deliver":

- Never confront. Instead say, "I am confused. Will you help me, please?" This is a way to change the energy about anything, as you are not going to be in control.

- Never validate. Don't say, "Oh, I know you are so busy. I am sorry to ask this." You are not sorry to ask. You are hoping the person will come around to realize he should and could deliver.

- Never explain or justify. You are doing whatever you are doing. That's all. If you are trying to justify or explain, you are trying to make it right. That's not a good place to live. If you try to justify why you made a choice, are you being present? No. Are you making a choice? No. You are trying to make it okay that you made a choice. What's the difference between making a choice and making it okay that you chose what you chose? If you try to make it okay and justify it under the guise that you can justify it, you think the other person has to accept it. But that's not the way it works.

If you are trying to do validation, explanation or justification, you have to live up to some image you have of you rather than the reality of what you want to create as a deal. If you do, "I am just a woman," is that an explanation? Yes. It is a justification. It validates the choice you made. None of that is being willing to be aware of what can get created with your choice.

Salon Participant:

I am aware that the ultimate "deal and deliver" is you to you, and it's not really possible to have deal and deliver with another person if you don't get clear about what it is for you.

Gary:

Exactly. That's what I am hoping all of you are going to get out of this particular class.

Is the Other Person Required to Be Conscious as Well?

Salon Participant:

In a conscious relationship, is the other person required to be conscious as well? Or is it that you stay conscious to get what you want out of them?

Gary:

If you stay conscious, you will not have any projections, expectations, separations, rejections or judgments. Conscious relationship has none of those.

Salon Participant:

What if the other person functions from those?

Gary:

That's fine, as long as you don't.

Salon Participant:

So, you remain conscious and you allow the other person to function where he is functioning from?

Gary:

Yup. In a conscious relationship, you are aware of what is going on with your partner. You are willing to recognize that you have to choose what is going to work for you, not in relationship to him, but because of you—not because of him.

Let's go on to some questions.

Thriving as a Woman

Salon Participant:

Can you talk more about thriving as a woman?

Gary:

Thriving as a woman is recognizing how to use your womanly wiles. For example, women have the ability to change their mind. Do men get the same choice? Not really. A man who changes his mind is considered weak-willed and insubstantial. A woman who changes her point of view is considered creative and enigmatic. She is someone who cannot be framed, put in a picture or a locked cage.

You have to learn how to use what you have as a woman. Ask, "Lover, will you please do this for me?" A friend of mine used to be in pain all the time. I told her, "You have to ask people to help you." She got it, and now when she's in the airport, she will ask, "Lover, will you please do this for me?" and guys will reply, "Sure, honey, I will get your bag for you. Which one is yours?" Men are willing to put themselves out for her.

As a woman, you have the right to ask a man to do things for you. Does a man have that right? No, not unless he is committed to you. He has to have decided he is going to marry you and live happily ever after with you in order for him to ask you to do something for him.

To thrive as a woman, you have to use all your worldly charms and also recognize that you are the warrior who will go to battle for creating a future that nobody else can see. You have abilities that other people can't see, which is pretty amazing.

To thrive as a woman is to recognize all the things you can ask for and none of the things you have to deliver. If you will use your worldly charms and what God has given you as a weapon, you can get a man to do things for you. You have to be willing to do that. But because you are so independent, you keep trying to prove you don't need anybody. You are correct; you don't need anybody—but why not use your womanly wiles?

Seeing Negative Realities

Salon Participant:

Can I ask about seeing things other people don't see and how the unwillingness to see negative realities plays into that?

Gary:

Most people try to see that everything is turning out well, especially when it comes to decisions, judgments, conclusions and computations. Let's say you decide you are in love with a man. Is that a judgment?

Salon Participant:

Yeah.

Gary:

You need to ask: What negative reality am I unwilling to look at here?

Before I got together with my ex-wife, I made a list of all the things I wanted in a woman I was in a relationship with. She had all those things. What I didn't make is a list of all the things I did *not* want in that person. So, I got everything I wanted, and I also got everything I *didn't* want. Was that awareness or choice? Or was I not willing to look at negative realities?

Salon Participant:

Not willing to look at negative realities.

Gary:

You always have to be willing to look at the negative reality of somebody if you want total awareness. Once you have done that, you can create a relationship with anyone. But if you are not willing to see the negative reality they live from, you will be disappointed, unhappy and miserable. You will decide that something is terribly wrong.

Salon Participant:

Could you talk some more about what negative reality is?

Gary:

There are people who live in conclusion. I know a lady whose whole reality is, "I am right and people need to see the rightness of my point of view." She's one of those people who write letters to the editor. She recently got kicked out her apartment because she decided her upstairs neighbor was not being respectful of her and she complained about him to the owner of the apartment. Well, the upstairs neighbor happened to be the grandson of the lady who owned the apartment. So, the righteousness of my friend's point of view that the neighbor was wrong and she was right and he should be gone and she shouldn't didn't serve her well. She was not willing to look at the negative aspect of what would be created by her choice. You have to be willing to see the negative reality. You have to ask: If I choose this, what reality will get created? You have to get that your choice will create a positive or negative reality in your world or other people's world.

Creating beyond This Reality

Salon Participant:

Can I change the direction? I recently read a book about the Viking times. It said that when a male chief was being elected, the candidates had to appear in front of a group of seven to nine women and present a vision of the future they wanted to plan for coming generations. If a candidate could give a vision that the women liked, he was chosen as the chief. What do you think about this sort of collaboration between male and female energies?

Gary:

That's the collaboration that should be, that currently isn't.

Salon Participant:

Yeah, I liked it when I heard it.

Gary:

Did you like it? Or did you recognize that it would work?

Salon Participant:

I liked the dynamic between male and female and that they were working together towards the long term. Government today is short term; it's for next four years till next election.

Gary:

Well, not even that far. They are thinking about whether they'll get elected in the next ten seconds.

Salon Participant:

Yeah, of course. I just thought I would mention it because we are talking so much about the dynamics between male and female energies here. I am sure we should be able to get there.

Gary:

Can we back up a little bit? What you described is not a dynamic. It is a creation. A dynamic is a given point of view, "This is the way it is and we cannot change it."

What you described is a creation. It is what would be created if people were willing to function from a bigger reality, a larger, more global perspective. People do not look far enough into the future to determine what their creation is going to create. I do. I look at what people are going to create with the choices they are making. There isn't one of you who doesn't have the capacity to see a bigger and greater possibility than ninety percent of people around you, but instead of choosing that, you keep trying to bring yourself back into this reality by choosing the man who will make your life perfect or the restoration of your family that will make your life perfect or some other thing that will make your life perfect.

What if you were generating and creating beyond this reality? Everything that doesn't allow that to show up times a godzillion, will you destroy and uncreate it all? Right and Wrong, Good and Bad, POD and POC, All Nine, Shorts, Boys and Beyonds.

What physical actualization of creation of future beyond the future of this reality are you now capable of creating, generating and instituting? Everything that doesn't allow that times a godzillion, will you destroy and uncreate it all? Right and Wrong, Good and Bad, POD and POC, All Nine, Shorts, Boys and Beyonds.

Salon Participant:

It feels so much lighter when you run that clearing. More exciting.

Gary:

It's not exciting because excitement is what you use to get you out of your doldrums. It is the enthusiasm of living.

Salon Participant:

Yeah, got it. You are better at describing energy with words.

The Willingness to See the Future

Salon Participant:

Earlier you said you are willing to see a future that is far beyond what other people are willing to see. Can you talk about what that looks like in your universe and in ours?

Gary:

Well, what it looks like in my universe is realizing what people will do—and not having a point of view about it. As an example, a woman who was very active in Access Consciousness has left Access. I knew this was happening a year before she left. I could see what it was going to create for her and what she would do with it, and I was hoping she wouldn't choose it. But she did. I looked at it and asked, "Is this going to create an adverse effect in my reality?" No.

You have to look at the choices other people make and how those choices are going to affect your reality. Ask: Is this going to change my reality? Change it? Yes. Affect it in a negative way? No. Is it going to expand my agenda? Yes. Do I know how? No. But I am willing to have the question of what can show up rather than come to a conclusion or decision or determination of what I need to do to deal with it. Does that help?

Comfort Is Not about Awareness

Salon Participant:

Yes. Thank you. How does the discomfort of total awareness play into that?

Gary:

Comfort is not about awareness. Comfort is about decisions, judgments, conclusions and computations that make you right in what you chose. Uncomfort is about living in choice; comfort is living in conclusion.

Salon Participant:

Can you talk about how that relates to having no point of view and being aware of everything?

Gary:

If you have no point of view, you can be aware of everything. If you have a point of view, you eliminate from your awareness anything that doesn't match your point of view. And when you do that, you give your power away to conclusion. You make conclusion your guru instead of choice or possibility.

I can look at something like that woman's choice to leave Access Consciousness. Is it what I would have liked? No, but it is her choice and I let it be her choice. Is it going to create everything she thinks it is? No. But I have to trust that if she wishes to destroy herself or create problems for herself, that's her choice and she must do it. I am willing to let people die if that's what they are choosing. If somebody is doing something that is killing them, I will let them do it. I won't stop them. Why won't I? Because it is their choice, not mine.

Salon Participant:

Unless they ask you a question, Gary?

Gary:

Yes, unless they ask me a question. But most people who destroy themselves do not ask questions. They avoid asking questions because questions can challenge the decisions, judgments, conclusions and computations they used to create the conclusions they have come to and decisions they have made.

Salon Participant:

When you knew that woman was going to leave, you asked, "Will this affect me?" You didn't go to conclusion. You didn't say, "Now I have to fix it or change her mind." You do something different than I do. When I perceive something in the future, I go into action.

Gary:

Rather than being aware, you do action. You are willing to have a do-do world not a be-be world.

Salon Participant:

Sometimes it's not a negative energy or a negative reality, but you know it's not going to be a happy ending for someone. Are you still willing to let the person do it as long as it doesn't affect consciousness?

Gary:

Consciousness cannot be beaten, no matter what. Is her leaving going to adversely affect the consciousness I am working on? No. Because she will always do what she will do.

I was talking with someone the other day about a system for supporting different facilitators so we could expand Access Consciousness. I have to put a system in place and I don't yet have all the pieces to the puzzle. I decided I would take five or six people and start with them until I could get a system that works.

Someone called and asked, "Why are you excluding me?"

I said, "I am not excluding you. I need someone who will follow directions and move in the direction things have to go so we can get the system in place. The one thing I know about you is you ain't going to follow anybody. You will always do whatever you want."

The person laughed and said, "Yeah, I would always do that."

You Can Be Right or You Can Be Light

Salon Participant:

Lots of times I want to ask you a question like, "What awareness do you have of me that would really blow my universe and expand my awareness?"

Gary:

To some extent, you have made a lot of decisions and conclusions about your life that are working. Yes or no?

Salon Participant:

Yes.

Gary:

What if you had to give all of those up? Every single one of them?

Salon Participant:

It feels light.

Gary:

Yes, but you won't choose that.

Salon Participant:

I won't choose the lightness?

Gary:

No, because you have a choice. You can be right or you can be light.

Salon Participant:

I feel like saying, "Yes, I would give it up."

Gary:

Don't delude yourself. Be real about it. What's true? Ask: Would I rather have the lightness or the rightness? Be bluntly honest with yourself. The only way you are going to create your future is if you are honest with yourself.

There was a point when Access Consciousness wasn't succeeding the way I would have liked. I was bluntly honest with myself in looking at that. I changed the way Bars facilitators work. I did away with all the royalties they had to pay, which goes against the way things are done in this reality. I took away all necessity of paying me for things.

What I made a necessity was that there be more consciousness. Every time someone runs Bars, 300,000 other people get free of what that person got free of at that moment. That was my original target with Access Consciousness, to create freedom for everyone on the planet. I am still working on that one.

Salon Participant:

So, I don't have a target?

Gary:

Yeah, you don't have a target. You have come to conclusion that you have achieved what you set out to achieve.

Salon Participant:

Yet I am asking questions.

Gary:

The one question you are not willing to ask yourself is: What would I really like to create as my life? That's about having a sustainable future. You need to ask: What would my life be like in five years if I chose this?

You can't have a defined point of view and conclusion, which is what you keep trying to come to. It's an awareness of energy. You can tell that by choosing it, you can generate and create more from there.

Salon Participant:

What do we have in place that keeps us from seeing the future with more ease?

Gary:

You buy into this reality's point of view. If you buy this reality's point of view, you are supposed to be the little woman who is pregnant and cooking for your man. That would work for you how well?

Salon Participant:

Not at all. I tried it.

Gary:

Yeah. You have to have a greater willingness to be a conqueror of the world and a creator of the future.

Salon Participant:

So, it's just that we are buying into the stories of this reality?

Gary:

Yes, this reality doesn't work for shit. Love it? No. Tolerate it? Yes. Is it what I want? No. Is it what you want? Probably not. But what choice did you have?

Salon Participant:

What choices do I have? Something different?

Gary:

That's what you have to be willing to have. Something different.

What physical actualization of the creation of the future beyond the reality of this future are you now capable of creating generating and instituting? Everything that doesn't allow that to show up times a godzillion, will you destroy and uncreate it all? Right and Wrong, Good and Bad, POD and POC, All Nine, Shorts, Boys and Beyonds.

Conquering vs. Excluding

Salon Participant:

I have a confusion between conquering and excluding. Can you assist me with that?

Gary:

In the old days when someone conquered a country, they had a choice. They could kill all the people and have the country or they could include all the people in their reality and use them to create more.

Salon Participant:

I have done the first one.

Gary:

To kill everyone?

Salon Participant:

Yes, I think I have.

Gary:

The good news is you get to have the country. You have it all by yourself and there is nobody to play with.

Salon Participant:

Yeah, that's where I am.

Gary:

Is that really in your best interest?

Salon Participant:

Not at all. Could you help me change it please?

Gary:

What stupidity are you using to create conquering as a way of excluding you are you choosing? Everything that is times a godzillion, will you destroy and uncreate it all? Right and Wrong, Good and Bad, POD and POC, All Nine, Shorts, Boys and Beyonds.

Apparently you are not the only one who has done this.

Salon Participant:

Thank you!

Salon Participant:

Is it correct that when people are doing superiority, they actually believe everyone is better than they are? Or are they trying to prove otherwise? Is this buying the lie that anyone is greater or less than us?

Gary:

No one is greater or less than anyone else; they are different! I don't see anybody as greater or less than me. We have different experiences and awareness. My point of view is:

- What do you know I can use for me?
- What do you know I can use for others?
- What do you know that you haven't exposed to me yet?

"How Do I Prove My Contribution?"

Salon Participant:

Something is sticking me. I have to write a very long essay for my lawyers about my last thirteen years with my ex to prove my contribution to the relationship and business so that I can get more than the thirty-one percent that is being offered to me. I have gone halfway through it and I'm wondering what I could do or be different in proving my contribution. I can't put my contribution into words so people can see it.

Gary:

"Fairy tales can come true, it can happen to you." You have to write a fairy tale if you want others to believe it.

Salon Participant:

I just need to do what is required?

Gary:

You are trying to tell the truth. Tell fairy tales everyone wants to buy.

Salon Participant:

What does that mean?

Gary:

That's the reason I gave you that song. Think about that song and write again.

Salon Participant:

Are you saying I have to write the fairy tale that was not?

Gary:

You have to write the fairy tale about how much you loved and how much you lost. How you did everything you could to support him and all the long conversations you had that were designed to get him to see the amazingness of him.

Salon Participant:

I did go there. Why did I get stuck?

Gary:

You decided it a was fairy tale, not reality. You should be able to deliver the fairy tale that people can hear.

Salon Participant:

Okay.

Gary:

Everything that brought up or let down for everybody times a godzillion, will you destroy and uncreate it all? Right and Wrong, Good and Bad, POD and POC, All Nine, Shorts, Boys and Beyonds.

Being What's True for You

Salon Participant:

Sometimes I come across to other people more forcefully than I would like. I am not sure whether to leave this or change it. I get a tightening around my throat quite often. What is this?

Gary:

It's your awareness of where the rest of the world is not willing to go. Every time you open the space of possibility, you will feel and sense the actualization of other people's limitations.

You have to be willing to be what's true for you. I won't lie if someone asks me about something. I will tell them the truth. I won't hedge because I discovered that every time I hedged and didn't tell people what was, it was just as good as telling them a lie. I am not interested in lying to people.

Salon Participant:

Is there anything else that would assist me in knowing what to say, how, to whom, when and how to say it with potency and clarity?

Gary:

Ask: What stupidity am I using to create the lack of silence I am choosing?

You may not be saying anything but you have a loud head. You have to have the clarity and ease of silence as much as anything else.

Ninety-nine percent of the time, silence will give you more control over people than talking.

Being in the Computation of Your Own Life

Salon Participant:

Can you tell me what I am doing to destroy my life, living and reality that if I would change that, would create a sustainable reality for me?

Gary:

It's not what you are doing; it is what you are not doing. You need to ask:

What can I be or do today to change my life and future to a sustainable reality for all eternity? Everything that is times a godzillion, will you destroy and uncreate it all? Right and Wrong, Good and Bad, POD and POC, All Nine, Shorts, Boys and Beyonds.

It is not something that you have to be or do. It's something you have to choose. Most of us have no idea what that is. Truth, how much of your life have you created based on you?

Salon Participant:

Zero percent.

Gary:

That's pretty much where everybody functions from. A lady who was helping us with Access Consciousness messed up a couple of things. I told her, "People usually mess up when they don't want to do things. So truth, do you not want to work for Access anymore?"

She said "No, I don't."

I asked, "What do you want to do? What would you like your life to be like?"

She said, "I have no idea."

I said, "That's because you have spent your whole life doing for your parents, your grandmother, your husband and your business—but not anything for you. How come you are not in the computation of your own life?" Not that this would apply to anyone else on this call!

What stupidity are you using to create the invention and artificial intensity of not being in the computation of your own life you are choosing? Everything that is times a godzillion, will you destroy and uncreate it all? Right and Wrong, Good and Bad, POD and POC, All Nine, Shorts, Boys and Beyonds.

Tempt Them, Teach Them and Send Them on Their Way

Salon Participant:

You once said to me regarding men, "Tempt them, teach them and send them on their way." I may have misidentified that as "teach them a lesson," and while that may be required at times, I am not sure that's what you meant. Can you explain and expand on this?

Gary:

"Tempt them, teach them and send them on their way" is the idea that you don't really want a relationship. You would like to have fun with someone. Teaching them is teaching them everything that is going to make them better men; it's not about teaching them a lesson.

Salon Participant:

What's wrong with chopping off men's balls and having them on the wall as a trophy?

Gary:

Well, that's cool, but if you do that, chances are you are not going to have many men coming to visit you. If they see balls on the wall, they won't have anything to do with you. Is that what you want to create with men? Is that the future you'd like to have?

Look at it. Ask: If I choose to cut off this man's balls, what would my life be like in five years? More expanded or more contracted? If I choose to leave this man's balls on his body and caress them and enjoy them and use him as much as I choose, what will my life be in five years? More expanded less expanded? Feel the energy and figure it out yourself.

The Real Pragmatics: Start with Choice

Salon Participant:

Would you speak about the pragmatics of being clear about what we really want to create and where we blind ourselves?

Gary:

Real pragmatics is: Start with choice. If I choose this, what will my life be like in five years? Ask:

- If I choose this, what would my life be like in five years?
- If I don't choose this, what would my life be like in five years?

You will start to energetically feel the difference between choice and not choice, and slowly but surely, you will begin to choose what works for you. You will get what each choice will make your life like in five years.

You can have the energy of it—but you can't define it. You have to get out of trying to define what you'd like your life to be like. People say, "I'd like to have millions of dollars, I'd like to do this, I'd like to do that."

"I'd like to do it" is not the same as creating and generating.

Generation, Creation and Institution

Salon Participant:

How do functionality and institution play into that? When you ask, "If I choose this, what will it create?" what happens to actualize it?

Gary:

You have to go to question. It will give you an indication of the energies you desire to create from. *Generation* is the energy that starts something into existence, *creation* is when you put it into actualization and *institution* is what you do to create a platform to build more.

I am giving you the system by which you can become clear about what you can create. It's not going to be a cognitive universe. If you could create a universe based on a cognitive point of view, you would have done it centuries ago.

You have to recognize that clarity comes from the awareness you create around what your choice creates. The choice is the source of creation—not decisions, judgments, conclusions and computations. If you try to function from decisions, judgments, conclusions and computations, you are functioning from judgments rather than possibilities.

You have two choices: You can buy this chair or you can sell this chair. What will your life be like in five years if you buy this chair? What will your life be like in five years if you sell this chair? You can feel the difference in the energy of what will get created.

Don't give up your awareness in favor of conclusion. Use this process:

- If I choose this, what will my life be like in five years?
- If I don't choose it, what will my life be like in five years?

You can get the difference between the choice that feels more expansive and the choice that feels more contractive. In order to create a sustainable future, learn how to feel the difference in the energy of what gets created with the choices you make.

You learn to create by the choices you make, because every choice creates something.

If you are a warrior woman who is out to do a battle to create a sustainable future, it's a different world. You have to be willing to look at that, choose that and be that and then all of this other stuff will turn around. Get that your choice creates.

Okay, ladies, that's it for tonight. Please go out and be the woman you are who can create a future that will be sustainable and magnificent. That's the gift you are to mankind.

11

Staying in the Power of Choice and Awareness

You invite a demon to come into your life
whenever you give your power to something other than awareness.

Gary:

Hello, ladies. Let's talk about what demons are and how they relate to you being a warrior woman who is out to do a battle to create a sustainable future.

Demons

A demon is any being or anything else that wants to have some control in your life. You invite a demon to come into your life whenever you give your power to something other than awareness. If you are looking for a relationship where someone will take care of you and you can be the follower, you are inviting demon energies to come into your life—because being a follower requires you to give away you and your awareness. Demons and entities want you to become a follower. So, that's one way you can invite them in. Fortunately, you guys are lousy at being followers! You're no good at following three paces behind your man.

The other way you can invite demons in is to give your power away to conclusion—because conclusion is the opposite of awareness. When you have a point of view, you eliminate from your awareness anything that doesn't match that point of view. You're giving your power to the conclusion rather than your awareness.

When you have no point of view, you can be aware of everything.

You also give your power away when you abandon your awareness in favor of someone else's.

Salon Participant:

I don't have a good sense of what demons are. Can you expand on this?

Gary:

Who or what do you give your power away to?

Salon Participant:

To others.

Gary:

Really? I don't think so.

Salon Participant:

To conclusion.

Gary:

Conclusion is one. Money is another. You have demons of conclusion in your life that tell you what to do or that there is a problem with money. They tell you that you have to come to conclusion.

It's about recognizing where you have invited demons into your life to control things for you. Demons tell you all the right things to do and say. They try to get you to give up your life in favor of what they choose. Whenever you come to conclusion, you are inviting demons of conclusion to make sure you get the right conclusion and conclude what's right.

Salon Participant:

What would it take to be clear about where I allow demons to take control of my relationships or sex? What will it take to deliver me from the demons that screw up my friendships and sex with men?

Gary:

Here is a process:

What stupidity are you using to create the invention, artificial intensity and the demons from which you must be delivered are you choosing? Everything that is times a godzillion, will you destroy and uncreate it all? Right and Wrong, Good and Bad, POD and POC, All Nine, Shorts, Boys and Beyonds.

That's working!

How much of thoughts, feelings, emotions, sex and no sex is actually the demon universe from which you must be delivered? Quite a bit. Everything that is times a godzillion, will you destroy and uncreate it all? Right and Wrong, Good and Bad, POD and POC, All Nine, Shorts, Boys and Beyonds.

All the demons of being woman, being feminine, being female, being *la femme* that require you to diminish you, will you now ask them to go back to from whence they came and never return to you or this reality for all eternity? Everything that doesn't allow that times a godzillion, will you destroy and uncreate it all? Right and Wrong, Good and Bad, POD and POC, All Nine, Shorts, Boys and Beyonds.

You Create Demons Rather Than Choice

This is the place where you have *demons* of what being female is rather than the choice of being what female is. You have to recognize the place where you, as the female, are the person who goes to battle for the creation of future. If you get that, your target in life is to be a futurist and not somebody who is willing to be the effect of the past, as though that is the creation of future. Everywhere that exists in the world, you create the demons of womanhood, womanizing and woman embodiment.

How many demons of woman embodiment can you now destroy and uncreate and return to from whence they came never to return to this reality or you ever again for all eternity? Everything that is times a godzillion, will you destroy and uncreate it all? Right and Wrong, Good and Bad, POD and POC, All Nine, Shorts, Boys and Beyonds.

Salon Participant:

In the clearing you said, "Return to from whence you came never to return to me or this reality for all eternity." What does whence mean?

Gary:

It's Old English for *when you came. A place from which you came.*

What if There Was No Greater Source of Power Than You?

Salon Participant:

Could you explain *demon-dominated Earth?*

Gary:

Anything that creates the power of demons is judgment. Demons have no power unless you align and agree or resist and react to their judgments. Their job is to exacerbate the judgment until you come to a place where you give up your power or potency in favor of their point of view. Wherever you are functioning from judgment as a sense of rightness or wrongness, you invite demons into your life to prove the rightness of your point of view. When you have no point of view, there can be no right or wrong and there can be no demons of judgment to exacerbate or exponentialize the wrongness of you in any shape or form.

How much energy are you using to create the wrongness of you, which is the domination on planet Earth by demons of judgment? Everything that is times a godzillion, will you destroy and uncreate it all? Right and Wrong, Good and Bad, POD and POC, All Nine, Shorts, Boys and Beyonds.

What stupidity are you using to create the absolute invention and total artificial intensity of the demon source and demon-dominated Earth are you choosing? Everything that is times a godzillion, will you destroy and uncreate it all? Right and Wrong, Good and Bad, POD and POC, All Nine, Shorts, Boys and Beyonds.

Humans Believe Demons Are a Source of Power

Salon Participant:

I work a lot with human females. It seems they are vicious; they lie and cheat to get whatever they want. Is this demons?

Gary:

Humanoids can recognize demons for what they are. Humans, however, believe demons are a source of power. Human women are interested in getting to a place where they have control over men in one way or another. Their life is dedicated to inviting demons to create control over men. How many of you have invited the demons that will create control over men?

Will you now demand that they return to from whence they came and never to return to you or this reality again? Everything that doesn't allow that times a godzillion, will you destroy and uncreate it all? Right and Wrong, Good and Bad, POD and POC, All Nine, Shorts, Boys and Beyonds.

Ladies, my target is to get you to the point where you have no judgments of you or anything you choose. It is to get you to the place where you have total awareness of how your choice is creating the future, because you are the source creating the future that never existed on this planet—if you will frigging choose! You keep trying not to choose as if you are waiting for somebody to come along and choose for you and tell you what to do. I love you all, and not one of you is not capable of following somebody else. Why the hell are you not following you instead of someone else? Why are you trying to find a man you can follow—or anybody you can follow? The good news is that I will never let you follow me because I will run away from you. You can't catch me no matter how fast you run.

Everything that is times a godzillion, will you destroy and uncreate it all? Right and Wrong, Good and Bad, POD and POC, All Nine, Shorts, Boys and Beyonds.

Salon Participant:

What's coming up for me lately is that I have given demons jobs to do over the last four trillion years. It has been their job to keep judgment, control and points of view in place. I have been saying, "Every job I have given you, take it with you and never return."

Gary:

You have to say: Go back to from whence you came, never to return to me or this reality for all eternity.

Salon Participant:

For me, a demon has always been a little black figure or something like that. Now it's more like a judgment that comes up is actually the demon.

Gary:

Yeah, it's about the judgments you create. If you see them as little black figures or red figures with horns and tails or any of that kind of stuff, you are conforming to this reality. You are insisting that this reality has the truth about demons.

Salon Participant:

Seeing demons in that way has stopped me from realizing where I have called them into my life and where I have been using them. Now there is a completely different energy on these demons, and I am in total gratitude for you.

Gary:

You invited them into your life, thinking that was the way to have power over something. But the ultimate power over anything is total awareness. What if there was no greater source of power than you?

Everything that doesn't allow for that to show up times a godzillion, will you destroy and uncreate it all? Right and Wrong, Good and Bad, POD and POC, All Nine, Shorts, Boys and Beyonds.

Judgment Is the Way You Invite Demons In

Salon Participant:

When you were speaking to me earlier, a bunch of energy came up for me. It was a, "Don't shut me up" kind of feeling. It was, "You are not going to listen to me. You misunderstood me." It was strange.

Gary:

Do you feel misunderstood?

Salon Participant:

Yes.

Gary:

Everywhere you decided what misunderstood means, will you destroy and uncreate it all? Right and Wrong, Good and Bad, POD and POC, All Nine, Shorts, Boys and Beyonds.

The whole idea of understanding is that someone must stand under you to support you. Do you like standing on top of people?

Salon Participant:

Not particularly.

Gary:

With or without high heels!

Salon Participant:

Wow! I see that all my questions have been trying to get you to align with the rightness of my judgments of me.

Gary:

Pretty much. Unfortunately I have no judgments of you, so it is hard for me to align with your judgments.

Salon Participant:

When I am interacting with people, I look for their judgments that align with something about me so I can get mad at them.

Gary:

No, so you can get mad at you. Are you dedicated to seeing the wrongness of you?

Salon Participant:

I have been realizing that I have these judgments.

Gary:

Everything you have done to create that times a godzillion, will you destroy and uncreate it all? Right and Wrong, Good and Bad, POD and POC, All Nine, Shorts, Boys and Beyonds.

What stupidity are you using to create the absolute invention and total artificial intensity of the demon source and demon-dominated Earth are you choosing? Everything that is times a godzillion, will you destroy and uncreate it all? Right and Wrong, Good and Bad, POD and POC, All Nine, Shorts, Boys and Beyonds.

Salon Participant:

I recently chose to do a project and I got a lot of work done around it. Then I didn't follow through on it, and I went into the wrongness of myself. Just now, listening to what you were saying, I got the awareness that I have been judging myself about the wrongness.

Gary:

Let me ask you a question. What is the value of going into the judgment of yourself?

Salon Participant:

There is no value.

Gary:

There has to be a value or you wouldn't go there. Judgment is the way you invite demons in. That's why humans judge others. Humans use judgment of others to take power over them. They get control over others by using their judgment to invite in demons who will create control. Judgment of self is the way you create the invitation.

All the places where you have judged yourself to invite demons, will you destroy and uncreate it all and return to sender? Right and Wrong, Good and Bad, POD and POC, All Nine, Shorts, Boys and Beyonds.

What would you like your life to be if you didn't bother to have judgments?

Salon Participant:

Enjoyment.

Gary:

How much energy are you using to create value with bothering to have judgments? Everything that is times a godzillion,
will you destroy and uncreate it all? Right and Wrong, Good and
Bad, POD and POC, All Nine, Shorts, Boys and Beyonds.

You bother with judgments.

Salon Participant:

What would it take for that to change so it's not something I
choose anymore?

Gary:

What stupidity are you using to create the invention, artificial intensity and demons of bothering with judgments are you
choosing? Everything that is times a godzillion, will you destroy
and uncreate it all? Right and Wrong, Good and Bad, POD and
POC, All Nine, Shorts, Boys and Beyonds.

Salon Participant:

In the clearing, you said, "artificial intensity". Can you talk about
what that is?

Gary:

Think about who does judgment of you. What part of that is
intense? Some? All? Or more?

Salon Participant:

All of it.

Gary:

You think that intensity is more valuable than awareness.

Everything that is times a godzillion, will you destroy and uncreate it all? Right and Wrong, Good and Bad, POD and POC, All Nine, Shorts, Boys and Beyonds.

Salon Participant:

Gary, I realize more and more as I see you and Dain work, that you have the ability and patience to only give people what they can hear, even though you know what they are actually capable of opening up to receiving at that moment, and only when they ask a question do you have a window to knowing where they are willing to go.

Gary:

Yeah, I am willing to look at the future you are willing to have.

Salon Participant:

By the questions we ask?

Gary:

Yeah.

Salon Participant:

I tend to give people the whole world when they ask a question.

Gary:

You keep trying to come to conclusion about what you can give them that will allow them to judge you the way you feel you deserve to be judged.

Salon Participant:

That I am someone valuable?

Gary:

That means what is valuable is your judgments of you.

Salon Participant:

Whichever way the judgment goes, where am I sticking myself here? It feels heavy.

Gary:

What lie are you making more real than you? Everything that is times a godzillion, will you destroy and uncreate it all? Right and Wrong, Good and Bad, POD and POC, All Nine, Shorts, Boys and Beyonds.

"No Point of View" Is Simply a Choice

Salon Participant:

Is it possible to choose to have no point of view and make that greater than decision, judgment, compilation and conclusion?

Gary:

Yes.

Salon Participant:

It's simply a choice?

Gary:

Yes, it is simply a choice.

What are you creating as choice that isn't choice that if you didn't create it as choice would actualize as total awareness? Everything that is times a godzillion, will you destroy and uncreate it all? Right and Wrong, Good and Bad, POD and POC, All Nine, Shorts, Boys and Beyonds.

Salon Participant:

What choices are available for us to create a totally different future?

Gary:

There is a tremendous amount of choice available. The problem is we spend our entire life trying to entrain to the no-choice universe, the demon-infested universe, which is equal to being real in this reality. What if you no longer had to be real in this reality? What choices would you have?

Salon Participant:

The process you just ran created so much space through my body. I am aware of somebody's contraction in their universe through my body, though it's not mine.

Gary:

Rather than being *through* your body, what if it's *with* your body?

Salon Participant:

What is the difference?

Gary:

Through your body is the idea that your body has awareness you don't have. *With* your body is when you expand what you and your body are aware of.

Salon Participant:

That process created more expansion of what my body and I are aware of. It's so cool. Thank you.

Salon Participant:

Is that what more space for the future is?

Never Wait for Anyone or Anything

Gary:

Yes, that's what you've got to have as space for the future.

Here's an example. We have someone who has created a beautiful logo for us, and everyone is trying to decide whether we should
make all our logos the same or whether we should all have a different logo. People aren't going forward. They are waiting until this gets
sorted out. I keep saying, "Never wait for anyone or anything."

You guys need to get this. If you are going to create a future, you
cannot wait for anyone—because then you're creating based on the
other person's future timeline, not what you're aware of.

Salon Participant:

When you said, "Don't wait for anyone," I realized how much I
disappear when I wait for people.

Gary:

The moment you go into waiting you cease to exist. You put you
on hold. It's like holding your breath and waiting until the next time
you can take a breath. Does that work? No.

When people wait for things, they are trying to get it right. It's
about judgment. Everything they do is choosing to get it right. That's
too slow.

Recently we were dealing with two people who are artists, and
when you are dealing with an artist, nothing is ever going to be right
or perfect, no matter what you do. It can always be improved. Artists
are never in question of what they are doing. They are always in
conclusion about what it should have been or they are judging what
it is not that they thought it would turn out to be.

I never wait for anybody, I just continue to create. I say, "You
know what? This is great. Let's go."

If you go slow, you are living life in this reality's universe of
correct behavior. This reality's correct behavior is to go as slow as
possible so you don't create waves. But you are wave makers. When
you were kids and got into the bathtub, you would slosh around and

make waves crash over the edge of the tub. Being sedate in the tub was not one of your points of view. It was, "How much fun is this? Let's make everything move." Standing still was not a reality for most of you, yet you keep trying to stand still as if you can do it. The thing is—you can't. Never wait for anyone. Start, go, and create. If you wait, you put yourself out of existence until someone else completes what they're doing and opens the door for you to be.

What stupidity am I using to create the waiting I am choosing? Everything that is times a godzillion, will you destroy and uncreate it all? Right and Wrong, Good and Bad, POD and POC, All Nine, Shorts, Boys and Beyonds.

When you wait, you give up your awareness in favor of someone else's completion. What if the people you are waiting for never complete? When do you get to be? When they die?

I have known people who were waiting for their parents to die so they could get their money, and their parents went on for years and years. When the kids finally got their money, it wasn't the amount they thought they were going to get. It didn't actually create anything in their lives, and they were pissed their parents didn't have more money! Why would you wait to create your life based on inheriting money or what you are going to have when you get it? Why don't you create your life now and enjoy yourself?

What is it that you are waiting for? Everything that is times a godzillion, will you destroy and uncreate it all? Right and Wrong, Good and Bad, POD and POC, All Nine, Shorts, Boys and Beyonds.

I have known people who were waiting for their retirement, thinking that once they retired, everything would be good. A friend of mine sent me a joke: Someone asks a retired guy, "What do you do now that you're retired?" The retired guy says, "Well, I have a chemical engineering background, and one of the things I enjoy most is converting beer, wine and whiskey into urine. It is rewarding, uplifting and satisfying. I do it every day and really enjoy it!"

Being a Futurist

Salon Participant:

What does it look like to be a futurist?

Gary:

To be a futurist, you have to be willing to see what it is that you are capable of that you have not yet chosen.

What creation of future are you capable of that you have not yet chosen, questioned and created as a possibility? Everything that is times a godzillion, will you destroy and uncreate it all? Right and Wrong, Good and Bad, POD and POC, All Nine, Shorts, Boys and Beyonds.

Salon Participant:

Could you talk about fate, spirit and destiny, please?

Gary:

If you are going to be the future, you have to be willing to recognize where you can be fate, spirit and destiny. It is about being the harbinger of future possibilities.

What stupidity are you using to avoid being the harbinger of future possibilities you could be choosing? Everything that is times a godzillion, will you destroy and uncreate it all? Right and Wrong, Good and Bad, POD and POC, All Nine, Shorts, Boys and Beyonds.

Salon Participant:

What is a harbinger?

Gary:

A harbinger is one who is capable of bringing into actualization what can exist. You are like the forecaster of what will be.

Salon Participant:

The question, "If I choose this, what would my life be like in five years?" has changed my whole focus and the choices I am making. I ask it with everything, and I'm much more aware of what I'd like my life and living to be.

Gary:

Exactly. That's why you need to ask that question. If you don't, you are creating the same thing you did in the past. You are not looking for what your agenda is, you are not looking for what would allow you to create your future. You will not just choose it. So, this is a trick question to get you to do that. I am giving it to you because you will not just choose. I have to trick you into consciousness. Sorry, ladies.

Salon Participant:

I am focusing on the present, not future. I have bought the idea that I have to be present, in the moment. I have to be *now*. So, how does that come in to future?

Gary:

You have to be willing to look at now *and* the future and recognize that the choices you make are creation of the future. You have to be willing to create the future. Focusing exclusively on the now is to avoid creation and generation.

Salon Participant:

So, where have I bought the idea of living in the moment?

Gary:

From some arsehole!

Salon Participant:

It has been a purpose of mine to live in the moment. I love you! This is huge for me. Living in the moment is actually stopping my future.

Gary:

You want to be present and live to create now and the future. If you don't, by the time you get to the future you will have nothing.

If you are living in the moment without creating the future, when you get to the future, you will have to live in the moment in order to not create the future so you can have the now you decided is a good now rather than a bad now, which means you are in judgment. The future you are creating is judgment. How is that working for you?

Salon Participant:

It is not. Thank you.

Gary:

Everything that is times a godzillion, will you destroy and uncreate it all? Right and Wrong, Good and Bad, POD and POC, All Nine, Shorts, Boys and Beyonds.

Salon Participant:

Can you explain what *conquer* is in the context of creation and oneness?

Gary:

If you are functioning from oneness and consciousness, *conquering* means you will conquer your own limitations and not try to conquer others.

In this reality, conquering is always about getting control over others. That's most often done with anger or judgment. So, judgment and anger are two primary sources to create control over others.

How many of you have dedicated your life to judgment and anger as a way of getting control over who and what you cannot dominate? Everything that is times a godzillion, will you destroy and uncreate it all? Right and Wrong, Good and Bad, POD and POC, All Nine, Shorts, Boys and Beyonds.

Choosing a Reality

Salon Participant:

At the moment, everything is opening up for me. I perceive that I am creating all my realities, one that is almost working for me and one that is like my old reality.

Gary:

It is not *almost*. You are having two realities. Now, what if you chose to go beyond that?

Salon Participant:

That feels exciting.

Gary:

I'd like to create a different point of view here. Excitement is the idea that you go out of something to create the *excitement,* the intensity you have defined as excitement. Out of the doldrums into something greater.

Try using *enthusiasm* instead. Ask, "What am I enthusiastic about?" not "What am I excited about?" If you start to function from the enthusiasm of things, you will be continuing, altering and changing possibility. If you function from excitement, then it always has to come to an end. That which is exciting must of necessity come to an end because excitement is only out of something, not into something. Enthusiasm is an into universe.

Salon Participant:

Thank you, I will do that. I feel there is an addictive quality to excitement. Can you clear that, please?

Gary:

It is not an addiction. It is an entrainment. You have learned to be excited. Excitement is something everyone assumes is a betterment of what they have. They think it's getting out of a limitation. That's enough for most people. But excitement is not an infinite possibility.

Everything you have done to create excitement as a betterment of what your limitation is rather than enthusiasm for greater possibilities, will you destroy and uncreate it all? Right and Wrong, Good and Bad, POD and POC, All Nine, Shorts, Boys and Beyonds.

Salon Participant:

Does excitement keep judgment in place, Gary? I see judgment all around me.

Gary:

Excitement maintains judgment as part and parcel of what you keep choosing.

Salon Participant:

So, the old reality is no longer required?

Gary:

Unfortunately, you have to choose, darling. Ask:

• If I choose this reality, what will my life be in five years?

- And if I choose the other reality, what will my life be in five years?

You will get clarity about what your real agenda is and what you would really like to create as your life. There is not one person on this call who was ever encouraged to choose something that would create a future. Has anyone noticed that?

Salon Participant:

Yeah, I am loving it. It's okay to let one reality go completely?

Gary:

Yes, or you can let both realities go completely and maybe find a third one.

Salon Participant:

Cool, so none of it is real.

Gary:

Reality means two or more people align and agree with your point of view.

Salon Participant:

I am not even aligning and agreeing with myself.

Gary:

Exactly! I don't align and agree with my own point of view; therefore, I don't have a point of view; therefore, I always get choice. Every choice creates possibility, every choice creates awareness and every choice creates a different future of possibility. I am interested in what choices I have and what possibilities I can create and generate here.

I look at everything in my life and I ask:

*   Do you still want to be in my life?

*   Is this working?

*   Is this actualizing what you would like to be and do in the world?

Even with my furniture, I look around and do this. Today a lady came to look at my house to see about the possibility of photographing it for a magazine, and she was overwhelmed. She said, "You have too much stuff in your house for us to photograph it."

I realized they would want to make everything as sparse as possible; that's what they would consider great possibility. If you have nothing in your shelf, nothing in your house and nothing going on except one thing, that means you are elegant.

It freaked her out when I said, "I love the antique stuff, as it comes from a time of greater elegance than what we have now. People don't like to live elegantly. People like to live sparsely." She didn't like that.

Before she left, she said, "We will come back to you in the fall, as that's when we use shots of indoor space. We do outdoor space in the summer."

I thought, "Wow, I have outdoor space in summer, spring, winter and fall. Why don't you?" I didn't say it. I was aware of it, though, because for me, it is not about having a point of view about anything, which creates the possibility for everything.

So, everywhere you took points of view to create and eliminate what you could have as a possibility, will you destroy and uncreate it all? Right and Wrong, Good and Bad, POD and POC, All Nine, Shorts, Boys and Beyonds.

She was taking a visually limited reality in order to create what she has decided is acceptable to people who will align and agree with her point of view. The majority of the world functions like that. They are eliminating future as a possibility.

Where have you aligned and agreed with someone else's point of view to eliminate the future possibilities you could be choosing? Everything that is times a godzillion, will you destroy and uncreate it all? Right and Wrong, Good and Bad, POD and POC, All Nine, Shorts, Boys and Beyonds.

Becoming a Source for Greater Possibility

Salon Participant:

Yesterday something in my universe shifted and I became willing to be aware of the future while being present in the now, as we have talked about. I have been asking, "What information is here that can be implemented now that will create that future?" Could you contribute more to that?

Gary:

If you don't have a point of view, you create a possibility. Every choice creates and every creation brings something into actualization. What choices are you making, what actualization are you choosing? What would it be like if you were willing to be the source for greater possibility?

What physical actualization of perceiving, knowing, being and receiving you as the source of greater possibility are you now capable of generating, creating and instituting? Everything that doesn't allow that times a godzillion, will you destroy and uncreate it all? Right and Wrong, Good and Bad, POD and POC, All Nine, Shorts, Boys and Beyonds.

Choice Is the Source of All Creation

Gary:

Possibility creates greater question, choice, possibility and contribution. These things are interrelated. And they are the source for creating a different possibility.

Salon Participant:

You said, "Every choice creates," and you asked, "What actualization are you choosing?"

Gary:

Choice is the source of all creation. That's why I am suggesting you ask: If I choose this what will my life be like in five years? You have been *doing* your life but not *being* what creates your life. If you make a choice based on being the future, you open the door to every possibility that is available to you, every choice you have never seen, every choice nobody has ever asked you to choose.

Your family tries to get you to choose between *this* and *that*. They say, "You can have chocolate ice cream or vanilla."

You say, "But I want strawberry."

They say, "No, you can have chocolate or vanilla."

You say, "No, I want strawberry."

They say, "But your choices are chocolate or vanilla."

You finally say, "Okay, I will have vanilla" or "I will have a little of each." You create "not choice" as the only choice you have in this reality.

Salon Participant:

I have a problem with the word *choice*. I heard you say all that, but it is not registering in my head at all. It's as if you are speaking another language.

Gary:

What is choice for you?

Salon Participant:

To me, choice is a decision. Either this or that. I don't see beyond choice.

Gary:

This means you are not willing to truly choose. You are only willing to see what is possible before you choose. You are stuck in right or wrong choice. What if there were no right or wrong choice, but just choice?

Salon Participant:

How is that choice? I hear you saying it as a singular thing. In my mind choice is a multiple thing.

Gary:

If you have multiple choices, you have to be willing to see which choice creates a future that works for you, which is why I ask: If I choose this, what will my life be like in five years?

Salon Participant:

What if you don't get an answer?

Gary:

It won't be an answer. The purpose of a question is not to get an answer; the purpose of a question is awareness. You may have misidentified and misapplied that choice is about getting an answer.

If we have the point of view that we are supposed to ask a question to get an answer or come to conclusion, decision or judgment, we are trying to create our life as a conclusionary reality. That's not the reality you want to live in.

Salon Participant:

I think that's what it is.

Gary:

Everywhere you have created questions and choice as answer, will you destroy and uncreate it all? Right and Wrong, Good and Bad, POD and POC, All Nine, Shorts, Boys and Beyonds.

Salon Participant:

I just realized that we ask, "What choice can we make?" as though it is about *doing* it; when actually, it's more like *being* the choice.

Gary:

Yeah, that's the reason I said you have to look at this from a different place. You have to ask:

- What kind of thing do I want to create?
- If I choose this, what would my life be like in the next five years?

Five years in the future is too long for you to define it or make it concrete. You can only have the awareness of what it will be like. You cannot have the awareness of the conclusions you can come to, the limitations you can create, and so on. All you can have is the awareness of what is actually possible.

This is the place where you have to be willing to see there is a different possibility.

I am trying to get you to choose different possibilities, because when you start to do this from the point of view of choice, question and possibility, everything is about creating awareness, not about coming to conclusions. Unfortunately, so much of this reality is created around the idea of conclusions.

How many conclusions do you have about what it means to be a woman? Everything that is times a godzillion, will you destroy and uncreate it all? Right and Wrong, Good and Bad, POD and POC, All Nine, Shorts, Boys and Beyonds.

How many conclusions do you have about what choices you have, what the purpose of choice is, what the value of choice is and what you are supposed to do with choice? Everything that is times a godzillion, will you destroy and uncreate it all? Right and Wrong, Good and Bad, POD and POC, All Nine, Shorts, Boys and Beyonds.

Seeing What Is Wrong vs. Seeing What Is Possible

Salon Participant:

I have become more aware of how manipulative, cruel, lying, violent and controlling my mother chooses to be, all behind the veil of niceness, fakeness and prettiness. From the time I was young, she has told me how lovely and beautiful I am and she has accused me of being mean, vicious, cruel and addicted. I used to believe those things about me and now I know that she is just accusing me of what she is doing.

Gary:

Yes, people only accuse you of what they themselves are doing.

Salon Participant:

I find her difficult to deal with. She wants someone to care about her and parent her, and I have tried to do that. I have also tried to help her to fix it.

Gary:

Stop being a man. Only men try to fix things.

Everywhere you have tried to be a man to fix the parents that don't work for you, all of you, will you destroy and uncreate it all? Right and Wrong, Good and Bad, POD and POC, All Nine, Shorts, Boys and Beyonds.

Salon Participant:

Gary, can you throw that into any relationship? To try not to fix anything in any relationship across the board, including marriage?

Gary:

Yeah, if you are trying to be the man, you are always trying to fix what is wrong, which means you have to focus on what? What is possible? Or what is wrong?

Salon Participant:

What is wrong.

Gary:

Yes, and whenever you focus on what is wrong, what do you see? More wrong. You don't get to see what is possible. The thing about being in the future is you are always capable of seeing, perceiving, knowing, being and receiving what is possible.

When you focus on what is wrong, how much of your energy are you using to destroy your capacity to perceive, know, be and receive what is actually possible?

Everything that is times a godzillion, will you destroy and uncreate it all? Right and Wrong, Good and Bad, POD and POC, All Nine, Shorts, Boys and Beyonds.

Salon Participant:

I'd like to clear and change that stuff with my mother.

Gary:

Ask: What stupidity am I using to create the mom I am choosing? Stop trying to support this stupid woman.

You Can Hate Your Mom or You Can Have Total Freedom

Salon Participant:

I hate her. I just frigging hate her.

Gary:

Do you hate her so much that you would create that much energy to hate her? That gives you total freedom, right?

Salon Participant:

I have obviously created somewhere I am buying into this, but I can't be anything else.

Gary:

You have two choices here. You can hate your mom or you can have total freedom. Which one would you choose?

Salon Participant:

Total freedom.

Gary:

Are you sure it's total freedom? It is so much more familiar to hate her, isn't it?

Salon Participant:

Yeah, I have done it for a long time.

Gary:

You have hated her. Has that created freedom for you?

Salon Participant:

I have hated her as a way of barricading myself against her.

Gary:

Are you barricading yourself in order to not have you, not be you and not choose you? Or is it to assume she is the reason you can't be everything you want to be?

Salon Participant:

That one.

Gary:

Everything that is times a godzillion, will you destroy and uncreate it all? Right and Wrong, Good and Bad, POD and POC, All Nine, Shorts, Boys and Beyonds.

Truth, were you her competition?

Salon Participant:

Yes.

Gary:

Did she like having competition?

Salon Participant:

She loves it. She likes fighting everyone.

Gary:

Which includes fighting herself as well?

Salon Participant:

Yes.

Gary:

Everywhere you tried to duplicate her so you wouldn't be like her, which makes you like her, which means you fight you all the time, will you destroy and uncreate it all? Right and Wrong, Good and Bad, POD and POC, All Nine, Shorts, Boys and Beyonds.

You got mad at K when she was laughing at something you said about your mom. Do you realize at that moment you were defending your mom against K's laughter.

Salon Participant:

Defending my mom against K's laughter? Yeah, that's what it was.

Gary:

Yeah, you buy your mom's point of view. Why? That is the entrainment to being a woman.

Everything you have done to entrain you to being a woman, to make you like your mom, who you hate, which means you have to like you or hate you? Or see you as good, bad or wrong? Isn't that cool? You hate your mom, so you duplicate her and become like her to make sure you won't be her, but that makes you her. Everything that is times a godzillion, will you destroy and uncreate it all? Right and Wrong, Good and Bad, POD and POC, All Nine, Shorts, Boys and Beyonds.

Salon Participant:

I have an intensity on my left side. It is in my chest and goes up my neck.

Gary:

Based on what? How much of you have you made wrong?

Everything you have done to make you wrong, and everything you have locked up into the left side of your body and all the demons you used to lock in the wrongness of you, will you destroy and uncreate it all? And demand that they go back to from whence they came never to return to this reality again? Right and Wrong, Good and Bad, POD and POC, All Nine, Shorts, Boys and Beyonds.

Feeling better?

Salon Participant:

Yeah.

Gary:

Every time you have something on the left side of your body, I want you to ask: Is this me or my mom?

Salon Participant:

And if I get it's my mom?

Gary:

Say: Everything I did to duplicate that, POC and POD it.

Most of us, when we have a parent who doesn't love us, try to duplicate who they are to get them to love us. Does it work?

Salon Participant:

No. Do they encourage us to be like them so they have something to judge ?

Gary:

No. You have already judged them. Your judgment of them might not actually be your judgment of them but rather your awareness of their judgment of themselves. And you think you have no awareness!

Salon Participant:

Thanks, Gary.

Gary:

Everything you have done to buy their judgments of them as your judgments of them so you can have the judgments of them so you are as judgmental of them as they are judgmental of themselves and they can be certain that they are right that they are wrong, and having to duplicate them in order to do that, you are right that you are wrong and that makes everything work right? Not really. Everything that is times a godzillion, will you destroy and uncreate it all? Right and Wrong, Good and Bad, POD and POC, All Nine, Shorts, Boys and Beyonds.

The Greatest Revenge

Be careful, T, things are starting to blow off. If you are not careful, you will be happy again. Can I tell you this? The greatest revenge on your parents is to be happy.

Salon Participant:

I'll have it.

Gary:

What physical actualization of the capacity to be, do, have, create and generate happy are you now capable of creating, generating and instituting? Everything that doesn't allow that times a godzillion, will you destroy and uncreate it all? Right and Wrong, Good and Bad, POD and POC, All Nine, Shorts, Boys and Beyonds.

All of you need to get that whenever somebody laughs about something you have made serious, it is because they see the humor in it. If you are angry about it, you are trying to defend the person you are angry at. You will have such freedom when you realize this. It is part of the comedy of this reality that our hate can only be judged or created based on our judgments of ourselves that we have consented to. If you are trying to be upset about it, you are defending the person you are upset with. That shows you care for them, but you don't want to know that you care for them.

Salon Participant:

If somebody hates you, how do you handle that?

Gary:

If someone hates you, intimidate them with the awareness of what they can be that they don't want to be.

Salon Participant:

How much fun can we have with that?

Gary:

No, you are not allowed to have fun! You have to be miserable.

Okay, ladies, I hope this has been fun for you. It has been really interesting to me. You always take me to places I was not planning on going to, whether I like to or not! Thank you.

12

Becoming a Free Radical of Consciousness

Consciousness is a liquid reality.
It is never solidified by limitation.

Gary:

Hello, ladies. Does anyone have a question?

The Easy Space of Possibility

Salon Participant:

I am trying to deal with something, and I am making myself smaller than the task. Please can you suggest a clearing that will help me to stay in the expansive, exuberant, easy space of possibility?

Gary:

What stupidity am I using to create avoiding the easy space of possibility I could be choosing? Everything that is times a godzillion, are you willing to destroy and uncreate it all? Right and Wrong, Good and Bad, POD and POC, All Nine, Shorts, Boys and Beyonds.

Apparently this will work on some other people as well!

What stupidity am I using to create avoiding the easy space of possibility I could be choosing? Everything that is times a godzillion, are you willing to destroy and uncreate it all? Right and Wrong, Good and Bad, POD and POC, All Nine, Shorts, Boys and Beyonds.

Salon Participant:

I am creating a business beyond this reality and I need some assistance. I need to be able to do ten hours of work each day and attract people with phenomenal capacities to help me, and I am choosing this. What clearing can I do?

Gary:

What stupidity am I using to avoid the ease of creation and generation I could be choosing? Everything that is times a godzillion, are you willing to destroy and uncreate it all? Right and Wrong, Good and Bad, POD and POC, All Nine, Shorts, Boys and Beyonds.

What stupidity are you using to create the invention, the artificial intensity and the demons of mathematical computation of the median ground for the institution of mediocrity as the formula for the creation of maximization of human reality with regard to sex, copulation, money and the other sex are you choosing in relationships? Everything that is times a godzillion, will you destroy and uncreate it all? Right and Wrong, Good and Bad, POD and POC, All Nine, Shorts, Boys and Beyonds.

Going Beyond the Standard Deviations of Human Reality

Salon Participant:

Can you explain what the maximization of human reality is, please?

Gary:

Maximization of human reality is when you allow yourself to have only certain amounts of what doesn't fit with human reality. You have moments where you shoot out and create wonderful things and then you go back to where we were before so you're "normal" and within the acceptable norm of human reality. You make a certain amount of money, but it is within the standard deviation from the norm, which is about never getting too big. You cap out on the amount of money you can make because of it. You're maximizing human reality.

You ask, "How can I maximize myself into something greater than this?" Maximization at this point is no more than two standard deviations from the norm. So you make yourself wrong, or you destroy what you have, or you get tired at the wrong time, or you don't like yourself creating more than that, or you go hang out with people who are slackers and lackers, and then you say, "I can't do it anyway." It's the way you make yourself satisfied with less than instead of more than. It's a total deviant point of view.

We refuse to go beyond the standard deviations of human reality.

How much of sex, copulation, relationship and money are you choosing based on never deviating more than two standard degrees of deviation from the norm? Everything that is times a godzillion, will you destroy and uncreate it all? Right and Wrong, Good and Bad, POD and POC, All Nine, Shorts, Boys and Beyonds.

What stupidity are you using to create the invention, the artificial intensity and the demons of mathematical computation of the median ground for the institution of mediocrity as the formula for the creation of maximization of human reality with regard to sex, copulation, money and the other sex are you choosing in relationships? Everything that is times a godzillion, will you destroy and uncreate it all? Right and Wrong, Good and Bad, POD and POC, All Nine, Shorts, Boys and Beyonds.

Consciousness is a liquid reality. It is never solidified by limitation, yet we are stuck with the computation for handling the median ground for human reality.

Salon Participant:

In this reality, we talk about maximizing our advantage. So, when you do that, you are only maximizing what you already know.

Gary:

Yeah, that's all you can do. You can never go beyond two standard deviations from the median ground. That's the only way you can fit in this reality.

What stupidity are you using to create the invention, the artificial intensity and the demons of mathematical computation of the median ground for the institution of mediocrity as the formula for the creation of maximization of human reality with regard to sex, copulation, money and the other sex are you choosing? Everything that is times a godzillion, will you destroy and uncreate it all? Right and Wrong, Good and Bad, POD and POC, All Nine, Shorts, Boys and Beyonds.

Human Reality Is Dedicated to Mediocrity

You are dedicated to mediocrity. Everything has to remain the same. That is pretty much human reality in a nutshell. Don't deviate too much on one side or the other. There are some people who deviate to a degree in that they have a whole bunch of money.

There are also people like S who are seriously deviant in relationships because they are willing to have more than what most people are willing to have. You have gone beyond the standard deviation, but you keep trying to see how you are wrong or how everybody else should choose what you choose, which is true, but they can't as long as they are stuck with this median ground.

What stupidity are you using to create the invention, the artificial intensity and the demons of mathematical computation of the median ground for the institution of mediocrity as the formula for the creation of maximization of human reality with regard to sex, relationships, copulation, money and body are you choosing? Everything that is times a godzillion, will you destroy and uncreate it all?

The median ground is the place where everything is balanced. You never catapult anybody, including you, into something different you don't know about. That's why you won't allow yourself to have a great relationship. You have that median ground you look for in each man. You don't allow yourself to have a man who will come into your life and catapult you off this reality into something greater.

Everything that is times a godzillion, will you destroy and uncreate it all? Right and Wrong, Good and Bad, POD and POC, All Nine, Shorts, Boys and Beyonds.

Salon Participant:

Where is awareness in this?

Gary:

There is no awareness in the median ground. That's the purpose of it—to keep you out of awareness.

Salon Participant:

When you say, "beyond the median ground" and "the other sex," what does it look like?

Gary:

I know women who have identified themselves as being masculine. They try to create themselves on a masculine edge, which causes them to create their body as not totally feminine. That's why we use the words *body* and *other sex* rather than *opposite sex*.

If you are willing to function out of the ordinary, you can have everything available to you instead of part of it. You can have all the masculine traits and be the most feminine looking woman in the entire world.

One of the biggest mistakes women make is they take over, they put themselves in charge, and then they hate the man. There is no space for the man to be anything except a slave, a whipping boy. As soon as he becomes a whipping boy, the women don't like him any-more. They go out and find another person they can whip into shape. Unfortunately, a lot of women have the point of view, "I can whip him into shape in a heartbeat." Why would you want to do that? Why wouldn't you want to expand his reality and yours?

Everywhere you decided you will whip some guy into shape, will you destroy and uncreate it all? Right and Wrong, Good and Bad, POD and POC, All Nine, Shorts, Boys and Beyonds.

What stupidity are you using to create the invention, the artificial intensity and the demons of mathematical computation of the median ground for the institution of mediocrity as the formula for the creation of maximization of human reality with regard to sex, relationships, copulation, money, body and the other sex are you choosing? Everything that is times a godzillion, will you destroy and uncreate it all? Right and Wrong, Good and Bad, POD and POC, All Nine, Shorts, Boys and Beyonds.

Salon Participant:

My parents taught me to receive from a man so that I can grow up to be a good wife and mother. I see how this stops the energy that I could generate. It keeps me from co-creating anything like relationships or co-facilitating classes. I pull back. Is that what this is?

Gary:

That's the mediocrity. It's the maximization of human reality. In human reality, what are you supposed to do?

Salon Participant:

Be a good wife and mother and have a small career.

Gary:

You did that?

Salon Participant:

No. I was not good at that. I feel like I have resisted and reacted to it my whole life. What am I missing here and not clearing?

Gary:

You have to get that you have been a great mother and also a great father. You have learned how to use men but you haven't learned how to enjoy them. If you like men, you use them as a stepping stone to expand their life as well as yours.

The reason many of you have chosen to stay single is that you don't need to have a man, but in this reality, that is what the maximization of human reality is. Do you want to live that life?

Salon Participant:

No, I want to generate and create the expansion of the planet with humanoid men.

Becoming as Deviant as You Would Like to Be

Gary:

I am hoping to get a process that will assist all of you to become as deviant as you would truly like to be. Being a deviant means you don't do things by the standards of this reality.

You don't look for the median ground. You aren't perfectly balanced on the teeter-totter of this reality.

When you come off the teeter-totter, you catapult you out of no choice and into possibility. You don't have to return to the state you were in before. In Access Consciousness, we have been choosing to get you off the teeter-totter so you can create and generate whatever you want. But as long as you try to go back to the median ground, you are trying to entrain to others. I want to get you un-entrained. I want to get you off the training wheels of your own reality so you can whip through life on a motor bike ride.

What stupidity are you using to create the invention, the artificial intensity and the demons of mathematical computation of the median ground for the institution of mediocrity as the formula for the creation of maximization of human reality with regard to sex, relationships, copulation, money, body and the other sex are you choosing? Everything that is times a godzillion, will you destroy and uncreate it all? Right and Wrong, Good and Bad, POD and POC, All Nine, Shorts, Boys and Beyonds.

Other Things Are Possible, but You Have to Ask a Question

Salon Participant:

I got divorced ten years ago, and I haven't been in a relationship since then. I see that I have not been willing to do something mediocre. So, what else is possible?

Gary:

That's the thing I'd like you all to get. Other things are possible—but you have to ask a question. If you find that you have a relationship that is mediocre and you go to, "I never want to do that again," you have to judge rather than being in the question, "What is possible to generate and create with this person?"

If you decide that you won't have anything mediocre, how many people can you let in your life? Only the mediocre ones. We continuously institute every limited point of view we have in our life. We make it the thing we always have to do.

When you say, "I'm not going to have something mediocre," you always have to look from the judgment, "Is this person mediocre?" rather than "What can I create with this person?" If you start to look from there, you can open doors to new possibilities that have never existed. This requires you to become a total freaking deviant.

What stupidity are you using to create the invention, the artificial intensity and the demons of mathematical computation of the median ground for the institution of mediocrity as the formula for the creation of maximization of human reality with regard to sex, relationships, copulation, money, body and the other sex are you choosing? Everything that is times a godzillion, will you destroy and uncreate it all? Right and Wrong, Good and Bad, POD and POC, All Nine, Shorts, Boys and Beyonds.

Recently a lady wrote to ask me about taking a detox supplement for the body. Did she ask her body about this? No, she determined that she needed to detox. She went into conclusion. That does not create a possibility.

This applies to everything in your life. If you are looking to create abundance and you are around other people who have a lot of lack, you have to ask: If I choose to be with these people, what will my life be like in five years? You could drop those friends because they aren't going where you are going. Trying to get them to go where you are going is like putting an anchor in the ocean. You keep trying to go forward, but you can't move from that place.

Salon Participant:

When you see what someone is doing and it looks like something you'd like, and you say, "I'll have some of that" or "I'll have the energy of that," is that still mediocrity?

Gary:

You're making it about what they can do. But the thing is: Are you looking to create a mediocre life?

Salon Participant:

No.

Gary:

Then start looking from:

•   How can I use this?

- What advantage can I get from this?

- What is it that I really want to create?

For the most part, when a mathematical computation is in place, you cannot create beyond two standard deviations from what everybody else has decided is the appropriate norm.

Salon Participant:

Is it what we have decided is the appropriate norm?

Gary:

No, it is what you have bought as the appropriate norm. It's what you have been taught from day one. For example, G said she was supposed to learn how to be a good wife and take care of a man. I would look at G and say, "No way that is going to work!"

Be Willing to See What Someone Is Going to Do

I have two daughters. One would be okay with being a mom as long as the guy is rich enough. The other one would be happy to stay at home and have children. That's her basic nature. You have to be willing to see what someone is going to do. Some couples have kids, but one of the parents is not into raising them. That just shows that the other parent didn't choose the best person in the world to have the baby with. That's the thing about going into a standard deviation.

A guy might be willing to be deviant enough to have a relationship and a baby, but he's not willing to be deviant enough to create what he really wants and to keep what he wants. He goes back to the standard point of view, thinking that someday he will find somebody that he could fit with. As soon as he realizes the woman he fits with isn't the one he really wants, he looks for a new one and it never works. Why? Because he is doing standard deviation.

Salon Participant:

Is it about the awareness that as soon as you buy something as true and real, you are stepping into somebody else's reality?

Gary:

Most people don't get that they are stepping into somebody else's reality, and they don't question:

- Am I stepping into somebody else's reality?
- Is this my point of view or is it something I am not willing to know, be or receive?

You have to look at that and ask: How will this work for me?

Salon Participant:

Rather than, "How can I make me work for it?"

As a Humanoid, You Are a Deviant

Gary:

Yeah. You have to ask: How do I get myself beyond the limitations of this reality?

What stupidity are you using to create the invention, the artificial intensity and the demons of mathematical computation of the median ground for the institution of mediocrity as the formula for the creation of maximization of human reality with regard to sex, relationships, copulation, money, body and the other sex are you choosing? Everything that is times a godzillion, will you destroy and uncreate it all? Right and Wrong, Good and Bad, POD and POC, All Nine, Shorts, Boys and Beyonds.

Are any of you looking at the fact that you actually have been pretty much a deviant most of your life?

Salon Participant:

Exactly! That's what I have been thinking. I remember in boarding school, the headmistress stood me up in front of everyone one night and said I was the black seed in the tomato that ruined the salad. She said I was a deviant, and they put me in solitary confinement for the rest of the semester. I actually enjoyed it. I could have my own room. Yeah totally, haven't we always been deviant?

Gary:

Yes. As a humanoid, you are a deviant. You try to make yourself like other people, like limited people and it doesn't work for you, which is why you came into Access Consciousness in the first place.

What stupidity are you using to create the invention, the artificial intensity and the demons of mathematical computation of the median ground for the institution of mediocrity as the formula for the creation of maximization of human reality with regard to sex, relationships, copulation, money, body and the other sex are you choosing? Everything that is times a godzillion, will you destroy and uncreate it all? Right and Wrong, Good and Bad, POD and POC, All Nine, Shorts, Boys and Beyonds.

Total Ease and Too Much Money

Salon Participant:

I had an awareness of the deviant with sex, body and copulation. I had the awareness of what that could be for me.

Gary:

I can tell you what it could be for you: Total ease and too much money. If you don't let yourself have total ease and too much money, you can go back to not being in a deviant category.

The thing I have noticed about you already is that you get involved with a man and you are cool and happy with it, then all of a sudden, you try to put it into a form where it's not about what you can create with him but rather, "How can I use this guy to my advantage?" and "What can I do to get everything I want?" You give up what you truly want in favor of becoming part of the standard reality here.

Salon Participant:

Yeah. You have told me that I would function better if I had a different man for everything I'd like to do.

Gary:

Yeah, you need a man who will buy you nice jewelry, find things for you and take you out for dinner.

Salon Participant:

How do I create more of that?

Gary:

Instead of saying, "Cool, I am going to create that as my reality," you went to, "How do I do that?" as though there is no place to go except the maximization of human reality, which is that you have to become a mistress.

What if you could create how you were in the world just by how you were in the world?

For years, people told me, "You are so weird, Douglas," then they'd ask, "Why don't you do this?"

I'd say, "Because I don't want to."

They'd say, "Yeah, but this is the way everybody else does it."

I'd say, "Yeah, but I don't want to live my life that way."

They'd say, "That's so frigging strange."

I'd say, "Yeah, I know that I am going to have a life I want."

A lot of that had to do with the fact my dad died when I was seventeen. The last few years of his life, he was doing things for himself for the first time. I realized he worked himself to death to create greater ease for his family. It was all about his family. He would work five days a week as well as the weekends to make money so his family could have a better life. Did we get a better life by having him die? No.

If he had followed his own knowing, he could have had so many possibilities. There were two times when he had an opportunity to turn himself into a multi-millionaire and my mother stopped him. She wanted a median ground, the institution of marriage and the institution of correct copulation. These are the things we institute. You keep looking at how you must be more realistic. No. You have to ask:

- How does this create my life?

- Is this really where I want to create from?

Yesterday a group of us went to a restaurant. We were the only people there. Just us and our waiter, who was a sweet man. Simone asked him a bunch of questions. He told us he was raised by his grandfather and hadn't seen his mother in ten to fifteen years. She was coming to visit. I said, "Here is $200 for you to give your mother a good time." He lost it. I did that for no other reason other than it worked for me.

What stupidity are you using to create the invention, the artificial intensity and the demons of mathematical computation of the median ground for the institution of mediocrity as the formula for the creation of maximization of human reality with regard to sex, relationships, copulation, money, body and the other sex are you choosing? Everything that is times a godzillion, will you destroy and uncreate it all? Right and Wrong, Good and Bad, POD and POC, All Nine, Shorts, Boys and Beyonds.

Salon Participant:

I am looking around to see what the standard deviation is rather than seeing what we require as a standard deviation.

Gary:

First of all, you don't need a standard deviation, you need to be a freaking deviant. You have to deviate from the middle ground. The middle ground is not a place to institute from.

Salon Participant:

I had in my head the image of a bell curve and the edge bits of the bell curve. That's where humanoids are.

Gary:

What if you were your own personal bell curve? Where would you land on the curve at any moment?

Salon Participant:

Wherever I chose, I guess.

Gary:

Exactly. You could go right, left, top or bottom. You would have the choice of anywhere on the curve of possibility. The standard deviation is finding the median line where the top of the bell curve exists, as though that's what is necessary.

What stupidity are you using to create the invention, the artificial intensity and the demons of mathematical computation of the median ground for the institution of mediocrity as the formula for the creation of maximization of human reality with regard to sex, relationships, copulation, money, body and the other sex are you choosing? Everything that is times a godzillion, will you destroy and uncreate it all? Right and Wrong, Good and Bad, POD and POC, All Nine, Shorts, Boys and Beyonds.

How you all doing? Anybody still alive out there?

Salon Participant:

There is such a joyfulness to all this. Thank you so much.

Gary:

What physical actualization of being the free radical of consciousness, kindness, generosity and possibility in sex, relationships, copulation, money, body and the other sex are you now capable of generating creating and instituting? Everything that doesn't allow that to show up times a godzillion, will you destroy and uncreate it all? Right and Wrong, Good and Bad, POD and POC, All Nine, Shorts, Boys and Beyonds.

Free Radicals

Salon Participant:

Can you explain about free radicals?

Gary:

In quantum physics, free radicals are the loose particles that do anything they want to do. They go places, they interact with other particles and they change what the result of something is going to be. Free radicals are always changing reality and what is possible.

When you become a free radical of consciousness, kindness, generosity and possibilities with money, sex and copulation, bodies, relationships and the other sex, you are not fixated on trying to figure out how to make something work. You ask:

• Okay, what else is possible?

• What can we create and generate?

• What would be fun here?

What stupidity are you using to create the avoidance of being as radically different as you could be are you choosing? Everything that is times a godzillion, will you destroy and uncreate it all? Right and Wrong, Good and Bad, POD and POC, All Nine, Shorts, Boys and Beyonds.

The purpose of maximizing human reality is so that people can be controlled. None of you have been good at being controlled. And you refuse to be controlling of others. A radically deviant point of view would be to recognize how and when to control and what you need to do.

We go into the judgment of, "Okay, I am going to control this guy and make him do this, this and this." That's a conclusion, not a question. And it's not creating and generating from possibilities. It's generating and instituting from conclusion. Most everything we institute in our life is based on conclusion—not on choice, question, possibility and contribution.

Everything that is times a godzillion, will you destroy and uncreate it all? Right and Wrong, Good and Bad, POD and POC, All Nine, Shorts, Boys and Beyonds.

Exit Stage Left

Salon Participant:

At the moment, my dad is dying. He has cancer that has spread everywhere. I have been asking: What else is possible here? I realize I have come to a lot of energetic conclusion around all of this. What are some of the questions I have not even considered?

Gary:

What stupidity am I using to create holding my dad in his body am I choosing? Everything that is times a godzillion, will you destroy and uncreate it all? Right and Wrong, Good and Bad, POD and POC, All Nine, Shorts, Boys and Beyonds.

Gary:

Have you done Exit Stage Left? Ask him (in your head): "Dad, what is it that you haven't completed that if you knew you had completed it, would allow you to leave with ease?"

I asked that of my mother, and the answer I got was, "I haven't taken life throughout the galaxy."

I said, "Well, Mom, at this point in time you can't do that from this planet because they don't have the technology or any other way of doing it, but if you work without a body, you might be able to." She died the next day. She knew she wouldn't succeed with the body she had.

We tend to maximize human reality. In human reality, you are not supposed to want anybody to die. In human reality, birth is great and death is horrible. Is it that way in nature?

Salon Participant:

No.

Gary:

Death is part of what is. In human reality, we say, "Oh, I love him so much. My life will be over when he dies." No, it won't! I know a family that lost a child, and the mother grieved forever, even after they had five other kids. I don't know how you grieve when you have five kids to take care of. I personally would be too busy.

Why don't you ask: What energy, space and consciousness can I be that would allow all of this to come to fruition with ease?

Salon Participant:

Thank you. That's nice and easy and simple.

Gary:

Yeah, I know you hate simple stuff. You want it to be complicated so you can stay in the maximization of human reality. If you make it complicated, then it must be right.

Everything that is times a godzillion, will you destroy and uncreate it all? Right and Wrong, Good and Bad, POD and POC, All Nine, Shorts, Boys and Beyonds.

The Ultimate Deviation

Salon Participant:

In the last week or so, what's coming up for me is separation or barriers, and today as you are talking, I am getting that I am not being a total deviant because that would mean separation.

Gary:

What's wrong with separating?

Salon Participant:

I have the idea that I don't want to be separate from anything.

Gary:

Except you are creating a separation by not being a total deviant. Ultimate deviation from maximization of human reality is oneness.

Salon Participant:

Yes, I am using separation as a reason to not be a deviant.

Gary:

That's the way you were entrained. You were entrained to believe that deviating from the norm is the worst thing you can do. Everything is about fitting in, being a part of, having your community, having your insane friends, having other people like you, having your peeps. What if you had no peeps? Life would not be nearly as sweet without your peeps.

What stupidity are you using to create the total avoidance of deviating from the maximization of human reality are you choosing? Everything that is times a godzillion, will you destroy and uncreate it all? Right and Wrong, Good and Bad, POD and POC, All Nine, Shorts, Boys and Beyonds.

Salon Participant:

Again, what came up for me was it would mean I have to separate.

Gary:

What would you have to separate from?

Salon Participant:

Them?

Gary:

Who are "them"?

Salon Participant:

I am getting an *it, them, reality* and so on.

Gary:

You have to separate from the limited reality—but the good news is you won't choose it, so you don't have to worry.

Salon Participant:

Ha! Liar, liar, pants on fire!

Gary:

Everything that is times a godzillion, will you destroy and uncreate it all? Right and Wrong, Good and Bad, POD and POC, All Nine, Shorts, Boys and Beyonds.

Salon Participant:

It feels like I have been asking to not separate myself from anything or anyone, and I am fighting as the deviant I am, all at the same time.

Gary:

That is called going back to the median. You have to fight against the options and possibilities that exist in life. You have to fight against choice, questions and what contributes to you.

Salon Participant:

Yes, to keep me busy so I don't actually create the possibilities that I know are possible.

Gary:

No, that's how you maintain and institute a constant state of action with only reaction.

What stupidity are you using to create the absolute and total aversion, rejection and repulsion of being total deviation to maximizing human reality are you choosing? Everything that is times a godzillion, will you destroy and uncreate it all? Right and Wrong, Good and Bad, POD and POC, All Nine, Shorts, Boys and Beyonds.

Salon Participant:

When K was talking about separating, I got that we are separating from the future.

Gary:

Yeah. Right now you are going through a divorce, and both of you are going to the norm to determine how to split your life. You are going to have a deviant relationship in which you and your husband have different houses to live in and you still have the kids. You have to create the relationship you want and not buy everybody else's point of view.

Salon Participant:

I am so enthused regarding being a future. Most of my life I have been told I am ahead of my time. Is this where I have been a harbinger of future possibilities?

Gary:

No, this is where you were being a foreseer of future possibilities.

Salon Participant:

Is this where I bought into that as a wrongness? Should I stop creating myself into the norm?

Gary:

Who doesn't make you wrong for being aware? That's why I did the norm process.

What physical actualization of being the total future I truly be am I now capable of generating, creating and instituting? Everything that doesn't allow that to show up times a godzillion, will you destroy and uncreate it all? Right and Wrong, Good and Bad, POD and POC, All Nine, Shorts, Boys and Beyonds.

Awareness has a lightness to it and judgment always feels like crap.

Okay, ladies, thanks for being on the call. Talk to you next time!

13

Recognizing the Gift You Are to the World

Everybody wants to assume that if you are conscious,
you get whatever you want.
No, being conscious means you have more possibilities than other people;
it doesn't mean you get what you want.

Gary:

Hello, ladies. Who has a question?

Being the Hedonist, Seductress and Voluptuary You Truly Be

Salon Participant:

I have a silly question about relationships. Sometimes I feel small, inadequate and judgmental of myself when I am with people who have been successful. I feel inferior. Please, could you give me a clearing so that I am free to be me?

Gary:

There is never a silly question about relationships. I had a similar question from another person on these calls. She said, "I see where I am a warrior and creator of future and then this thing creeps in with regards to relationships with men."

First of all, you have to stop considering that men are separate from you. Secondly, you have to see the gift you are. How often, when you feel inadequate, is it yours? And how often is it the man's? Men have the point of view about being inadequate too, ladies. It's not just women who have this issue.

Salon Participant:

I get lost in the sex phase of the relationship. I try to keep the guy or become someone I think he wants. The moment I do that, I can't see where I am a potent, amazing being. How do we do sex or relationship without getting lost in it?

Gary:

Here is a process that should assist all of you. Put this on a loop and listen to it non-stop:

What stupidity are you using to create the invention, artificial intensity and the demons of never being the hedonist, seductress and voluptuary you truly be are you choosing? Everything that is times a godzillion, are you willing to destroy and uncreate it all? Right and Wrong, Good and Bad, POD and POC, All Nine, Shorts, Boys and Beyonds.

Considering the amount of intensity on this process, I can say you ladies have been turning yourselves off pretty significantly. How's that going to create what you really want?

Salon Participant:

What do you mean by turning off?

Gary:

Not realizing you are a vixen.

Salon Participant:

What's a vixen?

Gary:

A *vixen* is a woman who is coquettish at the right moment, seductive at the right moment and disdainful at the right moment. She never functions from a point of view of what is supposed to be; she is always willing to see what else is possible.

A *voluptuary* is someone who enjoys the best of life. A *hedonist* likes the pleasure of life. How many of you have had pleasurable sex? You have a lot of sex but very little of it is based on the pleasure of it; it's based on the necessity of proving something. That comes from the male side as well.

A *seductress* is one who brings the man in and gets him interested. She doesn't have to do anything with that, but she can if she chooses. That's a whole different reality.

What stupidity are you using to create the invention, artificial intensity and the demons of never being the hedonist, seductress, voluptuary and the vixen you truly be are you choosing? Everything that is times a godzillion, are you willing to destroy and uncreate it all? Right and Wrong, Good and Bad, POD and POC, All Nine, Shorts, Boys and Beyonds.

Part of the problem of having been given the title of warrior, is that some women think it makes them better than men. You're not better than men—you're *greater*. *Greater* means you can go further and do more; *better* means that you are always in comparison and judgment of you and them. That doesn't sound like a good idea to me—but that's just my point of view.

What stupidity are you using to create the invention, artificial intensity and the demons of never being the hedonist, seductress, voluptuary and the vixen you truly be are you choosing? Everything that is times a godzillion, are you willing to destroy and uncreate it all? Right and Wrong, Good and Bad, POD and POC, All Nine, Shorts, Boys and Beyonds.

These are things that have been vilified about women throughout history. Women were not supposed to seek pleasure; they were supposed to seek pain to stop their basic nature of being someone who is a voluptuary and seductress. In order to stop that, you do things like vilify yourself, make yourself small and try to see how you are never supposed to be everything you can be. Throughout history, this has been the problem with women.

What stupidity are you using to create the invention, artificial intensity and the demons of never being the hedonistic, seductress, voluptuary and the vixen you truly be are you choosing? Everything that is times a godzillion, are you willing to destroy and uncreate it all? Right and Wrong, Good and Bad, POD and POC, All Nine, Shorts, Boys and Beyonds.

Salon Participant:

Do we cut off our receiving when we cut off being the vixen, the hedonist, the voluptuary and the seductress?

Gary:

Yes, wherever you cut off being these things, you cut off half of your receiving. Look at it from this point of view: Let's say you are selling something. If you are not the vixen, the hedonist, the voluptuary and the seductress, you are not going to induce anybody, male or female, into buying your product. Do women judge other women kindly or harshly?

Salon Participant:

Harshly!

Gary:

Yeah, women are incredibly harsh in their judgment of other women if those women don't fit what they have decided are the things a woman is or supposed to be and do. They determine what doesn't fit their reality—and that is what all women should not be doing or being.

Salon Participant:

I remember as a child, running around naked in the house. I loved it. But as soon as I began to develop, my parents told me I had to put my clothes on. They made being naked wrong.

Gary:

That's pretty much how it is done in this reality. It is wrong to be a seductress, a vixen, a hedonist or a voluptuary. You are supposed to be an ordinary sweet kind of girl who would stay home and mind the cats, which most of you couldn't do if your life depended on it. You could *have* a cat but not *mind* a cat—because a cat gives way too many orders.

What stupidity are you using to create the invention, artificial intensity and the demons of never being the hedonist, seductress, voluptuary and the vixen you truly be, are you choosing? Everything that is times a godzillion, are you willing to destroy and uncreate it all? Right and Wrong, Good and Bad, POD and POC, All Nine, Shorts, Boys and Beyonds.

The Turn-on You Could Be Choosing

You guys must be giving up a whole lot of yourself. One of the things I ran on the Gentlemen's Club call the other day was: What invention are you using to avoid the hard-on you could be choosing? Women won't do hard-on. What do they do? Turn-on.

What invention are you using to avoid the turn-on you could be choosing? Everything that is times a godzillion, are you willing to destroy and uncreate it all? Right and Wrong, Good and Bad, POD and POC, All Nine, Shorts, Boys and Beyonds.

So, if a guy turns you on, you immediately become a pile of debris. Have you noticed?

Salon Participant:

What does that mean?

Gary:

What if you were turned on by life and living? What if everything you wanted was the ability to be turned on to that degree? If you turn everybody else on, would more people be willing to receive you? Would more people be willing to gift to you? Would more people vilify you?

Salon Participant:

Probably all of those.

Gary:

Nope. Everybody would be inspired by your presence.

What invention are you using to avoid the turn-on you could be choosing? Everything that is times a godzillion, are you willing to destroy and uncreate it all? Right and Wrong, Good and Bad, POD and POC, All Nine, Shorts, Boys and Beyonds.

Salon Participant:

What came up for me was the judgment or the vilification of being turned on. Is that the lie I am using to stop myself?

Gary:

It's the lie that you are using to stop you. Rather than realizing, "I want something different," you go to "I need to be accepted by women." Very seldom are you accepted by women. Why would a woman not accept a woman? Because in this reality, competition is about making sure that you are greater than other women. Not greater than men.

The whole Women's Liberation thing created a giant confusion. In the past, women were willing to see that they needed to be better than each other; however, now they are willing to be better than men. So, how much judgment of themselves do they have to go into to be better than men?

Salon Participant:

A lot.

Gary:

You don't want to judge yourself. You want to choose what works for you. You gave up being a hedonist, a voluptuary and a seductress, all of the things that gave you control over men and control over women, in favor of being better than a man and never making yourself better than a woman.

Salon Participant:

For the last two weeks, I have been putting on weight. I don't feel sexy and I'm refusing sex.

Gary:

That's the reason I am running this process. These are all the places you are trying to cut off the energy you are that would give you everything you want. You might try running:

What invention am I using to create the body I am choosing to hate? Everything that is times a godzillion, are you willing to destroy and uncreate it all? Right and Wrong, Good and Bad, POD and POC, All Nine, Shorts, Boys and Beyonds.

Salon Participant:

I got sadness.

Gary:

Yes, you are inventing you are sad about this stuff.

Salon Participant:

I am not that?

Gary:

Sadness is or isn't an invention?

Salon Participant:

It is an invention.

Gary:

It's an invention to do what? Maximize human reality.

Everything that is times a godzillion, are you willing to destroy and uncreate it all? Right and Wrong, Good and Bad, POD and POC, All Nine, Shorts, Boys and Beyonds.

Keep running that.

Salon Participant:

Thank you.

Gary:

What stupidity are you using to create the invention, artificial intensity and the demons of never being the hedonist, seductress, voluptuary and the vixen you truly be, are you choosing? Everything that is times a godzillion, are you willing to destroy and uncreate it all? Right and Wrong, Good and Bad, POD and POC, All Nine, Shorts, Boys and Beyonds.

That's working well. How are you all feeling?

Salon Participant:

Sadness is still there for me.

Gary:

Sadness is an invention. You use it to make yourself less.

What invention, artificial intensity and the demons of thoughts, feelings, emotions, sex and no sex are you using to create a crap life you are choosing? Everything that is times a godzillion, are you willing to destroy and uncreate it all? Right and Wrong, Good and Bad, POD and POC, All Nine, Shorts, Boys and Beyonds.

Thoughts, Feelings, Emotions, Sex and No Sex

You guys don't seem to get that thoughts, feelings, emotions and sex or no sex are the lower harmonic of perceiving, knowing, being and receiving. You always go back to feeling sadness. You say, "I feel blah-blah" or "When I talk to a man I like, I turn into a pile of crap." All of these are about your thoughts, feelings and emotions. None of them are about being.

Salon Participant:

When I said, "The sadness is still there," it's more like an energy of sadness is there. It is not that I am sad.

Gary:

Do you ever ask, "Is this really mine?"

Salon Participant:

Yes, I do ask that. It isn't mine.

Gary:

So, why do you keep buying it as real? You don't have to buy it as real.

Salon Participant:

I am buying it as if I have to destroy and uncreate it.

Gary:

You don't have to buy it as real.

Salon Participant:

What is it that I try to fix?

Gary:

If you function from the point of view that you have to fix the sadness or get rid of it, you have made it real. You have made it more real than any other choice you have.

Salon Participant:

Even though I am telling myself I am not taking it on, it's there, so I feel I have to fix it.

Gary:

You have already taken it on if you feel you have to fix it. If you have to fix it, if you feel you have to change it, if you have to do something about it, you have made it more real than the capacity to perceive, know, be or receive.

Everything that brought up times a godzillion, are you willing to destroy and uncreate it all? Right and Wrong, Good and Bad, POD and POC, All Nine, Shorts, Boys and Beyonds.

Salon Participant:

Thank you, Gary. I get it. I am still making it real and claiming that it is mine.

Gary:

You are claiming it is not yours; you are claiming that somebody has it rather than it's a choice people choose to make. And why would they choose that rather than something different?

Salon Participant:

Thank you.

By What You Choose, You Create Greater Possibilities

Gary:

In my book, *Beyond the Utopian Ideal,* I talk about how, in order to create or generate anything, you have to function from choice, question, possibility and contribution. If you have choice, then by what you choose, you create greater possibilities. A possibility is always about levels of awareness; it's never about conclusions.

Every time you ask a question, you activate the quantum entanglements in the world to deliver to you. Quantum entanglements are the string theory that all things are interconnected. If you look at the universe, it's clear that each thing is interconnected with every other thing. Question, choice and possibility activate the quantum entanglements to create more possibilities, more choices and more questions, which bring into actualization whatever you desire, require and ask for. But instead of choosing that, you tend to choose according to somebody's point of view.

In this reality, people have made it that if you have a question, you are looking for a conclusion, if you have a choice you are looking for a right choice and a right conclusion, and if you have possibilities you are weighing and measuring what you have. You are not actually having more choice, more possibility and more questions.

What invention are you using to create the upset you are choosing? Everything that is times a godzillion, are you willing to destroy and uncreate it all? Right and Wrong, Good and Bad, POD and POC, All Nine, Shorts, Boys and Beyonds.

Defending Yourself against Something

Salon Participant:

Can you talk about being 100 percent comfortable? When I started Access Consciousness, I was four on a scale of ten; now I am six out of ten and I am choosing to be ten out of ten.

Gary:

You are defending a point of view. Whenever you see yourself as powerless or you make yourself less, you are defending yourself against something rather than being you.

Who or what are you defending for or against, that if you didn't defend for or against would give you all of you? Everything that is times a godzillion, are you willing to destroy and uncreate it all? Right and Wrong, Good and Bad, POD and POC, All Nine, Shorts, Boys and Beyonds.

Apparently you guys are doing a lot of defending.

Who or what are you defending for or against, that if you didn't defend for or against would give you all of you? Everything that is times a godzillion, are you willing to destroy and uncreate it all? Right and Wrong, Good and Bad, POD and POC, All Nine, Shorts, Boys and Beyonds.

Salon Participant:

You once said that anything that you defend, you cannot change. Can you talk about how to get out of that loop?

Gary:

Recognize that you are defending. Why would I defend any point of view?

A reporter from the *Houston Press* who was trying to write an article on Access Consciousness planned to vilify us. He left a message for C, telling her that the article would be about her. Why would he do that? Because C is a personality who is known in Houston, and if he can vilify her, he has done something good from his point of view.

Why is vilification of somebody a valuable product? Because it proves you are defending the rightness of your point of view. Most articles in the press are done to defend a point of view. They take a point of view and call it "true."

Salon Participant:

What's the difference between defending and judging?

Gary:

There's not much difference. You judge something to be so, then you have to defend the rightness of your judgment.

Salon Participant:

They are intertwined.

Gary:

Yes, without one, you cannot have the other. If you don't have a judgment, there is nothing to defend. If you have a judgment, then everything that comes within the purview of that judgment has to be defended.

Salon Participant:

Are you defending any time you are not in "no point of view" or "interesting point of view"?

Gary:

Pretty much. Functioning in "interesting point of view" or "no point of view" requires you to never defend anything. I never have to defend anything.

When I heard about the guy from the *Houston Press,* I thought about writing to him and saying, "I suggest you go ahead and sow your malice where you choose." Such maliciousness. Then I asked, "Is this going to change anything? Can I say or do anything to make this better? No. Okay, let it go."

There are people who take a fixed point of view, and there is nothing you can do about the point of view they have taken. You have to recognize there are certain things you have no control over. Everybody wants to assume that if you are conscious, you get what-

ever you want. No, being conscious means you have more possibilities than other people; it doesn't mean you get what you want.

I am always willing to go to the question, not to defend. When
you come out of question, you have to defend the rightness of any
point of view you take.

The same thing occurs with relationships. Most relationships
don't work because you try to defend something. I used to do this.
If someone had a point of view about me, I would try to defend
myself against it. I would not go to, "What is possible here?" I would
say, "This person won't like this about me," so I would defend that. I
would not let them see that part of me. I'd start cutting off parts of
me to create relationships. Does that work? No.

Who or what are you defending for or against, that if
you didn't defend for or against, would give you all of you?
Everything that is times a godzillion, are you willing to destroy
and uncreate it all? Right and Wrong, Good and Bad, POD and
POC, All Nine, Shorts, Boys and Beyonds.

Defining Who You Are

Salon Participant:

What comes up for me is "me". I say to myself, "That's ridicu-
lous," but it's not, is it?

Gary:

You have defined who you are. And when you define who you
are, you try to put everything into place so you can defend who you
are, so you can prove that who you are is who you are.

Everything that is times a godzillion, are you willing to
destroy and uncreate it all? Right and Wrong, Good and Bad,
POD and POC, All Nine, Shorts, Boys and Beyonds.

Salon Participant:

The thing that came up for me is the energy of past lives, where I have been defending who I defined myself as.

Gary:

If you define yourself as a woman, are you defending everything that a woman should be instead of just being who you choose to be? Yes. Being a defender is like living in a castle. You have to keep up the walls so nobody can get in. And nobody includes you.

Who or what are you defending for or against, that if you didn't defend for or against would give you all of you? Everything that is times a godzillion, are you willing to destroy and uncreate it all? Right and Wrong, Good and Bad, POD and POC, All Nine, Shorts, Boys and Beyonds.

Salon Participant:

When N talked about running around naked as a child and being told to put clothes on, was that about her parents' buying into others' reality?

Gary:

No. They were trying to defend their reputation. I have a question for you. Do you really think, given who your parents were, that they actually gave a damn about anything except how your behavior reflected on them?

They were doing it so you would not be a bad reflection on them. They were defending their reputation by what they made you do. How much of what you have been doing is based on your family's desire to defend their reputation?

There are a lot of things possible in this reality, but you can't get to that as long as you are defending anything. My ex-wife used to defend the point of view that our daughter Shannon never got as much as our other kids. She was always defending that point of view. Even though I could show her that Shannon had more presents at Christmas time than our other kids, my ex-wife's point of view was that Shannon never got enough.

Would that projected and expected point of view create an effect in Shannon's world? Would she come away thinking or feeling that she never got as much? That kind of thing is projected at you all the time. Most of you have experienced it.

How much of what you are defending about your parents, for or against, is based on projections and expectations they had—and had nothing to do with you? Everything that is times a godzillion, are you willing to destroy and uncreate it all? Right and Wrong, Good and Bad, POD and POC, All Nine, Shorts, Boys and Beyonds.

Salon Participant:

If I was told that I was wasting my talent, what am I defending against?

Gary:

If you decided your parents loved you, then you would have to defend for the fact that they loved you while defending against the fact that you have wasted your talent. Are you in a Catch-22? Does it give you many choices? Or does it start to take away your choices?

Salon Participant:

All of the above.

Gary:

Everything that is times a godzillion, are you willing to destroy and uncreate it all? Right and Wrong, Good and Bad, POD and POC, All Nine, Shorts, Boys and Beyonds.

"I Am Not That"

Salon Participant:

So, when I defend against something, I am trying to not make it real. I am defending so that this is not who I am. I defend that I am not that. And I am solidifying it by defending against it.

Gary:

Yes, because you are defending against it rather than being able to choose it or not choose it at will.

Salon Participant:

I am justifying by saying, "I am going to defend against, as I am not that."

Gary:

Yeah. Anything you say you are not, you are defending. My point of view is I am everything. So how could I defend anything?

"What could I choose that I haven't chosen?" is a different point of view. If you could choose anything, what would be available to you? Then it's a matter of, "What is really available to me now?" not "What do I have to choose?" "What is important for me to choose?" "What do I need to choose?" "What will make it real for me?" or "What will work for me?" All of those are defended positions.

When you get out of defending, the question becomes: What else is possible that I never knew I could choose?

Everything that is times a godzillion, are you willing to destroy and uncreate it all? Right and Wrong, Good and Bad, POD and POC, All Nine, Shorts, Boys and Beyonds.

Salon Participant:

When I find myself in a situation like that, I say, "That doesn't matter." I get that there is an energy to it. I do that with my father, for example. I say, "That doesn't matter." Am I lying to myself?

Gary:

"Doesn't matter" is defending against. If you really went to "interesting point of view that is his point of view," then it truly wouldn't matter and you wouldn't have to say anything else about it. "Doesn't matter" is to defend against. You are making yourself right. And by making yourself right, you are making him wrong. If you make somebody right or wrong, you are defending.

Salon Participant:

I am doing little things like that, that I think are expanding my awareness, but I am actually tricking myself in a lot of ways.

Gary:

Are you expanding your awareness? Is that true? Or are you defending a point of view to *prove* it is true rather than *allowing* it to be true?

Salon Participant:

I so like you!

Salon Participant:

I am able to be outside the human maximization, yet I am aware that I am trying to protect myself from being so different. What am I trying to protect myself from?

Gary:

You are defending you.

Salon Participant:

Why am I defending me?

Gary:

There is no reason; you just are. How many of you think that if you can find the why, you will be able to let it go, rather than just choosing something different? The why question is the defensive position you take.

How many defenses do you have to protect the *why* of your reality? Everything that is times a godzillion, are you willing to destroy and uncreate it all? Right and Wrong, Good and Bad, POD and POC, All Nine, Shorts, Boys and Beyonds.

Salon Participant:

To be able to justify something in case I need to.

Gary:

Yes, that is still defending.

Salon Participant:

So, what else is possible?

Gary:

That's the question! Now we are getting somewhere. If you ask, "What else is possible?" then what is possible is for you to have a different choice.

Defending against Human Reality

Salon Participant:

Is it totally okay to be outside human maximization all the time, no matter what?

Gary:

Why would you be outside of it? Why would you not be able to have awareness of it?

I don't have to be outside of it; I just know I don't have to buy it.

Salon Participant:

Ah, am I trying to create a different reality outside this human reality?

Gary:

Yeah, you are trying to defend against human reality by choosing outside of human reality rather than being willing to choose whatever works for you in whatever situation or reality shows up.

Everything that is times a godzillion, are you willing to destroy and uncreate it all? Right and Wrong, Good and Bad, POD and POC, All Nine, Shorts, Boys and Beyonds.

Salon Participant:

This morning my dad rang me. He had a fall and there was a lot of drama. I just asked, "What else is possible here?" and chose to be here on this call. The energy of that was expansive for me.

Gary:

That's choosing for you *and* this reality; that's not choosing what doesn't work.

Salon Participant:

That's being in the energy of, "What else is truly possible here?"

Gary:

When you ask, "What else is truly possible here?" the quantum entanglements go, "Oh, you want something different! We will show you how." They contribute to the creation and actualization of what you desire in life.

Most Men Are Pleasure Seekers

Salon Participant:

I find that sometimes I am more comfortable with men than women. Is that the competition you were talking about?

Gary:

Yeah. Men are usually easier to hang out with for women who like men. There is a possibility for a greater reality.

Salon Participant:

What is that with men, if we like to hang around with them? How do they perceive us?

Gary:

If they feel comfortable, they think you are a friend. They don't necessarily see you as a seductress or a voluptuary. You have to have it all. You can change them from friends to friends with benefits. How do you do that? The first way is to be the hedonist, voluptuary, seductress and vixen you truly be. How often do you use your hedonist capacity to enticement?

Salon Participant:

Not yet. Not often.

Gary:

Most men are pleasure seekers. If you use your hedonistic capacities, you feed them something that gives them pleasure and they say, "Oh, I haven't seen this side of this woman."

When it is easier to just hang out with men, it tends to be like doing business. You have to recognize there is a different possibility.

Turned On By Everything in Life?

377

. be willing to allow everything to turn you on? I was
.at everything becomes irrelevant and you are total space
.hoice and oneness.

Gary:

What invention are you using to create the turn-on you could be choosing? Everything that is times a godzillion, are you willing to destroy and uncreate it all? Right and Wrong, Good and Bad, POD and POC, All Nine, Shorts, Boys and Beyonds.

Salon Participant:

That's the opposite of everything we were told was the correct way to be.

Gary:

Yup. What is this whole correct way to be and all this proper and pious stuff? They all are inventions. They are invented to control you. Why would people want to control you? So they can get what they want from you. When you are not controllable, no one can confine you, define you or keep you separate from you.

What invention are you using to avoid the turn-on you could be choosing? Everything that is times a godzillion, are you willing to destroy and uncreate it all? Right and Wrong, Good and Bad, POD and POC, All Nine, Shorts, Boys and Beyonds.

The women who have people following them are the ones who are constantly turned on by everything in life. When you are not turned on, do you tend to be positive or negative?

Salon Participant:

Negative.

Gary:

Is that a turn-off for a guy?

Salon Participant:

Yes.

Gary:

When you are being positive about yourself and everything around you, you inspire people to the possibilities, which is the awareness that will give them you—if that's what you are choosing. You have to be willing to recognize what you choose.

You tend to choose men who won't choose themselves rather than men who would be fun to be with. You don't ask, "Who would be the funnest person to have sex with? Who would be the funnest person to have in my life? Who would expand my life and make it better?" That's a different reality. Instead you tend to say, "I want a man who loves me totally for me."

But if *you* don't love you totally for you, can any man love you totally for you? No. Because you are trying to cut off the parts and pieces of you to defend that you are not lovable, which is actually correct. You are not that lovable. You are more lovable than that, but you don't want to be loved that way because then you would be out of control and that would be bad based on what?

What invention are you using to avoid the turn-on you could be choosing? Everything that is times a godzillion, are you willing to destroy and uncreate it all? Right and Wrong, Good and Bad, POD and POC, All Nine, Shorts, Boys and Beyonds.

Salon Participant:

You said that with the reporter in Houston, you asked the question, "Is there anything I could do to change this?" and you got no. Is that where you use turn-on to create and generate something beyond it?

Gary:

That's where you realize that in everything, pretty much every time, it's only a choice to have something greater or less great.

Salon Participant:

And any time you defend, it stops creation and generation.

Gary:

What are you defending, that if you didn't defend it, would allow you to outcreate yourself? Everything that is times a godzillion, are you willing to destroy and uncreate it all? Right and Wrong, Good and Bad, POD and POC, All Nine, Shorts, Boys and Beyonds.

Salon Participant:

"Me" is coming up every time you run that process. Am I in competition with me?

Gary:

No. You created the "you" that you decided was you. That's the "you" you show the world so you don't have to be the real you, which you have defended against everyone so that even you can't find you.

Salon Participant:

Yes, I understood everything you said.

Gary:

Everything that is times a godzillion, are you willing to destroy and uncreate it all? Right and Wrong, Good and Bad, POD and POC, All Nine, Shorts, Boys and Beyonds.

Salon Participant:

I am agreeing with you. What else is possible? Where do I go?

Gary:

What if you were able to be something you have never chosen to be? What are you refusing to be, that if you chose to be it, would allow you to be everything you truly be? Everything that is times a godzillion, are you willing to destroy and uncreate it all? Right and Wrong, Good and Bad, POD and POC, All Nine, Shorts, Boys and Beyonds.

Salon Participant:

In the last call, you mentioned choosing someone who would catapult us off the teeter-totter of this reality. Is it possible to do that while we are doing defending?

Gary:

It is possible, but I doubt it would maintain itself. As soon as you catapult off your comfort zone, you defend the rightness of the comfort zone you chose.

Salon Participant:

Could you talk some more about what it looks like to choose someone like that?

Gary:

It's someone who is not defending a point of view, someone who is willing to be whatever point of view would create the greatest result.

Salon Participant:

Would it be functioning from, "What is this? What do I do with it?"

Gary:

You have to be willing to look at a different possibility.

Salon Participant:

I have just become aware that I am constantly making this reality greater or less than me. That's a judgment that is sticking me. It's a comparison thing. Can you give me a clearing for that?

Gary:

Ask: What am I defending that has created all this?

If you are doing comparison of any kind, you are doing judgment, which is something you are defending. You are operating from the rightness or wrongness of this reality, not the choice of this reality.

Choice, Question, Possibility and Contribution

Salon Participant:

Yeah, I can feel that. Thank you. Question, choice, possibility and contribution—are they simultaneous energetic states?

Gary:

Not quite. Yes and no. Choice is choice. You have to make a choice, and every choice creates another question, which creates another set of possibilities. Every possibility is a level of awareness you can have about something else. There are subtle levels of awareness that exist that will give you more space and possibility, which is more awareness, which gives you more choices, more questions and on and on. Every time a question comes up, it activates the quantum entanglements to give you more choices, more possibilities and more questions. It's all the things that contribute to creating and generating beyond this reality.

Salon Participant:

I feel cut off on the contribution. That's where I feel I withdraw.

Gary:

No, I think you are not cut off from the contribution and from giving what you can be, but from the gifting you can receive. You're cutting off the contribution of receiving from the quantum entanglements, which try to actualize anything you request. Do you ask for things—or not?

Salon Participant:

Not.

Gary:

Which means you are not willing to receive. How much of what you are doing is defending against receiving? A lot, a little or megatons?

Salon Participant:

Megatons.

Gary:

Everything that is times a godzillion, are you willing to destroy and uncreate it all? Right and Wrong, Good and Bad, POD and POC, All Nine, Shorts, Boys and Beyonds.

Salon Participant:

So, I am defending me not receiving?

Gary:

You are defending the way in which you receive. If you go to, "I can only receive this way" or "I can only receive a certain kind of person," you are defending the choices you have made in the past that didn't work.

Salon Participant:

Can we clear that, please?

Gary:

How much of your past are you defending to make you not wrong or to make you right? Everything that is times a godzillion, are you willing to destroy and uncreate it all? Right and Wrong, Good and Bad, POD and POC, All Nine, Shorts, Boys and Beyonds.

Salon Participant:

Thank you, Gary. The clearing that you did is the space of infinite possibility.

Salon Participant:

What does an infinitely receiving world look like?

Gary:

An infinitely receiving world is one in which you cut off no awareness. Regardless of what occurs, you are aware that there is a different possibility. You are always looking for infinite possibilities, and each possibility is the number of choices and awarenesses you can have, which are only expanding and not contracting.

Every Answer Is an Invention

Salon Participant:

Since I have been on this call, I have burning in my chest and throat, and I feel like I could throw up.

Gary:

What invention are you using to create the feeling you are choosing?

Salon Participant:

So, I am just making it up?

Gary:

I didn't say you were making it up. *Making it up* and *inventing* are different universes. When you *invent* something, you take a creation and decide it is so. You say, "This is the way it is." You invent from that point of view. *Creation* is a place where you realize there is a different possibility that you haven't chosen yet. You just stated, "I have this, this and this." Is that a question?

Salon Participant:

I was asking, "Body, what awareness am I perceiving?" and I did go to conclusion.

Gary:

Why is it necessary to come to conclusion?

Salon Participant:

To fix it or change it.

Gary:

That's the reason it is an invention.

What invention am I using to create the crappy feeling I am choosing? Everything that is times a godzillion, are you willing to destroy and uncreate it all? Right and Wrong, Good and Bad, POD and POC, All Nine, Shorts, Boys and Beyonds.

Salon Participant:

I still don't get what invention is. Is invention where we twist one thing to be something else?

Gary:

No, invention is where you come to a conclusion. The patent office closed down when they invented color TV because they said nothing else could be invented. Why would they do that?

Salon Participant:

They decided that's all there was. That was the answer.

Gary:

Yes, that's what happens with anything you invent. You say, "This is the answer. This is what it is." Everywhere you have gone into an answer, it's an invention. Nothing is an answer; it's only an awareness. Every answer is an invention.

What invention are you using to create the sucky life you are choosing? Everything that is times a godzillion, are you willing to destroy and uncreate it all? Right and Wrong, Good and Bad, POD and POC, All Nine, Shorts, Boys and Beyonds.

Keep using that.

Salon Participant:

Thank you.

Gary:

How are you all doing? Would you be willing to do a process about the last guy you had in your life who you thought was worth having?

What invention are you using to create the relationship you are choosing? Everything that is times a godzillion, are you willing to destroy and uncreate it all? Right and Wrong, Good and Bad, POD and POC, All Nine, Shorts, Boys and Beyonds.

Salon Participant:

With every call, I get how not screwed up I am and how much possibility is available every second. I can keep choosing something new and different. Even if I don't, that's also choice. Thank you so much.

Gary:

I like that you are finally realizing you are not as screwed up as you think you have to be. And I like that you see there is a different possibility.

Salon Participant:

All the inventions people think they have to function from—the upset, trauma, drama and problems—all of that is getting really funny. Thank you.

Gary:

Keep running this: What invention am I using to create the upset I am choosing?

Salon Participant:

Gary, if you could have anything from this call for us, what would it be?

Gary:

Freedom for you to recognize the gift you are in the world and to be that instead of trying to be what you be as a woman.

Okay, sweet ladies. Love you all. Goodbye.

14

Having the Greatness of You

*Most of you have spent your life looking at the wrongness,
the past and the things that don't work.
Seldom do you look at the future and what actually will work.*

*What kind of future would you like to create?
Why is your attention not on that?*

Gary:

Welcome, ladies. Are there any questions?

Do You Really Like Men?

Salon Participant:

Can you facilitate some clearings for my dislike of men, please? I allowed myself to be raped, used and abused by men when I was being a whore.

Gary:

What stupidity am I using to create the invention, artificial intensity and demons of being a used and abused whore am I choosing? Everything that is times a godzillion, will you destroy and uncreate it all? Right and Wrong, Good and Bad, POD and POC, All Nine, Shorts, Boys and Beyonds.

At one time or another, we all have been used and abused. You need to have an awareness of whether you actually like men. Ask yourself this question: Truth, do I really like men?

If the answer is no, does that mean you have to go to women? No, it just means you don't like men. So, you have to choose men who you don't have to ever become involved with. That's what someone does when she is choosing to be a whore: she chooses men she doesn't have to be involved with forever. You will always get the best quality men if you are being a whore or a hooker, because the best quality men always go for that. Oh yeah, not!

You have to be willing to function with the way everything works. How do you get everything to work? You have to choose a different possibility.

What stupidity am I using to avoid the choices for men or women I could be choosing? Everything that is times a godzillion, will you destroy and uncreate it all? Right and Wrong, Good and Bad, POD and POC, All Nine, Shorts, Boys and Beyonds.

The Pragmatics of Getting Everything to Work with a Man

Salon Participant:

Can you talk about the pragmatics of getting everything to work with a man?

Gary:

You have to come from the point of view, "What is going to make this work?" instead of "Do I love this man?" or "Do I like this man?" or "Is he good?" Those are judgments used to include or exclude. What if we didn't have to include or exclude anything? What if we could have anything? We have to get to a point where we recognize a different possibility instead of choosing a limitation.

Salon Participant:

Can you be more specific? When you say, "Get this to work," is this where you go with anything that is light?

Gary:

It can be where it's light all the time. The main thing is to ask: What's going to be the best way for something good to occur?

Salon Participant:

Oh, you mean for you and everyone else? The Kingdom of We?

Gary:

Yeah. You have to look at what is going to work for you and everyone else. What works for you oftentimes destroys so many others that in the process of going for that, you don't have a place where you include you in your reality. You have to be willing to choose you and your reality.

If you function as though there is a problem for you, you are going to create more problems. This is more important than anything else. If you have the point of view that there is going to be a problem, you will create a problem. Why would you create a problem? Because a problem makes everyone feel more real. Problems equal reality here on planet Earth; they don't create possibility. You want to have more possibilities than problems. Ask: What's going to create the greatest possibility? not What's going to create the greatest problem?

"Every Day I Want to Get a Divorce"

Salon Participant:

I have a wonderful relationship with my kids. We dance and sing, but in the meantime, my husband is constantly saying weird things like, "Why don't I have boys?" We are remodeling a house. He keeps asking me to be a partner and give up Access Consciousness so he can put money into this project. Every day I want to get a divorce. I was on my way to get papers today, but the office was closed. What am I defending here with this intensity?

Gary:

Are you defending the rightness of marriage?

Salon Participant:

I guess I'm defending all of it—family, marriage, relationships.

Gary:

Everything that is times a godzillion, will you destroy and uncreate it all? Right and Wrong, Good and Bad, POD and POC, All Nine, Shorts, Boys and Beyonds.

What if you said to your husband, "Obviously this marriage isn't working for you. Why do you stay married to me?"

Salon Participant:

I did. When I asked him that, he said, "It would cost me more to divorce you."

Gary:

Well, that's a good reason to stay married!

Salon Participant:

I know. That's why I am going in a circle.

Gary:

Why are you going down the rabbit hole of your emotions?

Salon Participant:

I am not clear.

Gary:

Emotions won't give you clarity. They will lock you in the same old place you always go, as though by going there, you will get somewhere else. Have your emotions ever gotten you to a place that was really good?

Salon Participant:

Not at all.

Gary:

So, maybe you should consider that your emotions are not a way of creating.

Salon Participant:

I fully agree.

Gary:

Everything that is times a godzillion, will you destroy and uncreate it all? Right and Wrong, Good and Bad, POD and POC, All Nine, Shorts, Boys and Beyonds.

Defending for or Against

Salon Participant:

Sometimes when I am attached to the outcome of something, I will be in an interaction with another person and I will get totally choked with fear. I'll compare myself, judge myself as less-than and screw up all the work I did before we had the meeting. Can you give me any clearings that will assist me to stay expanded without contracting and to be myself without apology?

Gary:

Use this:

Who or what am I defending for or against that if I didn't defend for or against would allow me to be all of me?

Do this about ten times before you go into any meeting or inter-action. If you are having an interaction and feel that you are becoming small, ask: Would an infinite being truly choose this?

If an infinite being wouldn't choose it, why would you? You have to start functioning from the ten commandments. If you haven't listened to the Ten Commandments calls, please get them and listen to them.

Choosing According to Other People's Choices

Salon Participant:

I have had an awareness during the last couple of days about how I choose according to other people's choices. Can you help me with that?

Gary:

Why are other people's choices more real to you than your choices?

Salon Participant:

Because I allow them to affect my life.

Gary:

Why?

Salon Participant:

Because these are the people I choose to be in my life.

Gary:

Oh, you mean you are choosing to *be them* in your life instead of choosing to be *with them* in your life. You said, "These are the people I choose to be in my life." You like to *be them* when you are with them, so instead of being *with* them, you are *being them*. You are not keeping you. You are destroying you to be with them.

To be them means you have to become them, which means you have to let them choose what works for you. You are stating exactly the way it is showing up for you. You are *being them* rather than *being with them.* When you *be* somebody in a relationship, you give up you in favor of them. Always.

Salon Participant:

Okay, so, when someone chooses something , how do I not have it affect my life? That's my target.

Gary:

Yes, but if you are being them, it has to affect your life.

Salon Participant:

Every time you say, "You are being them," an electric shock goes through me.

Gary:

What invention are you using to create the lack of you in every relationship you are choosing? Everything that is times a godzillion, will you destroy and uncreate it all? Right and Wrong, Good and Bad, POD and POC, All Nine, Shorts, Boys and Beyonds.

Salon Participant:

So, *being with* them would include everything and not affect my life?

Gary:

Being with them would not limit you or stop you.

Salon Participant:

What came up is, "That's the only way to have a relationship, Gary."

Gary:

Good idea. Not!

Salon Participant:

That's the only way I have been till this moment. Time to change it.

Gary:

What invention are you using to create the lack of you in every relationship you are choosing? Everything that is times a godzillion, will you destroy and uncreate it all? Right and Wrong, Good and Bad, POD and POC, All Nine, Shorts, Boys and Beyonds.

Salon Participant:

Something else is possible other than that? One more time, please!

Gary:

What invention are you using to create the lack of you in every relationship you are choosing? Everything that is times a godzillion, will you destroy and uncreate it all? Right and Wrong, Good and Bad, POD and POC, All Nine, Shorts, Boys and Beyonds.

Keeping You out of Existence

Salon Participant:

Is this also how I keep separation in existence?

Gary:

No, it's how you keep you out of existence.

Salon Participant:

Wow. Yes!

Salon Participant:

When K was talking just now, about how she chooses according to other people's choices, I realized I have done that too.

Gary:

When you decide you like someone, whether it's a man or a woman or a friend, how much of you do you have to divorce to create that? The lack of you.

Salon Participant:

And the you is what you choose?

Gary:

It's who you are in these ten seconds.

Salon Participant:

How do you divorce yourself when you like someone?

Gary:

You keep trying to prove that liking someone enough is all it takes. The reality is you have to more than like you. You have to do something different, like love you.

Salon Participant:

Are you saying that what I have been sensing is true, that there is no real love?

Gary:

Yeah, you are defending that love is real.

All of you who are defending the reality of love, will you destroy and uncreate that? Right and Wrong, Good and Bad, POD and POC, All Nine, Shorts, Boys and Beyonds.

That's the "what" you've been sensing. Who are you defending and what are you defending? You are defending that there has to be some rightness in the love you are choosing for each and every person you are choosing to love. Your choosing to love them is more important than being you.

Who or what are you defending for or against, that if you didn't defend for or against, would change all reality? Everything that is times a godzillion, will you destroy and uncreate it all? Right and Wrong, Good and Bad, POD and POC, All Nine, Shorts, Boys and Beyonds.

Allowance and Having the Greatness of You

Salon Participant:

Could you talk about allowance?

Gary:

If you are defending anything, are you in allowance of anyone?

Salon Participant:

No.

Gary:

Are you in allowance of you?

Salon Participant:

No.

Gary:

Why are you not in allowance of you?

Salon Participant:

Because I am not actually being me.

Gary:

No, because you are not having any part of the greatness of you.

What stupidity are you using to defend against the greatness of you are you choosing? Everything that is times a godzillion, will you destroy and uncreate it all? Right and Wrong, Good and Bad, POD and POC, All Nine, Shorts, Boys and Beyonds.

Salon Participant:

You said I am not having any part of the greatness of me. What's the difference between *having* and *being*?

Gary:

If you cannot *be* you, you cannot *have,* and if you cannot *have,* you cannot *be.* To *have* is the willingness to see anything and not have judgment of it. You choose who and what you have based on what you judge. That determines what you can *be.*

Salon Participant:

Wow, all of that is limiting.

Gary:

Yes, it is limiting, rather than being unlimited, where you can have anything. Once you know you can have anything, you actually have choice. When you can only have what others are willing to give you, you have no choice.

Salon Participant:

How does that play into, "I am not needing."

Gary:

Most people do, "I can have this" or "I need this."

When you can have, you don't need anything. You can choose. If you dislike men and you know that, it's not a matter of anything wrong. It's, "What would I like to choose here? Would I like to choose women? Would I like to choose not to have sex? Or would I like to choose something else?" Then you can get into the question of what you would really like to choose. But when you have the point of view that you have to have a man or a relationship or money to be complete, you are limiting choice in favor of not having. In order to not have, you have to not be.

Salon Participant:

You were saying "not need." I don't get it.

Gary:

If you have no need, can you have anything?

Salon Participant:

Yes.

Gary:

Now do you get it?

Salon Participant:

Oh! I see. I was thinking of it as a wrongness.

Gary:

I know. It is not a wrongness! You never listen to me. Are we married?

Salon Participant:

I get it. This changes so much.

Inspiring the Guy

Salon Participant:

When you are living with a man, how do you not pick up on all his stuff? How do we, as humanoid women who create our future, inspire our partners to create a different reality?

Gary:

You want to inspire the guy to think he is coming up with the idea that he is going to institute. So you say, "I have a feeling that this could be possible. What do you think, honey?" When he comes back and tells you he thinks it's a great idea, he will do it.

You have to be a little more circumspect in the ways you create things. Ask:

- What do I want to create here?
- What is really possible?
- What is he actually capable of that he hasn't acknowledged?

Not:

- What do I think I have to do?
- What do I need to do to inspire him more?

Salon Participant:

I noticed that I defend a negative belief about feeling like I am a fraud. I feel like I'm faking it.

Gary:

You are a fraud and you are faking it. That's not a wrongness. That's the way you start creating—by pretending to be able to do something that you don't think you can do…until you can do it. You are capable of doing more than almost anybody in the world and you keep acting like you can do less. Why? I keep trying to tell you, you guys are humanoids. That makes you a master of all trades and a jack of none. You have no problems. Why do you keep trying to create that you have problems?

Everything that is times a godzillion, will you destroy and uncreate it all? Right and Wrong, Good and Bad, POD and POC, All Nine, Shorts, Boys and Beyonds.

You Can't Create a Future by Focusing on Limitations

Salon Participant:

Can we talk about the body and creating a future that we would like to have? A lot of things are changing in my body from the classes I've done recently and from being in the question of what capacities I have to change any limitations.

Gary:

Limitations? Why are you focusing on limitations instead of what you are capable of?

Salon Participant:

That's what I said. What capacities do I have that would undo my limitations?

Gary:

Yes, but you are still looking at limitations. You want to look from: What capacities do I have that I have not yet instituted, generated or created?

We have a tendency to focus on limitations as though limitations are going to create. Limitations don't do anything except validate limitations. Creation only occurs when we are willing to step into creation. You have to look at: What am I capable of generating, creating and instituting physically that I have never even considered?

Salon Participant:

Thank you. That's what I was looking for. Can you speak about being out of definition with the body?

Gary:

If you are doing any kind of limitation, thinking there is some problem with your body or if you are looking for some problem or what isn't working for your body or what's wrong with your body, you are looking from limitation. You are not being out of control, out of definition, out of limitation, out of form, structure or significance, out of linearities and concentricities for all eternity.

What energy, space and consciousness can my body and I be that would allow us to be out of control, out of definition, out of limitation, out of form, structure and significance, out of linearities and concentricities for all eternity? Everything that is times a godzillion, will you destroy and uncreate it all? Right and Wrong, Good and Bad, POD and POC, All Nine, Shorts, Boys and Beyonds.

This is the place where you start to look at what might be possible instead of what you think is not possible.

Salon Participant:

My husband keeps saying, "I want you to change." He wants me to make money, but I see that everything I do contributes to our having the money we have. Am I defending something?

Gary:

He wants you to go get a job.

Salon Participant:

I have been playing that game for years. I have gone to get a job, then he complains about it. I am still not living life for me. Do

I need to ask a question like, "If I was really living this life for me, what would I be choosing?"

Gary:

That's a good question.

Salon Participant:

I know that I can make anything work in my relationship and life, but sometimes there are things I don't want to play with.

Gary:

What's the limitation here? You went to the past. You didn't start creating future. If you were going to battle to have a life from future, what would be valuable to you? What would you choose? What are you looking for? You want to be a warrior woman who is battling to create a future that has never existed here—that would be a sustainable world, not a conflictual world.

Salon Participant:

Just now when you were talking to N about the body, I got that everything that I start is based on limitation. I am not creating the future.

Gary:

That is correct. You are trying to create the future by creating from the past. You see limitation as greater than possibility. You are making limitation greater than possibility.

Salon Participant:

That's a lot of my life. Going on a diet, exercising, doing a business, taking care of my son. I see that I start from the limitation. I want to fix or cure the limitation and somehow leap from the limitation to the future, but I am actually getting stuck with the limitation.

Gary:

Yeah, because you have made the limitation real. You have not been willing to move to something greater.

Salon Participant:

If I don't start based on limitation, what's the question I should ask? If I am basing everything on the limitation, how am I doing that?

Gary:

What is it that you want to create?

Salon Participant:

I want to create a different reality for everything.

Gary:

Then why aren't you creating that instead of trying to undo the limitation?

Salon Participant:

That's what I thought I had to do.

Gary:

You want to get rid of the limitations when you come up against one, but you have to start creating the future or all you are going to deal with are limitations.

Salon Participant:

Thank you. In reality, it's not about getting rid of the limitation. It's about creating the future and dealing with whatever limitation when it shows up.

Gary:

Exactly, if you are not creating the future, you are choosing to give credence to that limitation and making it more valuable and real than your creative capacity.

Salon Participant:

Yes, that's very cool. Thank you

Gary:

Never fixate on the past. Create the future. As long as you fixate on the past, you are trying to solve the problem you created in the first place. Instead ask:

What invention am I using to create the problem I am choosing? Everything that is times a godzillion, will you destroy and uncreate it all? Right and Wrong, Good and Bad, POD and POC, All Nine, Shorts, Boys and Beyonds.

Always be the warrior of creating the future that does not exist. As long as you are looking to create a future that does not exist, you are on the creative edge of possibility. Be in the question. The question isn't, "What's wrong with me?" or "How do I get over judging me?" The question is: I would judge me for what reason? Why would you judge you instead of enjoying you?

If you are in a relationship you have to ask: Truth, what's going to make this person happy? You also have to get that there are some people who don't want to be happy. They have an illusion of what they think their relationship is supposed to be. When that's what's happening, my way of doing things is to say to that person, "Show me an example of a relationship that works the way you think relationships work."

You will be quite amazed at how few of the people you ask will be able to show you relationships that work the way they think relationships should work. That's because they are not using what would actually work in a relationship but what they think they should choose.

What stupidity are you using to avoid the future you could be creating and choosing? Everything that is times a godzillion, will you destroy and uncreate it all? Right and Wrong, Good and Bad, POD and POC, All Nine, Shorts, Boys and Beyonds.

What stupidity are you using to avoid the capacities of creation you could be choosing but are refusing to choose to make sure you don't have to actually be? Everything that is times a godzillion, will you destroy and uncreate it all? Right and Wrong, Good and Bad, POD and POC, All Nine, Shorts, Boys and Beyonds.

Getting Clear about What You Want

Salon Participant:

I'd really like to create a man in my life. Maybe sex. When I am around men, I ask, "What would this create in five years time?" and generally, I don't get anything expansive.

Gary:

Are you choosing men who would actually generate and create more in your life? Have you chosen that in the past?

Salon Participant:

Definitely not.

Gary:

Then you don't have a clear picture of what you want.

Salon Participant:

That's correct. You asked, "What if you chose someone who would take you out for dinner, treat you well and buy you jewelry?" That seems nice. It sounds different. It's kind of fuzzy. I really like men. I know that I have created yucky stuff in the past. I didn't have clarity.

Gary:

What stupidity are you using to create the avoidance of the awareness with men you could be choosing? Everything that is times a godzillion, will you destroy and uncreate it all? Right and Wrong, Good and Bad, POD and POC, All Nine, Shorts, Boys and Beyonds.

You have to recognize that a man does not create or destroy your life. Men are there to be an *addition* to your life. If you are not doing a relationship with a man as an *addition* to your life, are you being you?

Salon Participant:

No.

Gary:

You have to do that. Does that help? Run this process over and over again:

What stupidity are you using to create the avoidance of the awareness with men you could be choosing? Everything that is times a godzillion, will you destroy and uncreate it all? Right and Wrong, Good and Bad, POD and POC, All Nine, Shorts, Boys and Beyonds.

For all of you, if you haven't looked at what is true for you with men, more than anything else, you have to be honest with yourself. I know women who say, "I've got to have a relationship!"

One lady came to Access Consciousness, attended a lot of classes and then one day she quit. I asked her, "How can you quit?"

She said, "Because the one thing I wanted was the ability to know I was okay about not having a boyfriend and that I'd be able to handle that with my friends who were giving me crap about needing a boyfriend. With Access Consciousness, I discovered I didn't need or want a boyfriend. I am perfectly happy being alone."

I said, "Good."

She said, "I got what I came for."

That's the way you should look at it. Ask yourself:

- What am I really doing this for?
- What do I want?

Get clear about what you want. What do you really want in a relationship? Do you want male companionship? How can you get that? Get a boy friend. Do that, and you get the best of both worlds. You don't have to have sex with him and you can go shopping with him. You get to talk about anything with him, and what else is possible? What would it be like if you were willing to give yourself that?

You have to be willing to look at what's true for you. Then you can create a future with great ease. You will see that you're willing to have whatever you've got—or you will know it's not enough or that you want something greater or more. That too is valuable. It's: What do I really want to create here?

Salon Participant:

On the first call, you talked about the way we're entrained to the idea of riding off with the prince on a white horse. You said you didn't have a lot of clarity about what created that. Do you have more clarity now?

Gary:

No, it's a myth that exists in our society. If you can be addicted to the idea of the prince on the white horse, then you don't have to have you. If you are always looking for someone to save you, then do you have to save you?

What You Think Is What Shows up in Your Life

Salon Participant:

At the moment, I feel like there is a mix of great stuff happening in my life. I feel like I'm a crap magnet. I squashed the funnel of money that was coming towards me. What's your take on that?

Gary:

Was there a question in any of that? All you did was conclude, "I am a crap magnet. I create crap. Nothing is working." That works for you?

Salon Participant:

No, it doesn't. Thank you.

Gary:

"Why do I have all this crap in my life?" is not a question. It's a statement with a question mark attached. You should ask:

- What's it going to take to change this?
- What can I be different?
- What am I not choosing to be that if I chose to be it would change all of this?

You have to figure out:

- What is it that works for me?
- What is it that I like?
- What is it that I want to do and that makes life fun and good?

Have you looked at that?

Salon Participant:

Yeah, I have been looking.

Gary:

But you haven't found it. You can't find it as long as you think you are a crap magnet. What you think is what shows up in your life. You have made determinations and decisions that you are a crap magnet.

Everywhere you decided that you are a crap magnet, and all of you who are good at picking up crap men or women, will you destroy and uncreate it all? Right and Wrong, Good and Bad, POD and POC, All Nine, Shorts, Boys and Beyonds.

Congratulations, ladies, you have managed within a heartbeat to turn yourself into a pile of crap. Aren't you proud?

Salon Participant:

Thank you, Gary.

The Space of Being

Salon Participant:

There are times when my body feels really alive and turned on, and for a while I am quite present in my body. Lately, though, it seems like I have shut me down. I need some more clarity on this.

Gary:

What's the value of shutting you down?

Salon Participant:

I got that I am not dangerous when I'm shut down.

Gary:

What's the value of holding you down? Everything that is times a godzillion, will you destroy and uncreate it all? Right and Wrong, Good and Bad, POD and POC, All Nine, Shorts, Boys and Beyonds.

Salon Participant:

That process about the value of holding me down, is that what I have locked in my body?

Gary:

You have locked you and your body with that. Keep running it.

What stupidity are you using to create the inventions, artificial intensities and the demons of defending the state or place of being rather than the space of being are you choosing? Everything that is times a godzillion, will you destroy and uncreate it all? Right and Wrong, Good and Bad, POD and POC, All Nine, Shorts, Boys and Beyonds.

Salon Participant:

Can you talk a little more about that clearing?

Gary:

There are *places* and *states* and *times* of being. The *space* of being includes everything and judges nothing. The space of being brings you to the oneness you are and gives you more choice. You have to be willing to be the space of being, which means you have no definition. For example, some people have a sense of themselves, a sense of knowing they are being, when they are in the woods.

M was saying she feels like she doesn't have a definition of who she is anymore. That's because when you are being you, there is no definition of being you. You just is what you is and nothing else is possible, available or necessary.

Salon Participant:

I have been asking, "What else is possible here that I am not even aware of?" Is there another question I can ask?

Gary:

Ask: What space of awareness can I be today that would allow me to be all of me and never go away?

Salon Participant:

Gary, am I tapping into the oneness or am I disappearing?

Gary:

I can't answer the question. Give me more information.

Salon Participant:

When I sense absolutely nothing and feel nothing....

Gary:

If you are being the space of oneness and consciousness, you feel everything and nothing is important or relevant. If you don't feel anything, you are making yourself not existent.

What invention am I using to create the non-existence of me am I choosing? Everything that is times a godzillion, will you destroy and uncreate it all? Right and Wrong, Good and Bad, POD and POC, All Nine, Shorts, Boys and Beyonds.

Conflictual Universes

Salon Participant:

It seems like there is a fight or a desperation to exist, and I get really angry that I don't even have the desperation.

Gary:

I have a question. Are you bipolar?

Salon Participant:

I am getting a yes, but I don't know what that means.

Gary:

It means you have a positive universe that is negative, and negative universe that is positive. You are in constant state of conflict with yourself.

What stupidity are you using to create the conflictual universe you are choosing? Everything that is times a godzillion, will you destroy and uncreate it all? Right and Wrong, Good and Bad, POD and POC, All Nine, Shorts, Boys and Beyonds.

Salon Participant:

I try to be so normal. I don't know what I am.

Gary:

Why would you want to be normal?

Salon Participant:

These things seem to be bad and wrong. You just diagnosed me. No one has spoken to me and told me I am bad and wrong.

Gary:

No one has ever told you that?

Salon Participant:

No one has told me that. Should I be institutionalized? Why I can't be happy? When you said that, I felt such relief and yet....

Gary:

Run this process about the conflictual universe. This is where the man/woman thing comes in. There is a constant state of conflictual universe about men, women, copulation and relationships. They're totally conflictual universes. All of you are bipolar when it comes to that.

What stupidity are you using to create the conflictual universes you are choosing? Everything that is times a godzillion, will you destroy and uncreate it all? Right and Wrong, Good and Bad, POD and POC, All Nine, Shorts, Boys and Beyonds.

Salon Participant:

Is that also true with bodies?

Gary:

Yes, if you are in conflict with your body, the same thing is going on.

Salon Participant:

That's very cool. Thank you.

Gary:

What stupidity are you using to create the conflictual universes you are choosing? Everything that is times a godzillion, will you destroy and uncreate it all? Right and Wrong, Good and Bad, POD and POC, All Nine, Shorts, Boys and Beyonds.

Salon Participant:

Are you saying this is all a choice and a creation? That we're manufacturing it?

Gary:

You are creating conflict instead of possibility, aren't you? If you are in constant judgment of you, what are you creating? Are you creating or destroying?

Salon Participant:

Destroying.

Gary:

You get involved in these things and choose conflicts instead of possibilities. Instead look at the question, choice, possibility and contribution. You have to ask:

- What is possible here that I haven't even considered?
- What choices do I have that I haven't even thought of?

When you have to give up everything you want in order for someone else to have what he or she wants, that's a conflictual universe. You are in conflict with one another, which explains why most relationships are so difficult. Most of the time, you are trying to get the other person to agree with you so they see that you agree with them and they finally get what they want. Does that work?

Salon Participant:

No.

Gary:

To have a conflict between men and women requires you to cut off awareness. To have a place where you can create conflict in your own life, you have to cut off awareness. Whenever you have a place where you are trying to create something that doesn't work in your life, you are creating a conflictual universe. It is a conflictual universe because you are not in communion with all things and you cannot choose all things. You could choose anything if you really wanted to choose it, but you have to realize when you are creating conflictual universes and function from a slightly different place.

In my own life, when Dain would have someone over to spend the night, I would get all weird and conflicted. I wouldn't know what the conflict was. I would say, "Oh, I don't like him having people over here." Then I said, "Wait a minute, that makes no sense. That cannot be my world. What am I creating here?"

I realized I was creating a place where I believed that if I had a problem with it, then I had something I could deal with. The conflict that was going on was actually the conflict with the people he was with—because the people he was having sex with were conflictual about what they were choosing. *They* were conflictual about what they were choosing. Once I got that, I didn't have to feel conflicted. I had more clarity and I knew what was true for me. But I had to get over the idea that *I* had a conflict with it or that *I* had a problem. Anywhere you are doing, "I have a problem with this thing," you are functioning from a conflictual universe.

What stupidity are you using to create the conflictual universes you are choosing? Everything that is times a godzillion, will you destroy and uncreate it all? Right and Wrong, Good and Bad, POD and POC, All Nine, Shorts, Boys and Beyonds.

Bodies and a Conflictual Universe

Salon Participant:

Can you say more about bodies and a conflictual universe? How does that show up?

Gary:

If you judge your body, are you actually looking to have change? Or are you in conflict with it?

Salon Participant:

Conflict.

Gary:

Yeah, any time you judge your body, you are in conflict with it. You are not looking at what is possible, nor are you looking at what you can be or do that you haven't even considered.

Salon Participant:

Is there a specific process for the body besides the one you gave?

Gary:

The one I gave will be the best one.

Salon Participant:

Awesome, thank you.

Gary:

I like the questions you guys come up with.

Salon Participant:

As you run these processes, I get a burning in my chest. Is that something shifting?

Gary:

Yes, it's stuff shifting. You have a lot of points of view about what is going on with your heartfelt stuff.

What stupidity are you using to create the conflictual universes you are choosing? Everything that is times a godzillion, will you destroy and uncreate it all? Right and Wrong, Good and Bad, POD and POC, All Nine, Shorts, Boys and Beyonds.

Salon Participant:

What is the connection between *defense, invention* and a *conflictual universe?*

Gary:

A *conflictual universe* is something you create, thinking that is the way to be in this reality. You create it to keep polarity in existence. Whenever you have two things that are different and polarized, like men and women, it is a conflictual universe—not necessarily truth.

Defense is what you do once you decide that what you decided is right. You make the decision to keep the defense in existence. You have to fight for it or against it.

Invention is when you buy someone else's point of view. Say your parents tell you that you shouldn't do x, y and z. As soon as they say that, you try to invent it as your point of view, too. It is not created because it is not based on anything you chose; it's based on what you chose from others.

Salon Participant:

I am confused about the part where a conflictual universe is where you think you are supposed to choose something.

Gary:

No, a conflictual universe is where you try to maintain the polarity of this reality. Would an infinite being truly choose this?

Salon Participant:

No.

Gary:

Would you really choose to be in conflict with men or women?

Salon Participant:

Not at all.

Gary:

Are you sure?

Salon Participant:

If I weren't in a conflictual reality, I don't see why I would choose to be in conflict with men or women.

Gary:

You have to realize there is a different possibility available that you haven't considered. What is really possible that you haven't considered?

What stupidity are you using to create the conflictual universes you are choosing? Everything that is times a godzillion, will you destroy and uncreate it all? Right and Wrong, Good and Bad, POD and POC, All Nine, Shorts, Boys and Beyonds.

These are all the places where you have allowed yourself to be polarized in one form or another.

Salon Participant:

When you asked, "Are you sure?" what did you mean by that?

Women Who Compete with Other Women

Gary:

Most women are competitive with other women. You need to be very clear about this if you are not in competition with women— because when you are not in competition with women, and women do competition with you, you don't understand it or get it.

Salon Participant:

Yes, that reads as true.

Gary:

It's important for you to get that you don't do conflictual universes with women. You don't do judgment of women and competition with women. But you have to be willing to recognize women who do. When they do competition with other women, they are looking to prove that someone is choosing wrong or doing wrong. They are always looking to see how other women are wrong.

Salon Participant:

There is something sticky here for me, regarding competition with other women. What can we change regarding this?

Gary:

First of all, realize that women are generally very competitive. If you don't acknowledge that they are competitive, you will see how they must be right when they judge you. Or you will see how they must be right when they point out that something is wrong with you or when they say, "That's a pretty dress" and they don't mean it. You have to see when women are doing competition and not buy into it.

If you buy out of competition yourself, eventually it will go away with the people you are capable of being in connection with. But women will be competitive, and you have to recognize it. That's important.

When you don't do competition with women, if a woman chooses to come around you with her man, you don't feel the necessity of undoing her or outdoing her. You get that there is a different choice for you.

When women do competition for men, they put a sign or a mark on the men they are having sex with, and every time some other woman walks into the room, they slime all over the guy. They put their piss mark on their man. Women and male dogs have a lot in common.

Salon Participant:

What does it look like when you don't do competition and you recognize that other women do?

Gary:

When women do competition with other women, you cannot be friends with them. They can never be your friends. They can only be acquaintances. Friendships cannot occur with women who compete with women.

Salon Participant:

That's what most women do.

Gary:

If you are willing to have no competition, you can have a close friendship. You have to be willing to recognize what kind of women you can choose as friends and what kind you can't.

Salon Participant:

What about working with women like that?

Gary:

When you work with women who do competition with women, you have to keep men out of the computation; otherwise, they will always find a way to create a problem that allows them to compete.

Salon Participant:

Wow, this seems like a foreign topic to me.

Gary:

Yeah, you don't do competition with women, so you don't understand how they function.

Salon Participant:

No, I don't.

Gary:

You think they function like other people do.

Salon Participant:

Thanks for enlightening me.

Salon Participant:

I am so grateful for this series of calls. I hadn't realized how much change was possible. If you had to leave us with the top three top points of view about being a woman on this planet, what would you say?

What Kind of Future Would You Like to Create?

Gary:

I've talked about the need to recognize that you are capable of being a warrior for creating a different reality here. You are a warrior for future.

How many of you are looking at the future, and how many of you are looking at the past? Most of you have spent your life looking at the wrongness, the past and the things that don't work. Seldom do you look at the future and what actually will work. What kind of future would you like to create? Why is your attention not on that? Every day.

I am interested in creating a future. To the best of my ability, I am being a humanoid man with a womanly touch. I am willing to look at what's going to create a future and what kind of future I can create. I am always looking to create everything different. With my own business, every day I look at: What do I need to be or change to make this better, greater or different? It's not going to work till I am able to create something different. For me, to create something different is the greatest gift I can give to myself. It's always about creating a future that has not yet existed.

You have to start thinking about how to create a future that has not existed here. If you function from this question, a lot of the problems you are having with marriage and everything else will go away. You have to start looking from:

- If I was creating the future I would like to have, what would it look like?

- What would it feel like?

It's a different possibility. It has to be something greater. You have to be willing to choose that.

Well, ladies, please be aware, as awareness is the greatest gift you can give yourself.

I hope you all enjoyed these calls as much as I did. Thank you all for the gift of your questions.

Salon Participants:

Thank you, Gary.

Salon Participant:

So much gratitude. Thank you!

The Access Consciousness Clearing Statement®

You are the only one who can unlock the points of view
that have you trapped.
What I am offering here with the clearing process is a tool you can use
to change the energy of the points of view that have you locked
into unchanging situations.

Throughout this book, I ask a lot of questions, and some of those questions might twist your head around a little bit. That's my intention. The questions I ask are designed to get your mind out of the picture so you can get to the *energy* of a situation.

Once the question has twisted your head around and brought up the energy of a situation, I ask if you are willing to destroy and uncreate that energy—because stuck energy is the source of barriers and limitations. Destroying and uncreating that energy will open the door to new possibilities for you.

This is your opportunity to say, "Yes, I'm willing to let go of whatever is holding that limitation in place."

That will be followed by some weird-speak we call the clearing statement:

Right and Wrong, Good and Bad, POD and POC, All Nine, Shorts, Boys and Beyonds

With the clearing statement, we're going back to the energy of the limitations and barriers that have been created. We're looking at the energies that keep us from moving forward and expanding into all of the spaces that we would like to go. The clearing statement is simply short-speak that addresses the energies that are creating the limitations and contractions in our life.

The more you run the clearing statement, the deeper it goes and the more layers and levels it can unlock for you. If a lot of energy comes up for you in response to a question, you may wish to repeat the process numerous times until the subject being addressed is no longer an issue for you.

You don't have to understand the words of the clearing statement for it to work because it's about the energy. However, if you're interested in knowing what the words mean, there are some brief definitions given below.

Right and Wrong, Good and Bad is shorthand for: What's right, good, perfect and correct about this? What's wrong, mean, vicious, terrible, bad and awful about this? The short version of these questions is: What's right and wrong, good and bad? It is the things that we consider right, good, perfect and/or correct that stick us the most. We do not wish to let go of them since we decided that we have them right.

POD stands for the **p**oint of **d**estruction; all the ways you have been destroying yourself in order to keep whatever you're clearing in existence.

POC stands for the **p**oint of **c**reation of the thoughts, feelings and emotions immediately preceding your decision to lock the energy in place.

Sometimes people say, "POD and POC it," which is simply shorthand for the longer statement. When you "POD and POC" something, it is like pulling the bottom card out of a house of cards. The whole thing falls down.

All Nine stands for the nine different ways you have created this item as a limitation in your life. They are the layers of thoughts, feelings, emotions and points of view that create the limitation as solid and real.

Shorts is the short version of a much longer series of questions that include: What's meaningful about this? What's meaningless about this? What's the punishment for this? What's the reward for this?

Boys stands for energetic structures called nucleated spheres. Basically these have to do with those areas of our life where we've tried to handle something continuously with no effect. There are at least thirteen different kinds of these spheres, which are collectively called "the boys." A nucleated sphere looks like the bubbles created when you blow in one of those kids' bubble pipes that has multiple chambers. It creates a huge mass of bubbles, and when you pop one bubble, the other bubbles fill in the space.

Have you ever tried to peel away the layers of an onion when you were trying to get to the core of an issue, but you could never get there? That's because it wasn't an onion; it was a nucleated sphere.

Beyonds are feelings or sensations that stop your heart, stop your breath or stop your willingness to look at possibilities. Beyonds are what occur when you are in shock. We have lots of areas in our life where we freeze up. Anytime you freeze up, it's a beyond holding you captive. That's the difficulty with a beyond: it stops you from being present. The beyonds include everything that is beyond belief, reality, imagination, conception, perception, rationalization, forgiveness as well as all the other beyonds. They are usually feelings and sensations, rarely emotions and never thoughts.

Glossary

Allowance

You can align and agree with a point of view, or you can resist and react to a point of view. That's the polarity of this reality. Or you can be in allowance. If you are in allowance, you are the rock in the middle of the stream. Thoughts, beliefs, attitudes and considerations come at you and they go around you because to you, they're just an interesting point of view. If, on the other hand, you go into alignment and agreement or resistance and reaction to that point of view, you get caught up in the stream of insanity and you go along for the ride. That's not the stream you want to be in. You want to be in allowance. Total allowance is: Everything is just an interesting point of view.

Be

In this book, the word *be* is sometimes used rather than *are* to refer to *you,* the infinite being you truly *be,* as opposed to a contrived point of view about who you think you *are.*

Bars

The Bars are a hands-on Access process that involves a light touch upon the head to contact points that correspond to different aspects of one's life. There are points for joy, sadness, body and sexuality, awareness, kindness, gratitude, peace and calm. There is even a money bar. These points are called "Bars" because they run from one side of the head to the other.

CFMW

Certifiable Fucking Miracle Worker.

Commandment

In Access Consciousness, we talk about the Ten Commandments—or the Ten Keys to Total Freedom. "No form, no structure, no significance" is one of those Ten Keys (or commandments). More information about the Ten Commandments or The Ten Keys is available in the book, *The Ten Keys to Total Freedom* or in *The Ten Commandments* CD.

Distractor Implants

Distractor implants are the sticky negative emotions we spend our time stuck in, longing to get out of, and firmly convinced we cannot escape. The distractor implants are: anger, rage, fury and hate; blame, shame, regret and guilt; obsessive, compulsive, addictive, perverted points of view; love, sex, jealousy and peace; life, living, death and relationships, business, fear and doubt.

Elementals

The fact is that every particle and every molecule has consciousness in it. When you invoke or use the elementals, you are addressing the consciousness of every molecule and asking it for the contribution it can be to your life.

Energetic Synthesis of Communion

This is a process that Dr. Dain Heer does. Basically, the energetic synthesis of communion puts you in connection with all the molecular structures of the universe in a different way. You can find out more about this on Dain's website (www.drdainheer.com). He offers free "tasters," so you can get a sense of what it's like.

Exit Stage Left

Exit Stage Left is an Access Consciousness process that can help the being and the body remember that life and death are a choice.

Fealty and Comealty

A fealty is a promise from feudal times, such as when a serf swore his loyalty to a king in return for the king's protection. A comealty is a fealty that has actually melded into your physical structure, like a blood oath on steroids.

Generation, Creation, Actualization and Institution

Generation is the energy that starts something into existence, *creation* is when you put it into actualization and *institution* is what you do to create a platform to build more.

Humans and Humanoids

There are two species of two-legged beings on this planet. We call them humans and humanoids. They look alike, they walk alike, they talk alike and they often eat alike, but the reality is they're different.

Humans will always tell you how you're wrong, how they're right, and how you shouldn't change anything. They say things like, "We don't do things that way, so don't even bother." They are the ones who ask, "Why are you changing that? It's fine the way it is."

Humanoids take a different approach. They are always looking at things and asking, "How can we change that? What will make this better? How can we outdo this?" They're the people who have created all the great art, all the great literature and all the great progress on the planet.

Interesting Point of View

Interesting point of view is an Access Consciousness tool. It is a great way to neutralize judgment by reminding yourself that whatever the judgment is, it's just a point of view that you or someone else has at this moment in time. It's not right or wrong or good or bad.

Any time a judgment comes up, just say, "Interesting point of view." It helps to distance you from the judgment. You don't align and agree with it—and you don't resist and react to it. You just allow it to be what it is, which is no more than an interesting point of view. When you can do this, you are in allowance.

Killing Energy

Killing energy is the energy it would take for you to kill something if you were willing to do it without any judgment. It takes energy to kill a cow or a deer or anything you're going to eat. That energy, delivered at somebody the way you would deliver it if you were actually slaughtering an animal, is the energy that will change things for people.

Kingdom of Me

Most of us try to function from the Kingdom of Me, which is about figuring out what we want, as though it has to be a separation from everyone else. What if you could choose from a totally different place? What if separation is what keeps you from having everything you truly desire?

Kingdom of We

When you choose from the Kingdom of We, it's not about choosing for you and against the other person. Nor do you choose for you and exclude the other person. You choose for you and everybody else; you choose what will expand all possibilities, including your own. When you do this, people around you realize their choice will expand by your choice, and they will contribute to your choices, not resist them.

Life and Living

Life is the completion; *living* is the act of continuous creation moment by moment, day by day.

Lighter/Heavier

That which is light is always true, and you sense the lightness of it. That which is a lie is always heavy, and you sense that heaviness.

MTVSS

Molecular Terminal Valence Sloughing System is a deeply relaxing Access Consciousness body process that works dynamically on the immune system and creates a sense of spaciousness and ease in the body that's often not experienced elsewhere.

Omnisexual

Omnisexuals feel attraction towards people of any gender and orientation. They see people for their personalities rather than their genitals or gender identity.

Out of Control

Being out of control is not being uncontrolled. It's not being drunk, disorderly or illegal. Being out of control means nothing controls or stops you—and you don't need to stop or limit anyone else. When you are out of control, you are willing to function outside of contextual reality and conventional points of reference. It's about not letting the controls of other people's points of view, realities, judgments and decisions be the controlling factor in your life.

Being out of control is being totally aware. You don't try to control the way things are generated. It is only when you are not being totally aware that you try to control what occurs or what comes in and goes out. Being out of control means nothing can stop you.

Out of Concentricities

Being out of concentricities is being out of the place where you try to put everything into concentric circles so they join one another and create a constant state of contraction.

Out of Context

Being out of context means you no longer operate in reference to anything or anyone else.

Out of Definition

Being out of definition is about being free from the definitions and limitations other people impose on you. Their definitions exist—and you are aware of them—but you operate outside of them.

Out of Form, Structure and Significance

Being out of form, structure and significance is not being bound by rigid forms and structures that others have deemed highly important and significant. It's being agile, responsive and innovative.

Out of Limitation

Being out of limitation means that you do not operate within the limitations that others create for themselves.

Out of Linearities

Out of linearities means you are out of the place where you try to line everything up so it agrees with everybody else's point of view.

POD and POCing

POD and POCing is a short way of saying that you are going back in time to the point where you destroyed yourself with something or to the point of creation of something that locks you up.

Put on a Loop

This is something you can do on your computer, which allows you to listen to something over and over again.

Quantum Entanglements

Quantum entanglements are the string theory that all things are interconnected. If you look at the universe, it's clear that each thing is interconnected with every other thing.

With every question, every choice and every possibility, you're inviting the quantum entanglements of the entire universe to join with you to actualize what you desire. The universe wishes to support us, but we act like we're all alone. It's as if we think the universe is an ecosystem we have to exclude ourselves from. We think we have to do everything ourselves—yet we are part of the whole. If we will embrace ourselves as part of the whole without any judgment, we absolutely invite the whole to be part of us and we open to the universe, which gives us everything we desire.

Signs, Seals, Emblems and Significances

These are the badges you wear all the time that have nothing to do with who you are.

Sex and No Sex

In Access Consciousness, when we say sex and no sex, we're not referring to copulation. We're talking about receiving. We chose these words because they bring up the energy of receiving and not receiving better than anything else we've found.

People use their points of view about sex and no sex as a way of limiting their receiving. Sex and no sex are exclusionary universes—either/or universes—where you either make your presence known (sex) to the exclusion of everyone else, or you hide your presence (no sex) so that you cannot be seen. In either case, given the focus on yourself, you don't allow yourself to receive from anyone or anything.

Systems and Structures

A system is something that is malleable and changeable. It can be adjusted according to the moment. A structure is something you put in place that has laws, regulations and rules that you have to follow. The military is a structure; it's not a system. The law is a structure; it's not a system. A system adapts to what you want. In my life, my system is being the question. A system puts a question foremost in

your mind as the doorway to options and possibilities you haven't
considered.

The Ten Commandments
(also known as the *Ten Keys to Total Freedom*)

Please read the book or listen to the calls. You need it.

Thrival

Thrival is the act of thriving. It includes survival but goes beyond
simple existence into the place of creation of a greater possibility.

Trifold Sequencing Systems

This is a Möbius strip, which means you play an event that happened
a long time ago over and over again in your head as though it just
happened today. Trifold sequencing systems are basically the source
of PTSD.

Utopian Ideals

Utopian ideals are conceptual realities that have been dropped into
our existence. Utopian ideals are fixed ideas or concepts of how
things are supposed to be—or should be. We take them on rather
than functioning in the moment.

Index of Chapter Titles and Headings

Chapter 7: Giving the Gift of Possibility **183**

What Will Allow Everything to Be Handled with Ease?.......... 183

True Caring vs. Taking Care Of.. 185

You Have to Recognize What Is.. 187

Creation and Invention.. 188

You Have to Be the Energy That Shows the Possibilities......... 191

Which Are You Living By—the Reality or the Illusion? 192

What Would You Like to Create as a Future? 194

Choice Is the Dominant Source of Creation........................... 197

"I Want This Now"... 199

The Problem with Living in the Present................................. 202

Trusting You as the Creator of Your Future 203

Trusting the Awareness You Truly Be...................................... 205

True Wealth 206

Confidence.. 208

Nobody Can See You Except You 211

Chapter 8: Creating Peace Instead of War................... **213**

The Reversal of Men's Roles and Women's Roles 213

Your Battle Is for Creating a Future....................................... 215

Becoming the Warrior Woman... 216

Battling For vs. Battling Against 218

Possibilities and Choices 219

Conquering... 221

"I Would Like to Have a Man Seduce Me for
   Once in My Life!"... 222

Living for Other People.. 223

Visual Representations and Inventions 224

Chapter 11:
Staying in the Power of Choice and Awareness 301

What Is Access Consciousness?

Access Consciousness is a simple set of tools, techniques and philosophies that allow you to create dynamic change in every area of your life. Access provides step-by-step building blocks that allow you to become totally aware and to begin functioning as the conscious being you truly are. These tools can be used to change whatever isn't working in your life so that you can have a different life and a different reality.

You can access these tools via a variety of classes, books, teleclasses and other products, or with an Access Consciousness Certified Facilitator or an Access Consciousness Bars Facilitator.

The goal of Access is to create a world of consciousness and oneness. Consciousness is the ability to be present in your life in every moment without judgment of yourself or anyone else. Consciousness includes everything and judges nothing. It's the ability to receive everything, reject nothing and create everything you desire in life, greater than you currently have and more than you can ever imagine.

For more information about Access Consciousness, or to locate an Access Consciousness Facilitator, please visit:

www.accessconsciousness.com   **www.garymdouglas.com**

Scan for more information   Scan for more information

Divorceless Relationships
By Gary M. Douglas

A Divorceless Relationship is one where you don't have to divorce any part of you in order to be in a relationship with someone else. It is a place where everyone and everything you are in a relationship with can become greater as a result of the relationship.

Joy of Business
By Simone Milasas

If you were creating your business from the JOY of it—what would you choose? What would you change? What would you choose if you knew you could not fail? Business is JOY, it's creation, it's generative. It can be the adventure of LIVING.

Scan for more information

For more Access Consciousness® Books go to www.accessconsciousnesspublishing.com

About the Author

Gary Douglas

Best-selling author, international speaker and a sought-after facilitator, Gary Douglas is known for his intensity of awareness and his incredible capacity to facilitate people to *know what they know.* He chooses to embody consciousness in everything that he does, which inspires others to choose to become more conscious as a result.

Gary came with an exceptional level of awareness into the Midwest middle class "white bread" family and lived the *Leave It to Beaver* childhood. He has a very different view on life and realized that he was very different from most of the people he knew when he was only six years old. He became aware of this difference by watching people create their lives and seeing that none of it was about the joy and the possibilities—it was always about the wrongness of everything. Gary knew there had to be more than this reality was offering, since there was nothing about it that was magical, joyful or expansive. So, he began seeking deeper awareness to life's mysteries at an early age. Along the way, he uncovered a new way forward—one that would create change in the world and in people's lives. He discovered that magic is all around us; it's something we create—it's consciousness. He recognized that the capacity to be more aware and more conscious was every person's gift if they were willing to choose it.

Over time what he recognised as the gift he was, was his intensity of awareness and his capacity to invite people to consciousness and to recognise that everything is possible and nothing is impossible. His gift is his ability to look at life, the universe and the consciousness that we all are, as well as the possibilities that are an intrinsic part of it from a space that no one else has ever chosen.

Empowering People to See Different Possibilities

Gary has become an internationally recognized thought leader in transforming lives and creating different choices—willing to empower people to see different possibilities and to recognize what is truly possible for them. Gary is acknowledged worldwide for his unique perspectives on personal transformation that is unlike anything else in the world. He is not aligned with any particular religion or tradition. Through his writing and workshops, he gifts processes and tools that bring within reach the ease, joy, and glory of life, and the magic of happiness that expands into more awareness, joy, and abundance. His simple, yet profound, teachings have already facilitated countless people throughout the world to *know what they know* and to realize what they can choose that they never realised they could choose.

At the Core of His Teachings Lies the Transformation of Consciousness

After recognising that greater consciousness in people can change the direction of their lives and the future of the planet, the creation and expansion of Access Consciousness by Gary has been primarily driven by a single question, "What can I do to help the world?"

He continues to inspire others, inviting the awareness of a different possibility across the world and making an immense contribution to the planet. He facilitates people to know that they are the source for creating the change they desire and creating a life that goes beyond the limitations of what the rest of the world thinks is important. He sees this as an essential aspect to creating a future that has greater possibilities in it for everyone, as well as the planet. This is a priority not only for personal happiness but also for the ending of violent conflict endemic on our planet and creating a different world. If enough people choose to be more aware and more conscious, they will start to see the possibilities of what they have available to them and change what is occurring here on planet earth.

Author

Gary Douglas is the author of the best-selling novel *The Place,* about people knowing that all things are possible and choice is the source of creation. Gary is also the co-author of a variety of books on the subjects of money, relationships, magic, and animals, with internationally renowned Energy Transformation virtuoso Dr. Dain Heer.

Inspiring People Worldwide

Gary pioneered a set of transformational life-changing tools and processes known as Access Consciousness® over twenty years ago. These leading edge tools have transformed the lives of thousands of people all over the world. His work has spread to forty-seven countries, with 2,000 trained facilitators worldwide. Simple, but so effective, the tools facilitate people of all ages and backgrounds to help remove limitations holding them back from a full life.

CPSIA information can be obtained
at www.ICGtesting.com
Printed in the USA
FSOW03n1724100216
16699FS